THE HISTORY OF THE FLEET AIR ARM

WID

THE HISTORY OF THE
FLEET AIR ARM
FROM KITES TO CARRIERS

Bill Finnis

Photographs supplied by Philip Jarrett other than the following:
Page 28 – BAE Systems; *Page 38* – BAE Systems; *Page 51* – Imperial War Museum NYP 68075; *Page 60* – Imperial War Museum CM 164; *Page 62* – Imperial War Museum A 6332; *Page 63* – Imperial War Museum Q 65690; *Page 68* – Imperial War Museum A 11201; *Page 69* – Imperial War Museum GM 1480; *Page 71* – Imperial War Museum A 15963; *Page 76* – Ron Ayrton; *Page 79* – BAE Systems; *Page 81* – Imperial War Museum HU 381; *Page 85* – Imperial War Museum HU 35743; *Page 88* – Imperial War Museum A 9423; *Page 91* – Imperial War Museum A 27217; *Page 95* – Imperial War Museum A 23576; *Page 100* – Imperial War Museum A 15365; *Page 101* – Imperial War Museum HU 2627; *Page 105* – Imperial War Museum MH 60145; *Page 118* – Imperial War Museum A 29167; *Page 121* – Imperial War Museum A 28007; *Page 130* – Imperial War Museum ABS 225; *Page 131* – Imperial War Museum MH 2095.

First published in the UK in 2000
by Airlife Publishing Ltd

British Library Cataloguing-in-Publication Data
A catalogue record for this book
is available from the British Library

ISBN 1 84037 182 X

Typeset by Servis Filmsetting Ltd, Manchester
Printed in England by Butler & Tanner Ltd, Frome & London.

Airlife Publishing Ltd

101 Longden Road, Shrewsbury SY3 9EB, England
E-mail: airlife@airlifebooks.com
Website: www.airlifebooks.com

Contents

Bats

CHAPTER ONE

In the Beginning

It is impossible to be dogmatic about the exact date on which the Royal Navy became interested in 'aircraft' if we use the word in its broadest possible sense. In the early stages it seems that the Air Arm 'like Topsy, she just growed'.

In about 1903 three methods of getting airborne were claiming the interest of a number of enthusiasts, man-lifting kites, lighter-than-air craft and heavier-than-air machines and the Navy experimented with each of them in turn.

A limited number of naval officers could see something of the potential offered by an Air Arm and although they would doubtless be astonished to see the advances that have been made since their day, they must be given credit for getting the idea off the ground, often against indifference and sometimes even downright hostility from the upper echelons of their own Service. The very first tentative official steps were directed towards the exploration of the potential of kites and lighter-than-air craft.

Samuel Franklin Cody, not to be confused with the showman of the same name, but in his way an equally colourful extrovert with a wide range of interests in matters aeronautical, was a designer of kites, airships and aeroplanes, and probably the first to give the Admiralty its earliest nudge towards an interest in aeronautical matters. It was his kites that first brought him to the notice of the Admiralty. He wrote to them on 6 February 1903 to tell them of a kite that he had designed that was capable of lifting a man 'for reconnaissance, signalling or spotting the fall of shot', claiming that in practice flights he had reached heights of up to 1,200 feet with kites towed by ships. He had some twenty of these kites for sale.

The point was that if an observer's height of eye could be raised by this means he would be able to see a great deal further than a man on the bridge of a ship. For example, with a height of eye of 40 feet an observer would have a horizon of 7.4 nautical miles but at 400 feet his horizon would be extended to 23.4 miles. An advantage of this kind could clearly be very valuable in an engagement at sea and indeed ashore. This could also influence the distance over which radio messages could be sent. Wireless telegraphy, as it was then called, was in its infancy and a factor that limited its range was the height to which it was possible to raise the aerial. The kite was seen as a means of lifting an aerial to greater heights than the masthead, thereby increasing the range over which a radio signal could be sent and received.

Five weeks after Cody's letter had been received a demonstration was staged by him on Woolwich Common and Capt. R. Tupper, Assistant Director of Naval Ordnance, reported very favourably on its potential for supporting an aerial for wireless telegraphy purposes.

On 18 March, Prince Louis recommended that the Navy begin their own experiments with both of the above possibilities (radio and reconnaissance) in mind. Mr Cody was to be asked to send his kites to Portsmouth where the Captain of HMS *Vernon*, a shore base, was to carry out trials with an eight-foot kite flown from a gunboat or a destroyer, with a view to lifting an aerial wire.

The Captain of HMS *Excellent*, the Gunnery School on Whale Island, was instructed to carry out trials with the man-lifting kites. If successful these could then be repeated from a ship under way.

Twelve days later the trials were started at *Vernon* with various sizes of kites that had been sent for test purposes and on the following day other tests took place on Whale Island during which an aerial was lifted to a height of 600 feet. Sea trials were carried out in HMS *Hector*, a

6,710-ton cruiser and HMS *Starfish,* a torpedo boat destroyer. These tests were completed on 4 April 1903 and three days later Captain Edgerton submitted a favourable report to the Admiralty.

Further trials with man-lifting kites took place at Whale Island and on 13 April one of Cody's sons reached a height of 500 feet. Three days later the kites went to sea in HMS *Seahorse* to continue the trials and in perfect weather it was repeatedly demonstrated that the kite could lift a log weighing 140 lb.

Sadly perfect weather at sea is something that cannot be relied upon to appear when it is most needed and in gusty conditions the kites could hardly be expected to lift a man to several hundred feet and keep him there in safety. This series of trials ended on 18 April and a report was prepared to that effect for submission to higher authority. It went on to say that perhaps with improvement kites might be relied upon to keep a man safely aloft in less than perfect conditions. The report had no reservations concerning the kites' ability to raise an aerial to extend the distance over which radio signals could be sent and received.

When the tests were completed and the reports had been studied Prince Louis recommended to the First Sea Lord that the Admiralty should purchase Cody's patents and employ Cody as a civilian kiting instructor. When this was put to Cody he overplayed his hand and asked the Admiralty for £25,000 for his patents plus a salary of £1,250 a year. He also wanted a clause written into his contract that would guarantee him a 'golden handshake' of £25,000 if the kites were still satisfactory when he was discharged. These were very large sums of money for those times.

On 20 May the Admiralty replied that his offer was unacceptable. It was obvious that Cody had asked too much for his gear and services because despite turning him down it was clear that the Admiralty retained an interest in kites inasmuch as they purchased four sets, each consisting of a pilot kite, two lifters and a carrier with controls and basket. These were supplied to HM Ships *Good Hope, Majestic, Revenge* and *Doris.*

The advantages that it was hoped would accrue from the use of kites for the Royal Navy were likely to be more readily obtainable for the Army working in the more stable conditions that would be found ashore. Probably for this reason the Royal Engineers in co-operation with the Balloon Factory had continued to take an active interest in kites long after the Navy had refused to employ Cody.

By 1907 the design of man-lifting kites had been perfected and the army had engaged Cody as their Chief Kiting Instructor. This reawakened the Admiralty's interest and Their Lordships sanctioned a new set of trials to ascertain their value when towed by HM Ships. These trials were conducted by the Gunnery School, *Excellent.*

A man-lifting kite being flown from the deck of one of HM Ships

Apart from some short breaks away at Farnborough, where he was working on his own aircraft, Cody spent his time from 17 August to 7 October 1908 on *Excellent* helping with the latest set of trials that were held on HM Ships *Grafton, Revenge, Fervent,* and *Recruit.*

On one occasion Cody, ever the showman, delighted a ship's company by arriving on the jetty for sea trials dressed in full cowboy gear, including a ten-gallon stetson.

An accident that occurred on 31 August caused Cody to crash into the sea from a height of some 800 feet. At the time he was borne aloft by a kite that was being towed by *Recruit.* A version of the incident that has been repeated by a number of writers has the CO of *Recruit* turning downwind so causing Cody to crash. The officers and men involved in this mishap had trained at Farnborough where kites were both designed and made and it really is very difficult to believe that they could have committed such an elementary mistake. Furthermore, the Navy at this time relied on small sailing vessels, mostly cutters and whalers, to carry out much of the work that would be done by power boats today and sailing is a pastime that requires a constant awareness of the wind's direction and strength.

The true facts of the matter would seem to be that Cody was aloft flying a combination of the pilot kite and four lifting kites when *Recruit*, which was towing him, ran out of the lee of the Isle of Wight causing a strong southerly wind to strike the kiting array with the result that it promptly went out of control and deposited Cody, unharmed fortunately, into the sea. The basket floated and Cody clung to this until he was picked up.

Again it was decided that the man-lifting kite was, because of its uncertainty, too dangerous and no further experiments in this area were sanctioned by the Admiralty.

While the Navy was experimenting with Cody's kites interest was also being shown in dirigibles. This interest in lighter-than-air craft not only took place at about the same time as the experiments with kites but for much the same reasons, namely as an aid to artillery and reconnaissance, and this interest was rather longer-lived than were the experiments with kites.

A committee on military ballooning was set up on 8 June 1903 to study the matter, probably in response to the campaigning of Rear Admiral Lambton. The committee produced their specification for a navigable balloon. It had to be able to operate at an altitude of 5,000 feet, be capable of flying for three days with a crew of three and maintain a speed of at least sixteen knots.

On 3 November of the same year, William Beadle demonstrated his idea of a navigable balloon at Alexandra Palace. Beadle's balloon was fitted with two propellers. One propeller was fixed in the fore and aft line and its purpose was to drive the balloon forward. The other was designed to swivel to give some directional control to the balloon.

Beadle's demonstration so impressed the pioneering airship company of E.T. Willows that they collaborated with him to improve and strengthen the design and to give it more power. The prototype that emerged from this co-operation, Willow No. 1, was ready for its test flight by early September 1905. This went well and lasted for 85 minutes in the course of which an altitude of 120 feet was reached. Not quite what the committee's specification demanded but a decided step forward. Clearly the Navy were impressed because they ordered a Willow non-rigid airship or blimp.

A blimp consists of three principal parts, the gas bag, the power plant and a gondola. The shape of the gas bag is maintained by keeping the pressure within the bag just slightly higher than the ambient atmospheric pressure. The power plant and the gondola, often united as one, are slung beneath the gas bag.

It has been said that the name 'blimp' arose because when, in its very early days, it was being inflated as part of a demonstration of its virtues, someone was heard to refer to it as 'bloody limp'; the obvious contraction followed. How true that is I do not know but it seems possible and it would be rather nice if it were true. The blimp was the forerunner of the airships that followed later.

Those senior naval officers who had admitted

The History of the Fleet Air Arm

Three Sea Scout blimps showing the use of the fuselage of a BE2c aircraft as a gondola

that there might be a place for aircraft in the service of the Navy were convinced that the future usefulness of an air arm lay in the operation of lighter-than-air craft. It was felt that because airships were able to adjust their speed to that of the fleet when the need arose, and because their load carrying ability and their endurance were vastly greater than that of the current breed of heavier-than-air machines, airships must be the right way to go.

In fairness it must be said that the heavier-than-air machines of the day were rather fragile and limited in their performance but could no one in the upper ranks of the Navy foresee the developmental possibilities?

Development of non-rigid dirigibles continued until it culminated in the North Sea type, which was the last of the non-rigids to be built for the Royal Navy. The gas capacity of these craft was at

first 210,000 cubic feet, a considerable increase in size on the earlier 'Coastal Type' airships which had a gas capacity of 170,000 cubic feet. Late in 1916 a number of even bigger North Sea class airships were built with a gas capacity of 360,000 cubic feet. The gondola, which was suspended below the gas bag, was built of a framework of timber covered with a skin of duraluminium. From the gondola a gangway extended aft and ended in two gantries that each supported a Rolls-Royce engine of 250 h.p.

The next step in sophistication was the semi-rigid airship. The semi-rigid was still a large gas bag, just like the blimp, but it was fitted on its underside

with a keel from which the power plant and the gondola were slung, thereby avoiding the need to suspend the gondola and power plant from the gas bag.

Most of the rigging was within the gas bag itself which brought the car, etc. closer to the envelope, so giving a cleaner shape and air speeds of 44 knots were common at quite low r.p.m. helping to increase endurance to about 24 hours.

By the end of World War One the Admiralty had about ninety-five SS (Sea Scout) airships in service and they had proved useful in reconnaissance and anti-submarine patrol work. There was considerable variation in size and power amongst these airships but many were about 145 feet long with a maximum diameter of some thirty feet. The gondola problem was solved in some airships by slinging the fuselage and undercarriage from a

Coastal class non-rigid airship

North Sea class of non-rigid dirigible

BE2c aircraft below the envelope. The 75 h.p. engines installed in some of the earlier types gave a maximum airspeed of 46 knots at 1,600 feet with an all-up load of 1,434 lb and an estimated endurance of 8 hours. Typically an airship of this kind would have a gas capacity of 60,000 cubic feet.

Later models were fitted with 100 h.p. engines which increased their airspeed to 49 knots and extended their endurance to about 12 hours.

Throughout the war years and after its conclusion, improvements continued to be made and in 1919 NS11 flew 4,000 miles in 101 hours, an endurance record for non-rigids, but without more details like the wind speed and direction experienced and the direction steered throughout, the figures do no more than underline the steady and considerable improvement that had been made in performance.

There were a number of problems that were common to all these lighter-than-air craft. The three most pressing were: the loss of gas through the fabric; the loss of ballast and gas in the constant juggling required to keep the airship in a state of equilibrium in the changing atmospheric pressures through which it moved; insufficient power to overcome head winds. The problems created by the loss of ballast and gas were greatly exacerbated by the loss of weight due to burning fuel in the propulsion unit. As fuel was used so the airship became lighter, which required that adjustments be made to gas and ballast to compensate for the loss of weight to maintain altitude. When a method of recovering the water from the exhaust gases was perfected the weight of the water saved went a long way towards counterbalancing the loss of weight caused by burning the fuel.

The final design was the rigid airship. This had a frame that was covered by a fabric envelope. The

The rigid airship was the final design. R25 displays the 'keel' to which the gondola and engine pods were attached in some versions. The overall design was basically a copy of the German Zeppelin with variations introduced by the various constructors

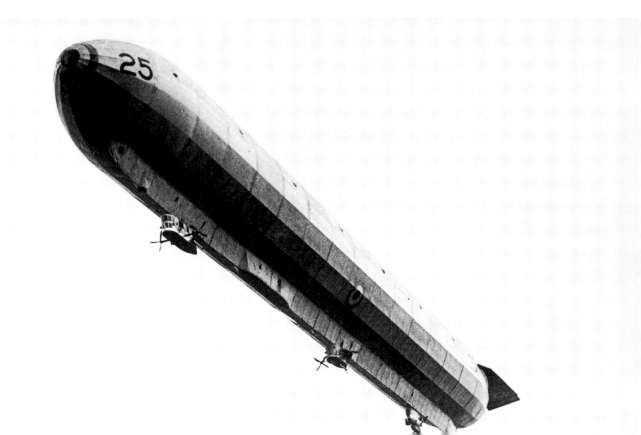

This photograph shows the massive size of the R Class airships and the size of the crew needed to handle one of them on the ground

airship's shape, being maintained by the frame, did not change when the gas bags, which were carried within the frame, were inflated or deflated. The gondola was carried largely within the main structure.

The rigid design gave the added bonus of simpler mooring than either of the other two designs. An airship that was so big and unwieldy was prone to problems created by unhelpful wind conditions and the non-rigid and semi-rigid types must, at times, have been absolute beasts to secure.

As greater load-carrying capacity and endurance was sought so, inevitably, the size of airships grew, eventually to more than 500 feet in length. The last of the rigid airships, the R Class, had a gas capacity of 1,500,000 cubic feet and R33 and R34 had a volume of 2,000,000 cubic feet.

Engines too increased their capacity to keep pace with the size of these huge craft. R34 and R35 were both powered with four 350 h.p. Sunbeam engines.

Almost 400 airships were built and between them they flew two and a half million miles with the loss of only forty-six crew members. In a pioneering venture such as this it is a remarkable tribute to the airmanship of the men concerned that there were so few casualties. It is even more striking when it is realised that a number of those forty-six casualties were inflicted by the enemy.

It must have taken a very special sort of courage to fly one of these dirigibles. The gas used to inflate them was hydrogen which is so highly inflammable that perhaps it should be described as explosive. Added to which there was no means of escape for the crew should it be ignited. The effectiveness of the parachute had yet to be demonstrated and this was not done until February 1917 when a Colonel Maitland stepped out of an airship at an altitude of 1,000 feet and landed safely. What confidence!

After the end of the war lighter-than-air craft were still commanding attention but now it was rather more in the field of commerce than the armed forces. In July 1919 R34 crossed the Atlantic from East Fortune in Scotland to Long Island (USA) and back. The 3,130 miles of one crossing, whether outward bound or return I cannot ascertain, took 108 hours 12 minutes, an average speed of about thirty knots.

The Germans had not been idle in the sphere of airships and indeed made much use of their huge Zeppelins during World War One. After the war they in particular took a commercial interest in lighter-than-air craft, carrying passengers across the Atlantic to the USA. This came to an abrupt end when one of their Zeppelins, *Hindenburg*, burst into flames as it was being connected to a mooring mast in America, killing thirty-five of the ninety-seven people who were aboard.

Whilst the use of kites and lighter-than-air craft was being investigated and developed, a similar interest was being shown in heavier-than-air craft but in this case by individuals rather than the Navy, at least in the earlier years.

There were a number of people experimenting with flying machines but the Wright brothers are generally given credit for the first successful powered, heavier-than-air flight. This was made in December 1903 when the Wrights' machine took off with one of the brothers aboard and flew 120 yards at an altitude of about ten feet. The two brothers continued to experiment and build improvements into their aircraft and finally in October 1905 they were rewarded by making a flight of twenty-five miles.

When the Wright brothers offered to sell their patents to the Admiralty in 1907 they were turned down because the Admiralty felt that they would be of no practical use to the Naval Service. It seemed there were very few, if any, senior officers who had the vision to foresee the possibility of improvement in heavier-than-air craft nor the future potential for their employment with the Fleet. Fortunately there were officers of lesser rank who could understand the possibilities and continued to work for the establishment of an air arm where heavier-than-air machines would have a place.

Undaunted by the Admiralty's lack of interest the Wright brothers continued working to improve their flying machine and on 12 September 1908 they achieved a flight of fifty miles and a reasonable degree of lateral and vertical control.

The Army authorities were not much better than the Admiralty. They formulated a specification for a flying machine in which they stated, amongst other things, that the machine must rise from the ground under its own power without assistance from special starting devices.

The Wright brothers' aeroplane had no undercarriage. In place of an undercarriage their pioneering plane had skids and took off along a well-greased inclined monorail. It seems that this offended the official specification and that no one had the foresight to see that wheels could be substituted for skids!

Running parallel with his interest in kiting Samuel Cody had been working on his own plane in Britain and eventually made his first flight, a distance of 1,390 feet, on Farnborough Common on 16 October 1908. Three weeks later Squadron Commander Dunne, an RN officer, flew 40 yards at Blair Atholl in Scotland.

At about this time air races were to be held at Rheims and the hierarchy of the Navy dropped its guard so far as to send a Captain R.H. Bacon to France to report on them. Races of this kind were usually very low level, timed events with the planes flying in turn around a course indicated by beacons on the ground.

Captain Bacon was impressed with what he had

"LEFÈVRE" SUR AÉROPLANE WRIGHT

One of the earliest Wright brothers' planes in flight

seen and on his return set about the uphill task of persuading 'the powers that be' to establish a number of administrative groups that would have the development of aircraft in the service of the Navy as their aim.

The RN's first qualified pilot was G.C. Colmore, who completed his training in June 1910, at his own expense. By April 1911 Britain had a total of six qualified military pilots. The French showed much more official interest in flying: by 1912 the French Navy alone had about 300 officers who had qualified as pilots.

In April 1911 a Lieutenant W. Parke, who had never flown an aircraft before, flew an Avro type D biplane, powered by a 35 h.p. Green engine, the length of the aerodrome and declared it stable, easy to fly and without vices. Later the wheels were removed from this plane and a combination of skids and floats were installed in their place. After trials the floats were modified so that the underside was stepped and on 18 November 1911, during taxying trials, the seaplane lifted off its step and reached a height of about twenty feet where it

remained for a short time and then dropped back onto the water with an expensive noise. The pilot, Commander Oliver Swann, was unqualified at the time. But what a beautifully apt name for the pilot of a seaplane!

For me these two examples typify the carefree atmosphere in which so much of this new pastime was conducted.

Today aircraft are so sophisticated, speeds so great and the engines deliver so much power that there is no room on the design side for anyone who has not undergone a long and highly technical training. This was not so in those early days and the men who were privileged to be involved must have had a field day.

I can recall the airspeed indicator on a Tiger Moth that I flew in the early 1940s. It consisted of a flat plate of metal about eight inches by two with a short length of rod welded to it. The top of the rod was attached to the apex of a quadrant of metal so that it could swing back and forth across the face of the quadrant whilst the plate remained at 90 degrees to the quadrant. The whole lash-up was mounted on the wing strut close to the port side of the cockpit so that the plate faced forward. A spring was fixed to the plate so that pressure was required to push the plate back across the quadrant. The bottom edge of the quadrant was marked off in knots. The pressure was supplied by the wind produced by the plane's forward motion, the greater the speed the greater the air pressure on the plate which was forced further and further back across the quadrant registering ever greater speeds. Many of the advances of the very early period of flying were of this order.

The turn and bank instrument in use in the years between the wars and in World War Two was in effect a spirit level but the small tube that contained the bubble was curved. If the turn was perfectly executed, i.e. it was not marred by the pilot causing the plane to side-slip or to skid across the sky, the bubble showed its approval by remaining in the centre of the tube. Its forerunner was a piece of string tied to a wing strut close to the cockpit. Normally the string would stream aft in line with the fore and aft line of the plane but if the plane was subjected to slipping or skidding it would respond by streaming to one side. When pilots began to fly planes at night the string was anointed with luminous paint.

In the final stages of a night landing the pilot needs to have some idea of just how high he is in relation to the ground. Without any form of runway lighting, not even kerosene smudge pots, the early pilots at one stage tried lowering a weight on fifty yards of line. When the weight struck the ground the drag created triggered a light switch in the cockpit.

On 1 July 1911 a Frenchman won the Gordon Bennet International Speed Race flying a Nieuport monoplane and Gerrard, a Royal Marine officer who was learning to fly, was sent to Pau to learn how to handle this type of plane. Before he was able to start, however, the Admiralty and the War Office banned the use of monoplanes because of several fatal accidents that had occurred and

this unqualified test pilot(!) had to return.

January 1912 saw some of the earliest experiments involving flying aircraft off HM Ships. A staging and trackway had been erected on the foredeck of the battleship *Africa*. Whilst she was at anchor at Sheerness Lt C.R. Samson successfully flew a Short biplane off this makeshift flight-deck without the help of the wind over the deck that would have been created if the ship had been under way.

Four months later Lt Gregory succeeded in flying a modified Short 27 from a platform that had been constructed over the fo'c'sle of HMS *Hibernia*. This time the parent ship was moving: *Hibernia* made ten and a half knots steaming directly into a two knot wind giving twelve and a half knots of wind over the flight-deck which obviously shortened the take-off run.

Later in the same year this performance was repeated aboard HMS *London* whilst she steamed at twelve knots into a force three wind. With the increased wind speed over the deck to help it the Short lifted off after a run of only twenty-five feet. The planes used in these experiments were float planes and for their take-off they were mounted on a trolley that fell away as they became airborne. When they had completed their flight the planes had to alight on the sea close to their parent ship to be hoisted aboard by the ship's crane.

In 1912 the flying school at Netheravon offered to train up to 180 officers a year. This was a private arrangement inasmuch as these students were required to pay their own fees but those who passed their final examinations were able to reclaim the £75 it had cost them to learn to fly. Once qualified they had the choice of naval or military flying, or alternatively they could choose to join one of two kinds of Reserve. In one they simply committed themselves to be available in time of war and in the other they were paid a small retainer on the completion of a few cross-country flights each year.

For those involved this must have been a very exciting time. Flying was a truly hands-on kind of pastime with many of the enthusiasts at least helping to maintain and modify their planes. Regulation was almost non-existent.

A Commander Newton wrote and published the first work devoted specifically to aerial navigation. The *Daily Mail* prize for the first cross-Channel flight from Calais to Dover was won in a time of thirty-seven minutes.

The Royal Aero Club offered to teach Naval Officers to fly and qualify in the Royal Aero Club's aircraft. An Admiralty Fleet Order which asked for volunteers was published and the response was enormous but out of over two hundred officers who volunteered only five were selected, three from the Royal Navy and two from the Royal Marines.

Instruction was far from easy: dual controls were unknown of course and the pupil had to crouch behind the instructor and get the feel of the controls by reaching over his shoulder. Training usually took place at dawn, to take advantage of the calm conditions that often prevail then but if the wind speed was over ten knots no flying took place.

In straight flight the height was often only feet above the ground and it was not unknown for observers to lie flat on the ground to make sure that the aircraft really did leave it. Many of the machines used were fitted with 50 or 60 h.p. engines, yet others were as low powered as 35 h.p. and in some cases were little more than powered kites. It was not unknown for the combined weight of the instructor and pupil to be too great for the size of the engine, causing the plane to have difficulty in getting off the ground!

It is tempting to think of the present day microlight planes as something of a highly sophisticated hark back to those days.

March 1912 saw Winston Churchill installed as First Lord of the Admiralty. Fortunately for the future of the Fleet Air Arm he was a man with vision enough to see some of the possibilities of naval aviation and he had the influence and ability to push through the changes that were needed. Things became rather easier for those pioneering spirits who had not lost faith. However, even under Churchill the role of naval aircraft was still visualised as a less than aggressive one; they were to detect mines, locate subs and direct gunfire. Others fortunately had different ideas.

Lieutenant Hugh Williamson, a submariner who had qualified as a naval pilot, submitted a paper to the Admiralty in which he proposed the use of aircraft for the purpose of detecting submarines and destroying them with bombs that would explode under water – a suggestion that eventually led to the aerial depth charge.

Others worked on the beginnings of a bomb sight and still other enthusiasts worked to design and produce a Wireless Telegraphy set that would be suitable for use in aircraft.

Improvements were being made in reliability and endurance and in March 1912 a Lt Longmore flew 181 miles in 3 hours, 15 minutes. Later in the summer of the same year the Short 541 biplane fitted with single step mahogany floats successfully completed its trials off Portland and was taken into service by the Navy.

On 7 May 1913 HMS *Hermes* was commissioned as the headquarters and parent ship of The Naval Wing. She was equipped to carry seaplanes but her speed of ten knots destroyed any hope of her operating with the Fleet where speeds of up to thirty knots were commonplace. This all important and, one would have thought, self-evident fact, seemed to take a long time to register with the Admiralty.

In the late summer of 1914 *Hermes* had been refitted and recommissioned as a seaplane carrier. Her upper deck was flush and clear of all obstructions from the stem to within one hundred feet of the stern. Further aft there was a large hatchway that gave access to a big hold with workshop facilities built around the hatch on the upper deck. A crane was fitted on either side of the deck to facilitate the handling of the aircraft.

An experimental feature was a fore and aft trackway that was intended to aid the launching of the ship's aircraft. An 80 h.p. Caudron amphibian was successfully flown off a number of times using a wheeled trolley on this trackway. Once the plane was airborne the trolley was left behind. *Hermes* carried and launched two seaplanes in this manner. This idea quickly gained favour with pilots and came into more general use.

On 31 October 1914, shortly after she was recommissioned, *Hermes* was returning to the UK having delivered a number of aircraft to the seaplane base at Dunkirk when she was torpedoed off Calais.

Ark Royal, the first ship of that name to grace the Fleet Air Arm, was launched on 5 September 1914 and was later renamed *Pegasus*. She was still in service during World War Two. Originally she was laid down as a 7,500 ton merchant ship but before she was launched she was converted to carry up to ten aircraft. Her engines and bridge were placed aft together with a hangar (130 feet by 45 feet) for the accommodation of her seaplanes. Although she had an uninterrupted deck 352 feet long by 51 feet wide and a further 130-foot long flush deck forward, there was no provision for flying off aircraft. Unfortunately her speed of just over ten knots was insufficient to create enough wind speed over the deck for successful flight operations and for this reason she carried only seaplanes, lowering and recovering them by crane.

Many of these hasty conversions proved to be far too slow to allow them to operate with the Fleet. Not only must a carrier generate enough wind over her flight-deck to enable planes to fly on and off but she must also be able to regain her position and keep pace with the fleet with which she is operating and this they were not able to do. Add to this the need to stop and crane seaplanes back aboard, operations that could be carried out only in a relatively calm sea, and it becomes apparent why these misconceived ships were of little value to the Fleet.

Thirteen of these early seaplane carriers saw service between 1914 and 1918 and it is true to say that the experience gained laid the foundations for the design and building of more modern carriers, but their active service contribution to the conduct of World War One was negligible.

Now that it had been demonstrated that it was possible to fly off the deck of a carrier the next step was clearly to develop the ability to land the plane back on to avoid the delay caused by stopping to lift it inboard, but it was to be five more years before the first steps were taken towards that goal. It was to be even longer before a suitable ship was produced to make landing on a matter of routine.

At about this time three fast cross-Channel packets, *Empress, Engadine* and *Riviera* were converted to handle seaplanes. Despite their speed no attempt was made to build flush decks on these vessels in the course of their conversion. Instead they were fitted with hangars for seaplanes with derricks for hoisting them into and out of the water. These ships took part in the early bombing raids on Cuxhaven and Wilhelmshaven and *Engadine* operated a Short 184 in the course of the Battle of Jutland.

A further three conversions were *Ben-My-Chree, Vindex* and *Manxman*. Of these, perhaps *Ben-My-Chree*, an Isle of Man packet, is the best-known. Just over 350 feet long with a beam of 46 feet she was armed with two 4-inch guns, and a 6-pounder and had a top speed of some 24 knots. Her hangars housed four 2-seater Short 184 seaplanes powered by 225 h.p. Sunbeam Mohawk engines. Each plane was able to carry a 14-inch torpedo slung between its floats making *Ben-My-Chree* the first ship to operate torpedo-carrying aircraft.

Viking, a 2,900-ton Isle of Man steamer, was converted in September 1915 to operate aircraft and was renamed HMS *Vindex*. She had a speed of 22 knots. Her 64-foot flight-deck and forward hangar were intended for the use of the two fighters she carried. The after hangar housed one small and four large seaplanes.

A major step forward in carrier history was the conversion of an 18,000 ton liner to carry seaplanes. *Campania*, as she was named, was commissioned on 10 April 1915. With a length of 600 feet, she had a speed of 23 knots, carried ten aircraft and was armed with six 4.7-inch guns and a 3-inch AA gun.

Unfortunately *Campania* was found to be unsuitable for operations, her 120-foot long flying-off deck being too short and it was back to the routine of stopping to launch her seaplanes. To overcome this she was modified in 1916. The forward funnel was split into two and the original flight-deck of 120 feet was lengthened to 200 feet, passing between the funnels. With the lengthened flight-deck seaplanes could be launched from a trolley which was discarded when the plane became airborne.

In August 1917 Commander Swann of *Campania* was complaining about the lack of training new pilots had received before being posted to his ship. It would seem they had little knowledge of handling engines, lacked flying experience, had never taken a passenger up in training and their knowledge of the compass and its place in navigation was distinctly lacking.

Commander Swann was not one to be content with complaining. He suggested a design for what must rank as the earliest simulator in which pilots could receive part of their training without leaving the ground. It was to consist of the fuselage, engine and undercarriage of a plane mounted on a turntable. With the engine running at a suitable speed the slipstream would cause a movement of the rudder to turn the fuselage and its platform and give the embryo pilot a feel for the controls. The fuselage was to be fitted with all that would be built into a reconnaissance aircraft.

By 1917 at last there were people in the RN who were seriously considering landing a plane onto a ship that was under way. It is difficult to believe now but not everyone considered this to be a desirable achievement.

Lieutenant Samson was one of those who were anxious to try their hand at landing an aircraft back onto the parent ship. When this came to the notice of an aviation writer he extolled Samson's manifold virtues and then went on to say, '. . . he should not therefore be permitted to risk his life on what is, after all is said and done, simply a dangerous trick of no practical value whatever'. One hopes that the writer lived long enough to eat his own words!

Furious was originally built as a light battle cruiser. In 1917 she underwent a major refit and conversion to enable her to handle aircraft. Her forward gun turret had been removed and a flying-off deck 228 feet long by 50 feet wide had been built in its place. Not yet a full length flight-deck but a definite step forward and successful flying-off trials had been carried out. Her complement of aircraft at this time was three Short seaplanes and five Sopwith Pup landplanes. *Furious* could maintain a little over thirty knots, a decided improvement on the speed of earlier aircraft carriers.

Lieutenant-Commander E.H. Dunning who, like Samson, had been involved in flying aircraft from HM Ships, also suggested that it might be possible not only to launch wheeled aircraft but to land them back on again. The advantages of being able to both fly off a ship at sea and land back on again were obvious and permission for a trial was quickly granted. *Furious* was with the Grand Fleet at Scapa Flow at the time and on 2 August 1917 a number of high-ranking officers gathered on her deck to watch Dunning's first attempt at a deck landing.

Dunning used a Sopwith Pup for the demonstration and he took off whilst *Furious* steamed steadily into the wind at twenty-six knots. The wind at the time was blowing at some eleven knots which, with the wind created by the ship's speed through the water, gave a wind speed over the deck of thirty-seven knots making a relatively slow landing approach possible.

The approach had to be made from one side as the flight-deck of *Furious* did not extend for the full length of the ship. Dunning chose to approach the vessel on the port side. As soon as he was clear of the ship's superstructure he successfully side-slipped down and centred up low over the flight-deck. A party of officers rushed out and pulled the aircraft down to the deck and held her there by means of special toggles that had been attached to the wings of his aircraft for this purpose.

Five days later further trials were carried out. Conditions on this occasion were less favourable, the wind being somewhat gusty. The first landing went well enough, considering the gusting wind, but in the course of the landing minor damage was caused to the elevator and Lieutenant-Commander Dunning reverted to his original aircraft. This time his approach was too high which meant that he would touch down rather further forward, maybe too far forward to be able to stop in time. Dunning, realising this, waved the deck party away and started to go round again. Unfortunately as he increased the throttle setting to climb away the engine choked and the aircraft stalled. It dropped heavily onto the starboard wheel, and started to slide over the side of the ship. The deck party made a dash for it but having been

Lieutenant-Commander Dunning's successful deck landing on HMS Furious

His second attempt ended in his death

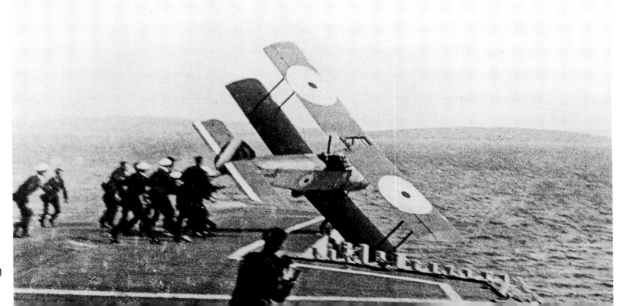

waved away were too far off to reach it in time to be able to help.

It was not possible to lower a safety boat: at the speed at which *Furious* was steaming, it would have been swamped, almost certainly with loss of life. It took the ship twenty minutes to turn around and return to the spot. It was too late. Dunning had evidently been knocked out when the aircraft ditched and, sadly, had drowned by the time he was recovered.

A ship the size and weight of *Furious* steaming at twenty-six knots takes time to stop or to turn. The only possible 'safety boat' available in those days would have been either a whaler or a cutter, both sailing or pulling boats, and the parent ship would need to come to a stop to be able to lower them safely. It must be supposed that it was deemed more likely to be faster to use the parent ship than to stop and lower a much slower craft to the water to effect a rescue. I know that we are all blessed with 20/20 hindsight but I do wonder that something like a destroyer, so much more manoeuvrable and fast enough to keep up with the parent vessel, was not in attendance.

Now that the feasibility of flying off and landing an aircraft onto the deck of a moving ship had been demonstrated the next logical development was a carrier with an uninterrupted flight-deck. It was also realised that some means of stopping aircraft once they had touched down would be needed.

The first true arrester gear was tried out on the American warship *Pennsylvania* which had had a timber deck of 110 feet by 30 feet constructed over her stern. The gear consisted of twenty-two ropes set across the deck at three-foot intervals, each rope having a 50-lb sand bag attached to either end. In January 1911 Eugene Ely landed safely on the deck coming to a halt after catching the last twelve ropes. This predates Dunning's demonstration by some six years and was much closer to the real thing.

The same pilot had earlier taken off from a platform that had been constructed over the bows of the American cruiser *Birmingham* so it would seem that single handedly he had made the case for flush deck aircraft carriers . . . if only someone would dispense with all that equipment between

Retrieving the wreckage

the two platforms!

The first step to be taken by the RN towards this end was to construct a flat deck on the after end of *Furious*. In the course of this work arrester gear similar to that used by Ely in 1911 was installed. Transverse wires fitted with sandbags at each end to add their weight to the stopping power of the wires were rigged. Fore and aft wires were also rigged about nine inches above the deck. Twin horns fitted to each aircraft's undercarriage were intended to engage these wires which would hold the aircraft on a straight line should it attempt to veer to one side of the deck after landing. The thought of landing a plane on this deck with the normal midship structures such as the bridge, funnel, etc. at the immediate end of the 'runway' must have given some cause for concern!

Furious underwent further modification in the course of which the after turret, mainmast and superstructure were all removed and replaced with a 300-foot long flight-deck beneath which was the hangar. Despite the length of the flight-deck, landing remained fraught with serious difficulties primarily caused because the flight-deck stopped well short of the bow and

HMS Furious, WWI. *She was described as an Aerodrome Ship*

therefore created a great deal of turbulence. These problems made it clear that future carriers just had to have a continuous full length flight-deck.

With a top speed of a little over thirty knots, *Furious* was a considerable improvement on most of the earlier carriers, but she had her teething troubles too and the overall result was a series of protracted flying trials which meant that throughout World War One the Grand Fleet had no effective aircraft carrier to operate with it.

Island Carriers had been proposed as early as 1909, 1912 and again in 1915 but the idea was too much for the Admiralty that had so many calls on its finances. A ship with a full-length flush deck was not to appear until September 1918 when HMS *Argus*, the world's first flush deck aircraft carrier, entered the service of the Royal Navy.

Argus was built on the hull of the Italian liner *Conte Rosso* which was purchased by the Admiralty in 1916 and launched in December 1917. She was given a 550-foot long flush deck in an attempt to overcome some of the landing problems that arose with her predecessors. The gases produced by the ship's engines were expelled by fans through horizontal ducts reaching well aft.

Not only were there two lifts for striking down the aircraft but the deck superstructure could be lowered to give a clear deck for flying operations. The hangar below decks was subdivided by fireproofed screens into four sections to accommodate the twenty aircraft she carried. Other areas were allocated to workshops, armament stores and so on.

Argus was fitted with a pair of fore and aft wires similar to those that had been fitted in *Furious*. Transverse wires and landing hooks were not yet part of her landing gear although a rope net was rigged forward to stop planes overrunning the deck and ending up in the sea under the bow. As the planes lacked brakes the rope barrier must have been a comforting addition.

In 1919, at last, *Hermes*, specifically designed as an aircraft carrier, was launched. The hull was constructed at Elswick in 1919 and then towed to Devonport for fitting out, which was completed in November 1924. She was the first ship in the world

HMS Hermes, *the first Royal Naval ship to be designed as an aircraft carrier, circa 1923*

to be specifically designed as an aircraft carrier and her design incorporated many of the lessons that had been so hard won in the past years. For her day *Hermes* was of a reasonable size, fast enough and with a wide enough radius of action to be able to operate with other naval vessels. Unfortunately her armament was limited and she had to rely on screening warships for her defence. It was to be some years before it was realised that the best defence for an aircraft carrier was in fact its own aircraft. That had to wait for all sorts of advances – larger carriers, better fighters, radar and doubtless many other improvements too. Although she was still in service at the time, *Hermes* played no part in the Pacific war as she was too old and too small to be of value to the Pacific Fleet.

Eagle was yet another conversion, this time it was the hull of the former Chilean battleship *Almirante Cochran* that was under construction in

1917 that was used. The *Almirante Cochran*'s stem was fitted with a ram as was quite usual in battle-ships of her day. When her conversion was completed she looked rather like an aircraft carrier above the waterline whilst below the waterline she resembled an ancient Greek Galley. She was equipped with lifts and a full-length flight-deck with an island to starboard and was commissioned in February 1924.

Courageous, commissioned in 1925, and *Glorious*, commissioned two years later, were virtually sister ships. They both had an upper flight-deck that ran from aft for about three-quarters of their length, which was intended to serve the needs of the heavier aircraft they carried; the torpedo, reconnaisance and spotter planes. Beneath this upper deck was a smaller flight-deck that ran from the interior of the ship forward and was intended to be used for flying-off the lighter fighter aircraft carried by these ships.

By the early 1930s the landing speed of carrier-borne aircraft was increasing as newer types came into service with the result that the friction type of arrester gear originally fitted to *Courageous* was becoming less than satisfactory and experiments had continued in order to improve the system. The main difficulty was the lack of control as the wire was pulled out when the aircraft's hook engaged it. The problem was finally solved by fitting *Courageous* with a hydraulic system during her refit at the end of 1932. This equipment was proved

in trials early the next year and was later fitted to other carriers.

By the early thirties the authorities were beginning to understand just how vulnerable lightly built aircraft carriers were and work was started on heavier and more powerful vessels like the *Ark Royal, Illustrious, Victorious, Formidable, Indomitable, Implacable* and *Indefatigable*, ships that were to play such a vital part in World War Two. These carriers broke new ground in many ways, large enough to take 70 or more aircraft, armoured flight-decks, a wide range of anti-aircraft armaments, a speed of about 30 knots, and at 23,000 tons with an overall length of about 750 feet, larger than anything that had gone before.

CHAPTER TWO

The Bureaucratic Battles

For something like twenty-five years the pioneers of the FAA had to contend with everything from indifference to open hostility from the many senior officers who could see little virtue in these new fangled contraptions called aeroplanes. And then, when converts were won in high places another battle had to be fought at the bureaucratic level to ensure that the control of its own air arm was in the hands of the RN and not the RAF. This sometimes bitter, bureaucratic power struggle was to rage for a good many years and doubtless retarded the earlier development of the Service.

The Royal Flying Corps was formed on 13 April 1912 and very shortly afterwards it was divided into two wings, Military and Naval, but the RFC retained responsibility for both forms of flying. Even at this early stage it was obvious that there was a measure of friction between the two services. The RFC was a land orientated service and lacked interest in matters nautical. However, they were in charge and not surprisingly the Naval Wing was relegated to a back seat. Some two years later, just one month before the outbreak of World War One the RN was given control of the Naval Wing and renamed it the Royal Naval Air Service. Under the impetus of war the RNAS began to expand, not only in the area of personnel and equipment but also in its field of operations.

The loss of the Naval Wing did not please the RFC and the Wing's expansion did nothing to improve matters. By 1916 the relations between the two air arms had become so bad that even the politicians became aware of it. Their response was typically political; they set up a committee.

An Air Board was appointed on 17 May 1916 in an attempt to bring some sense and harmony into what was fast becoming a chaotic situation. The Board was only advisory with no executive powers and not surprisingly it had very little success in

sorting out the disputes. For example, in August 1916 the Admiralty, without consulting the Air Board, persuaded the Treasury to sanction the spending of more than two million pounds on the expansion of the RNAS. This of course outraged Lord Curzon who headed the Air Board and he protested most vigorously to the Admiralty. The First Lord gave him a very salty reply to the effect that they had no intention of adjusting Naval policy to suit the Air Board. The Board did its best to fight back and proposed that the RNAS should be separated from Admiralty control with supply, design and finance invested in the Air Board. The First Lord's reply was terse and to the point, simply saying, 'I do not propose to discuss the constitution of the Admiralty. It was created some generations before the Air Board.'

In 1916 the Admiralty created a long-range bombing force and operated it from the French sector of the Allied front, attacking industrial targets far behind the German lines, a move not calculated to win the hearts and minds of the members of the Air Board! By November 1918 Naval aircraft had operated from the Dardanalles to East Africa, the Mediterranean and France.

With the end of the war it was made crystal clear that the hatchet had indeed been buried in a shallow, well-marked grave because on All Fools' Day 1918 (was there some significance in that date I wonder?) the RNAS was incorporated into the newly formed Royal Air Force and the Naval element was very quickly, drastically run down. From its very modest beginnings the RNAS ended World War One with almost 3,000 aircraft, more than 100 airships and between 55,000 and 65,000 officers and men. One year later the RNAS had been reduced by the RAF to a single spotter-reconnaissance squadron, part of a torpedo-bomber squadron and one flight each of fighters, seaplanes and flying boats!

On 4 December 1918 the Admiralty held a conference at which proposals for post-war naval aviation were discussed. It was decided that *Argus, Furious, Nairana, Pegasus, Vindex* and *Vindictive* were to be retained, with *Eagle* and *Hermes* completing their fitting-out some time in 1919. It was also agreed that all fully manned light cruisers should carry one light aircraft and battleships and battle cruisers carry two. Agreement was one thing, implementation was something else. Lacking the impetus of war, progress was very slow and many experienced observers felt that the Admiralty would be only too pleased to be rid of their problem child. The Board was still dominated by men who hankered after the 'glory of the big gun engagement' and were unable, or unwilling, to see a viable role for the air arm.

The desk-bound battle for control of the air arms of the three forces continued unabated. A snippet from the White Paper of 1919 mentioned almost as an afterthought that 'within the framework of the Royal Air Force there will be a small part of it trained to work with the Royal Navy.'

For the next nineteen years the ridiculous situation prevailed whereby planes in the service of the Royal Navy were controlled by a land-based, non-naval authority that clearly had no understanding of the needs of the Fleet nor the least wish to enlighten themselves in those matters. The Admiralty achieved the first small step back to the control of its own air arm in 1921 when it was agreed that Naval Officers could be trained as Observers. Later this was to provide a foundation on which to rebuild the naval air arm.

In 1924 a further compromise was reached when the FAA of the RAF was created under the operational control of the Admiralty. The Navy and the Royal Marines would provide seventy per cent of the pilots and all the Observers and Telegraphist Air Gunners. Naval aircraft were to be built to Admiralty requirements by the Air Ministry and the RAF was to continue to be responsible for administration, accommodation ashore, training facilities and for the balance of the pilots and all maintenance staff. Naval Officers who qualified as pilots were still required to hold a commission in the RAF since only officers with Royal Air Force

commissions were allowed to fly. This dual control worked only through the good will and the good sense of the officers and men of the two services.

Compromise is obviously no way to run a war machine and in 1938 the decision was taken to give the Admiralty absolute control of its own air arm complete with the necessary shore bases. Not surprisingly the Navy lacked sufficient numbers of trained ground staff and in a move that seemed to herald a new era of co-operation the RAF allowed volunteers to transfer to the Navy and loaned an additional 1,500 senior air artificers, fitters and mechanics. At the same time the Navy started training maintenance ratings who gradually freed the RAF NCOs. The airfield at Lee-on-Solent became HMS *Daedalus*, the headquarters and the barracks of the Fleet Air Arm ashore.

The title 'The Fleet Air Arm of the Royal Air Force' obviously could not stand and it was decided that it would be changed to the Air Branch. In practice the Navy never dropped 'The Fleet Air Arm' as a title and in 1953 it was officially re-adopted. One further common sense change remained to be accepted and on 24 May 1939 the Admiralty was given operational control of Coastal Command. Under this arrangement the Admiralty stated the tasks that were to be carried out by Coastal Command aircraft whether they belonged to the RAF or the RN. It took the Navy twenty years to regain control of its air arm and, at times, the fight had been a hard and an extremely bitter one.

Because the FAA had been under the control of the RAF and had been treated as a poor relation for so long, when war broke out in 1939 it found itself ill-equipped for the tasks that were to be demanded of it. Many of the aircraft the FAA was required to use were all too often adaptations of semi-obsolescent land-based RAF planes which did not necessarily make them suitable for work with the Fleet. There are many reasons why planes need to be specifically designed for work at sea; to give just one example, an undercarriage that has been built to withstand the stresses of landing an aircraft on a concrete runway or a grass field could well prove to be inadequate for the more rigorous conditions

A Gloster Sea Gladiator, obselete but welcome

often met when landing a plane on the heaving deck of an aircraft carrier at sea. The Seafire was a case in point. The Spitfire was modified by adding an arrester hook and was then called a Seafire. Unfortunately the undercarriage of the Spitfire was too narrow and not strong enough for carrier work and resulted in a significant number of accidents. Fine plane that the Spitfire was, its range was scarcely sufficient for operations at sea.

The Gloucester Sea Gladiator came into service with the Fleet in 1938. It was yet another RAF cast-off, this time a modification of a totally obsolescent RAF machine. The simple fact that the Navy was glad to have this outmoded plane is an indication of the paucity of its equipment at this time. One wonders why the RAF fought so long and so hard to retain control of the FAA when it showed so little interest in equipping it for the specialised role it had to fulfil. One is also given to wonder how

many lives were lost unnecessarily because of the inadequate equipment forced upon the FAA by the power struggle that dominated its formative years.

Fortunately for Britain, whilst the RAF and the RN were bickering over who should control the Navy's air arm the Americans had a more realistic understanding of the purpose of air power. They had no equivalent of the our RAF. Both the army and the navy had their own air forces, a system that worked well for a long time. They had equipped the United States Navy Air Force with a real understanding of the function of a naval air arm and the FAA was to be able to take advantage of this fact.

Once the RN had gained control of its air arm it

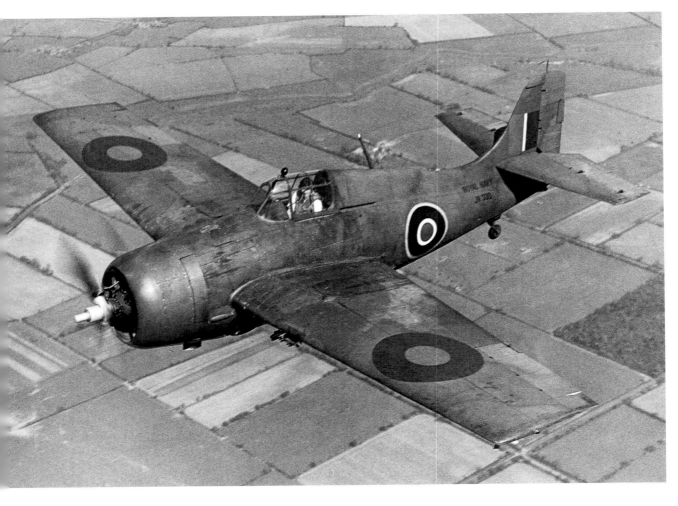

The Grumman Martlet, later renamed the Wildcat – a USN fighter supplied to the Royal Navy under the Lend-Lease Agreement

sought help from the USA and quite soon the FAA was able to purchase from the United States aircraft that had been designed specifically for service at sea. Planes like the Avenger and the Hellcat were bought in their hundreds and helped to overcome some of the deficiencies created by the years of deliberate neglect.

A few British-built aircraft of this vintage gave a surprisingly good account of themselves. Prominent among them of course was the Swordfish, affectionately known in the Service as the Stringbag. This wood and fabric biplane was due to be replaced when war broke out and was still in first line service six years later when the war came to an end. Its successes during World War

Two were legion. To mention just two, the night raid on the Italian Fleet at Taranto that put a major part of that Fleet out of action and the numerous operations that contributed so much to the sinking of *Bismarck* in the Atlantic. It was said that German gunners could not believe that a plane would be flying so slowly – top speed about 135 knots – and therefore gave too much aim off and missed. A happy thought, if true! Certainly anti-aircraft fire that hit a Swordfish would often pass through the

fabric and timber construction without inflicting more than superficial damage.

Another successful plane of this vintage was the Walrus, an unlikely-looking aircraft if ever there was one. The Walrus was an amphibian biplane with a radial pusher engine and two open cockpits with a third enclosed. The undercarriage was wound up and down by hand with no fancy electronics to confirm that it was locked in the chosen position; the thump that rang out when the wheels were either up or down was confirmation enough. The cockpits were connected by tunnels that usually contained the detritus appropriate to its years of service! Its Service nickname, the Shagbat, somehow seemed so appropriate for this plane that always made me think of dinosaurs whenever I clapped eyes on one! Nevertheless the Shagbat was not an aircraft to be underestimated. There is on record an account of an air/sea rescue that was

A Supermarine Walrus catapulted into flight from HMS Resolution

carried out in the North Sea in the course of World War Two when, having landed and picked up the ditched aircrew, it was found that the sea was too rough to allow the Walrus to take off. Nothing loath, the plane was safely taxied some forty miles back to its base. On another occasion, a Walrus that was in the air when the disastrous Russian convoy PQ17 was ordered to scatter, not surprisingly failed to find its parent ship but landed close to another escort vessel. Its crew was taken off and the plane was towed more than 400 miles to the Russian port that was their rescuer's destination!

HMS Newcastle's Walrus being hoisted onto the catapult after landing on the sea nearby

CHAPTER THREE

World War One

War with Germany commenced on 4 August 1914 and for the RNAS it started with a large measure of confusion about just what its role should be. This is not surprising, I suppose, in a service so young whose development had been dogged by such controversy and confusion.

Initially the RNAS had been given the responsibility for the air defence of the whole country but had been instructed to keep reconnaissance flights to a minimum to avoid unnecessary wear and tear on the planes involved. This was all changed on 8 August after a German minelayer had planted mines around the Norfolk coast. The Admiralty now required the RNAS to mount a complete coastal patrol from Kinnairds Head, about forty-five miles north of Glasgow, to Dungeness in Kent with orders to report any ships, submarines or aircraft they spotted. Two squadrons of the RFC were to assist, but not for long; they were soon needed elsewhere. Once the two RFC squadrons were withdrawn there were not sufficient planes to give the cover the Admiralty had originally required. It was decided therefore to restrict the coastal patrols to dawn and dusk and to restrict the coastal area to be covered to that between the Thames Estuary and the Humber.

For much of August naval aircraft flew additional patrols over the area Ostend to Kent to give some protection to the ships transporting the British Expeditionary Force to Europe. At the same time two airships patrolled the Dover Straits.

Winston Churchill pressed hard and successfully for a considerable expansion in the numbers of planes to be supplied to the RNAS. Many of those supplied were existing designs but the Admiralty also asked that there should be a number of float-plane fighters and planes capable of carrying and delivering a torpedo. At this stage of development the best that could be hoped for was a plane that could carry a 14-inch torpedo. The price the Navy had to pay for these planes was the loss of five airships that were about to be built.

To a large extent the Germans had placed their faith in their Zeppelins – large rigid airships – and in 1914 they were building them as fast as they could. In an effort to counter this, four RNAS aircraft flew from an airfield near Antwerp on 22 September to attack the airship sheds at Dusseldorf and Cologne. The only plane to find its target failed to do any damage. A second raid was mounted on 8 October and this one was more successful, destroying a Zeppelin and its shed. A further abortive raid was carried out on the airship sheds at Frichshafen.

So far the raids had been carried out by RNAS planes from airfields. The German Zeppelin sheds at Cuxhaven were to be the target of the next raid but they were beyond the reach of land-based aircraft and so it was decided to use carriers to get seaplanes within range of their targets. On 25 October the seaplane carriers with their escort were in place but the raid had to be aborted as it was raining so hard that the planes were unable to get airborne. The scheme was revived in December 1914. Nine Short seaplanes from *Empress*, *Engadine* and *Riviera*, three from each ship, were to be used.

The three seaplane carriers and their escort sailed on 24 December in two groups. *Empress* and the light cuiser *Undaunted* with four destroyers made up one group and *Engadine* and *Riviera* with the light cruiser *Arethusa* and four destroyers the other. The two groups made their way to a position twelve miles north of Heligoland which they reached by 0600 the next day.

At the same time the Grand Fleet took station in the middle of the North Sea with ten submarines deployed closer to the enemy coast in the hope that

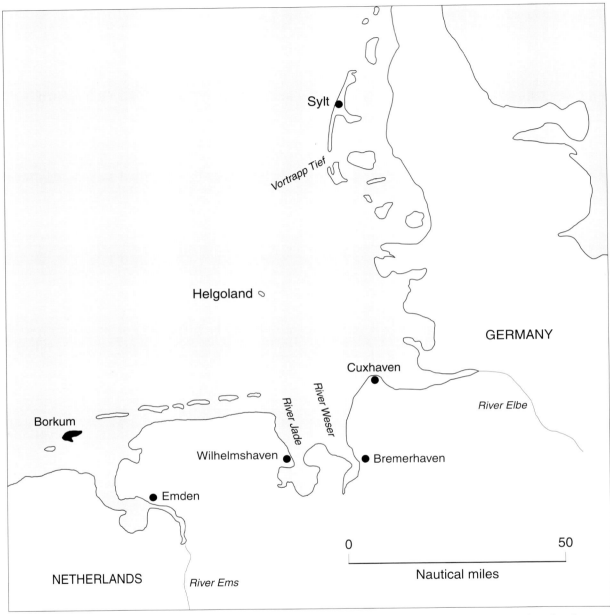

the German High Seas Fleet would venture out and might perhaps be brought to action. On Christmas Eve the carriers were escorted from Harwich by the two cruisers and eight destroyers to a position twelve miles north of Heligoland where the seaplanes were to be launched at 0600 the next day. In the course of the approach to the launching position the British force was spotted by

Heligoland – the first ever air strike carried out by planes transported to the scene by ship was conducted in this area

a U boat and after daybreak when they were in position they were seen again, this time from Heligoland. The Germans responded by launching Zeppelin L6 and then hauling L5 from her shed and preparing her for take-off; a solitary seaplane also took off and headed for the British ships.

Meanwhile the RNAS seaplanes were lowered to the water. Seven of the nine aircraft in the strike force lifted off and headed for Cuxhaven but two others failed to become airborne and were left behind.

When the German seaplane arrived over the escort vessels she dropped four bombs on the ships but missed. In return every gun that could be brought to bear from rifles to main armament was fired at the seaplane. A number of hits were registered and although the pilot was able to nurse his plane back to his base the damage inflicted was such that the plane was written off.

The airship L6 arrived on the scene and dropped a 110-lb bomb that was aimed at *Riviera* but missed. Again everything that could be brought to bear was fired, this time at the Zeppelin. *Undaunted* managed to explode a 6-inch shell close enough to L6 to persuade her that things were unhealthy for her and she returned to the Schillig Roads to report and then on to Nordholz to land where she found that she had acquired a number of bullet holes.

It had taken about an hour to prepare the second airship for flight and when she was airborne she crossed paths with three of the RNAS seaplanes on their way to their target. Shortly after crossing the coast the British aircraft encountered thick fog with the result that just one of them found the Zeppelin base at Nordholz. This seaplane attacked the installation that produced the hydrogen for the dirigibles but failed to do any real damage.

Of the seven RNAS planes that started out, two returned to their parent ship, one landed near a destroyer of the escort group, one made a forced landing due to engine trouble and the pilot was picked up by the crew of a Dutch fishing vessel. The remaining three aircraft ran out of fuel and alighted on the sea, their pilots being rescued by two nearby British submarines.

This, the first ever air strike by planes that had been transported by sea close to their target was, on the face of it, a failure but these were early days and much needed to be learned. The pilots were convinced they could have succeeded if they had not run into dense fog and lost their way. Certainly

the Germans could not claim to have driven off the strike force and it would have been interesting to see the result if the weather had not been so unhelpful.

Not only was this the first air strike of its kind but it was also the first time ships had fought off an air attack and it was obvious ships could deal with Zeppelin attacks just as long as they had room to manoeuvre.

The middle of January 1915 found the newly commissioned seaplane carrier *Ark Royal* on her way to the Dardanelles complete with eight aircraft. The performance of the planes was quite inadequate for the tasks they were to be allotted: if the sea was choppy or if there was a flat calm they were incapable of taking off. In the higher temperatures their maximum ceiling was such as to expose them to ground fire which made it unreasonably dangerous for them when they undertook the role of spotting for the fall of the ships' gunfire. Despite these deficiencies the aircraft made themselves useful with reconnaissance flights and others in which they attempted to locate mines; they also did some spotting for the Fleet but because of the limit on their ceiling it remained dangerous work.

The Admiral in charge, Admiral Carden, made an urgent request for more suitable planes and by the end of March eighteen RNAS planes had arrived and began to operate from an airfield that had been constructed on the island of Tenedos. At the same time the Admiralty had a merchant ship converted to enable it to handle a balloon which was to be used for observation and spotting for the ships' gunners. Its success was such that other ships were similarly converted and used to good effect in the Dardanalles campaign.

The balloon ships and the handful of planes from Tenedos and *Ark Royal* continued to give support to the ground forces throughout the campaign. Towards the end of May a German submarine arrived in the area and it was considered too dangerous to expose the *Ark* with her limited speed to the possibility of attack and so she was used in protected positions; harbours and the like. About three weeks later *Ben-My-Chree* arrived to support *Ark Royal*: she was smaller and faster than the *Ark* and it was considered safe for her to move more freely.

On 12 August 1915 Flight Commander C.K. Edmonds from *Ben-My-Chree* sighted, and torpedoed from the air, a Turkish merchantman that had been put out of action earlier by the British submarine E14. Not content with being the first man in the world to torpedo a ship from the air, albeit a sitting duck, he repeated the feat on the 17th when he sank a Turkish supply ship off Ak Bashi Liman, this time without the aid of a submarine. Aircraft of this vintage did not have enough power to carry a full-size torpedo and were forced to use a 14-inch torpedo, small perhaps but still a powerful weapon. The Short 184 used in this attack could only lift even this small torpedo if it reduced its supply of petrol to the point where just enough was carried for three-quarters of an hour's flying time.

Squadron Commander Bell Davies flying a single-seater Nieuport fighter landed behind Turkish lines to pick up Flight Sub-Lieutenant Smylie who had been shot down. With Turkish troops advancing on them, Smylie first destroyed his aircraft and then secured himself to the struts of Davies' plane which took off with its additional load and landed safely back at base.

Another remarkable and perhaps unique first was achieved by Flt Lt Dacre flying a Short 184, again from the *Ben-My-Chree*. An engine defect caused him to make an emergency landing on the water. After he had carried out the necessary repairs he was taxying on the water prior to taking off when he spotted and torpedoed a Turkish tug without taking to the air.

Unconsciously in keeping with the spirit of the aircrews were the Standing Orders for number 3 Wing issued on 4 December 1915. They stated that pilots were '... to be armed with a revolver or pistol and carry binoculars and a safety device, either a waistcoat, patent lifebelt or a petrol can'! Observers were always to carry a rifle but they were warned not to open fire '... until you are sure it is a German. You must on no account open fire until you have seen the markings on the enemy plane.'

In September 1914 a German light cruiser, *Königsberg*, had retreated up the River Rufiji in what is now Tanzania in east Africa, roughly seventy miles south of Dar es Salaam. Shore batteries had been established at the mouth of the river and mines had been laid in the approaches. The RN sank a ship in the mouth of the river in an attempt to ensure that *Königsberg* stayed there but there were doubts as to the total efficiency of the measures and a blockade had to be maintained to make sure that she did not break out and go on a commerce-raiding spree in the South Atlantic. While the blockade had to be maintained ships that could well be used elsewhere were tied up. As she was out of sight to the blockading force it was decided to try to put her out of action from the air. To this end two Curtiss flying boats were purchased in South Africa and shipped in the Armed Merchant Cruiser *Kinfauns Castle* complete with their former pilot, to the mouth of the River Rufiji. The pilot was given a commission in the RNAS to make it all legal.

It required five flights to locate *Königsberg* in the delta of the river. Unfortunately on the fifth flight engine failure made it necessary for the pilot to force-land which wrecked the machine and caused the pilot to be taken prisoner. A request was sent to England for seaplanes to bomb the enemy ship. In February 1915 two Sopwith seaplanes reached the blockading force but it was quickly found that the high temperatures made the planes so inefficient as to be almost useless. In April three Short seaplanes arrived and their performance was a little better. They found *Königsberg* but as they could climb no higher than 600 feet they were too vulnerable to rifle fire to be used to attack it. Four more planes were sent out and this time one of them managed to climb to 6,000 feet from where a bombing run was made on the German ship but no hits were registered.

Two months later two monitors, *Mersey* and *Severn*, joined the blockading force and once they were made ready they opened fire on *Königsberg* with the aircraft spotting for them. One of the aircraft was shot down and one of the monitors was damaged but *Königsberg* was destroyed. Although their bombing was ineffective their ability to locate the enemy ship which the attacking force could not see, and their spotting for the guns of the monitors made the success possible.

Flying over Ostend in a Morane Parasole on 7 June 1915 Flight Sub-Lieutenant R.A.J. Warnford spotted Zeppelin LZ37 flying high above him. He gave chase and climbed until he was above his quarry which was flying at 10,000 feet. For planes of that day this was a considerable height. Having climbed above the LZ37 Warnford released his 20-lb bombs which hit the airship. The resulting explosion of the highly inflammable gas with which the Zeppelin was inflated threw Warnford's monoplane onto its back. Warnford was able to regain control but a fuel pipe had been broken and he was forced to land behind enemy lines. He repaired the damaged fuel line, took off again and returned to his base at Dunkirk. For this successful attack Warnford was awarded the RNAS's first Victoria Cross. Sadly he was killed in a flying accident a short while later. The remainder of the aircraft from Warnford's squadron later bombed the Zeppelin installation at Evère and destroyed the dirigible LZ38 complete with the shed that housed it. On 22 November 1915 a second RNAS pilot was awarded a Victoria Cross.

Zeppelin activity in and around the North Sea was being stepped up as more of them came into service and RNAS aircraft were made responsible for finding and attacking them. No fewer than seventeen sorties were made by German airships against targets in Britain between March and the beginning of July 1915. Naval planes had little success against them as the raids were made at night making it somewhere between difficult and impossible for the defending planes to see their quarry.

Seaplane carriers attempted on four occasions to stage raids on the Zeppelin bases hoping to catch the dirigibles in their sheds but each time the state of the sea made it impossible for the seaplanes to get airborne or if they did manage to take off they encountered thick fog either en route or over their targets. Naturally the 'I told you so' brigade made the most of these failures to bolster their arguments.

The Sopwith Schneider seaplane came into service with the RNAS early in 1915 and its speed and ability to climb was such that it had a realistic chance of catching a Zeppelin in flight. *Ben-My-Chree* was fitted with a launching platform on her forward deck. The intention was to have the carrier cruise in the North Sea and when an airship was spotted a plane would be flown off to attack it. On 11 May the one and only attempt to fly off a Sopwith Schneider from this platform proved that it was too short to do its job. The pilot's comments do not appear in the report!

Instead of making a longer platform, and in the face of all the evidence, it was still hoped that seaplanes would be able to get off the water once a Zeppelin was spotted, and to this end a number of other vessels were modified to accommodate a plane or two, but the weather frustrated most of the attempts. Fortunately for its morale and reputation, at about this time RNAS planes in Belgium destroyed three German airships which was hailed as a great achievement. Good news it may have been but it was using aircraft as land-based machines, not as an adjunct to the Fleet.

Despite the difficulties experienced by float planes that attempted to get airborne in the rough waters of the North Sea it was decided to try yet another approach which ignored the fragility of the seaplanes then in service. The plan was for *Engadine* and *Riviera* to cruise in the vicinity of the Ems and Borkum in the hope that German airships would be sent out to deal with the intruders. The planes could then be launched to attack them.

As the carriers were approaching their chosen position unbeknown to them they were seen and reported by a German submarine. Six Zeppelins were ordered into the air at daybreak to attack the small naval force. So far everything was going to plan. Those aboard the carriers were not aware of the German dispositions and so, as planned, they lowered three reconnaissance planes to the water. One plane had engine trouble and had to be hoisted back inboard but the other two climbed away to trail their coats in front of the enemy defences in an effort to get the Zeppelins into the air where they would be drawn away towards the guns of the three Sopwith Schneiders that were about to be launched.

Soon four of the six Zeppelins were seen approaching the group of carriers and another was soon to be on the scene. In response the three Schneider seaplanes were launched into a rough sea; two smashed their floats and were lost before they could lift off and the third was so badly damaged by the seas that all thought of getting off the water had to be abandoned. The Zeppelins were driven off by gunfire from the ships. Of the two reconnaissance planes, one returned safely and the other lost its way and had to ditch. Its pilot was was picked up by a Dutch fishing boat only to be interned by the Netherlands authorities.

Both sides in this mini-conflict were pleased with the outcome. The Germans were convinced they had beaten off an attack, but the British knew their basic scheme had worked only to be frustrated by the frailty of the aircraft then in use. At last this lesson was learned by the RN and it was to be at least six months before any more offensive operations would be attempted by seaplanes in the open sea.

Despite the considerable increase in the numbers of planes and airships that were made available to the RNAS in the first year of the war there was little to show for it, certainly in Home Waters; the land-based planes on the continent were the exception. Further afield, at the Dardanalles and in east Africa they had a little more success, particularly in the realm of spotting for the guns of the Fleet. The great weaknesses were still the same, the fragility of the seaplanes in rough seas and the inability to launch and recover aircraft directly from a flight-deck.

Throughout 1915 the strength of the RNAS continued to grow. A replacement for the Sopwith Schneider appeared, named the Sopwith Baby, a fighter seaplane capable of 100 miles an hour and with a ceiling of 10,000 feet

Improved torpedo planes that had a much increased range and the ability to carry an 18-inch torpedo were coming onto the scene, but they were still seaplanes.

In January 1916 two raids involving *Vindex* were mounted against the Zeppelin base at Hage but both had to be aborted. The first because of dense fog and the other because U boat activity threatened the safety of *Vindex*.

The Royal Flying Corps undertook the responsiblity for the defence of Britain in February 1916 but the RNAS retained the task of tackling German dirigibles over the sea.

German battle cruisers supported by the German High Seas Fleet bombarded Lowestoft on 25 April. The Admiralty had prior knowledge of this raid and moved as many planes into the area as possible. When the bombardment started planes took off from Felixstowe and Yarmouth and bombed the German ships without success. A U boat was attacked and to show their impartiality the British aircraft also attacked a British submarine!

A Zeppelin reported the approach of the Harwich Force. Shortly afterwards she was tackled by two BE2c aircraft from Yarmouth; unfortunately the bombs they dropped missed and the Rankin Darts, specially designed for use against Zeppelins, had no visible effect and she moved away apparently unharmed. Other planes from Yarmouth chased two airships for sixty-five miles out into the North Sea but they too did their quarry no harm.

The attempts by the RNAS aircraft to bomb the German ships were ineffective because their aim was poor and the bombs were too small to do serious damage to armoured vessels. We know now that torpedoes have a better chance of doing significant damage to a moving warship than do bombs, especially small bombs. There were some aircraft available for torpedo dropping at both Felixstowe and Yarmouth but they were not used.

Towards the end of March *Vindex* was involved in a raid on Tondern which failed to destroy any Zeppelins but it did bring the German High Seas Fleet out into the open. This event prompted the planners to set up a second raid for the beginning of May, ostensibly to destroy German dirigibles and installations ashore but with the primary purpose of enticing the German High Seas Fleet out so that it could be brought to action by units of the Grand Fleet. *Vindex* and *Engadine* were to be escorted by the First Light Cruiser Squadron and a screen of sixteen destroyers. This was to be the bait. Submarines were to be in position to attack the German Fleet if it came out. Mine fields were laid in strategic positions and the Grand Fleet was to be further out but in a position where they could intervene if all went to plan. The two carriers embarked a total of eleven of the new Sopwith Baby seaplanes. These aircraft were basically fighters but they could also carry two 65-lb bombs. In what appeared to be first class conditions the eleven planes were lowered to the sea ready for take-off. Eight planes damaged their propellers by striking the chop of the sea and had to be hoisted inboard again, one flew into the mast of a destroyer and plunged into the sea, another had to return with engine problems and the remaining aircraft flew on to Tondern, dropped its bombs on the sheds but missed and then flew back to its carrier.

Zeppelin L7 took to the air at Tondern and started a search for the ships that had brought the aircraft. Once the crew of the airship spotted the British escort force they turned for home but were fired upon by the ships. _Galatea_ and _Phaeton_ gave chase but the Zeppelin drew away from them until a very long-range shot from one of _Galatea_'s 6-inch guns struck the dirigible and set it afire. The survivors were rescued by a British submarine that was on hand. The destruction of L7 saved the raid from being a complete failure but yet again it has to be said that the failure was the fault of inadequate equipment rather than the concept.

Throughout 1916 the Admiralty encouraged a programme of building rigid airships that were to be stationed around the coast. These lighter-than-air craft were inferior to the airships used by the Germans and it was not until two events occurred that improvements could be made to bring them up to something approaching the quality of the German airships. Early in May _Agamemnon_ brought down the Zeppelin LZ85 at Salonica. The wreckage was recovered and shipped home in one of the Kite-Balloon ships that was serving there. At about the same time a Swiss citizen who had been working on the design of dirigibles in Germany made his way to Britain and offered his services to the Admiralty. With his help it was possible to improve the lift available to the airships under construction by some three and a half tons but their endurance was still not enough to allow them

to be used for the longer scouting and raiding sorties that were commonplace to the Zeppelins.

The completion of _Campania_'s refit allowed her to rejoin the Grand Fleet in April 1917. It had been the practice to launch fighter planes from her flying-off deck by mounting the seaplanes on a trolley which was left behind when the aircraft became airborne: now with the deck increased in length to 200 feet she was able to launch the heavier reconnaissance seaplanes in the same way. On their return the planes had to alight on the sea and if it was rough the aircraft might well be a write-off. Hopefully the crew would be picked up.

Campania had also been fitted with a balloon and the gear required to handle it. The intention was to use the balloon for spotting the fall of shot for the guns of the Fleet and to give an overall picture of the battle area. Although she was ready in time, circumstances dictated that she should take no part in the Battle of Jutland and in fact the part played by the RNAS was negligible and did nothing to influence the course of the engagement.

The Germans had almost doubled the size of their newest Zeppelins to the point where they could carry three and a half tons of bombs at 64 knots for 1,200 miles. Their ceiling of 17,700 feet was beyond the range of most anti-aircraft fire and greater than many contemporary fighters, which, if they could reach those heights, would take up to an hour to get there and not be in a fit shape to inflict damage on the Super Zeppelin.

Manxman, a passenger ferry, had been converted along the lines of _Vindex_ and came into service in January 1917. Her intended complement of planes was four scouting seaplanes and four Sopwith Baby seaplanes which were to serve as fighters. _Manxman_'s captain asked that the Sopwith Baby seaplanes should be replaced by the Sopwith Pup aeroplanes. He argued that the Sopwith Pup was one of the few aeroplanes that had the performance needed to reach and destroy the latest Zeppelins. The Pups could be flown off _Manxman_'s deck and when their task was completed, if they could not reach the shore, they would ditch in the sea close to the parent vessel and if it was the pilot's lucky day he would be picked up. His point was that the Pups would

A Sopwith Baby seaplane

always be able to get airborne but seaplanes could become airborne only in the most favourable conditions. Furthermore it was quite usual for seaplanes to break up on landing in anything but ideal conditions so the pilots of the Pups would be no worse off than most of the seaplanes' pilots. His final piece of logic was simply that the loss of one aircraft would be a small price to pay for the destruction of one Zeppelin. His arguments were accepted and the Sopwith Baby seaplanes were swapped for Sopwith Pups. Once this had been accepted it was recommended that *Campania*

should also exchange her six fighter seaplanes.

In the United States, H12 Curtiss flying boats had been under development for a year or more and in April 1917 they came into service with the RNAS. Based at Felixstowe and Yarmouth these flying boats were much stronger than the current breed of seaplane and could safely operate in much rougher conditions. Larger than the

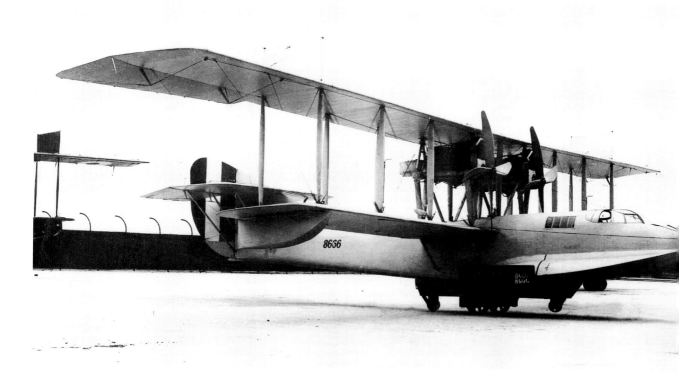

A Curtiss H12 flying boat. Its 8 hour endurance allowed it
to be land-based

seaplanes they had an endurance of eight hours and represented a real challenge to the German airships. Their first success came on 14 May when a Curtiss shot down a Zeppelin that was escorting a group of minesweepers off Terschelling. A second was destroyed by an H12 Curtiss flying boat on 5 June and thereafter the Germans ordered their Zeppelins to operate at or above 13,000 feet, despite which further successes followed. These huge airships were not difficult to shoot down once an aircraft armed with a machine-gun and incendiary ammunition was within range; the difficulty was getting there.

June 1917 found the light cruiser _Yarmouth_ back in service after a refit in the course of which a flying-off platform for a Sopwith Pup aeroplane had been built over the forward turret. The platform was so designed that it could stay in place if the cruiser went into action. Trials showed it to be so successful that it was decided to build similar platforms on four other light cruisers.

Furious joined the Grand Fleet in the July of 1917.

As a conventional warship she was a formidable weapon, being armed with one 18-inch and eleven 5.5-inch guns, however she was more than a heavily armed warship. She had been fitted with a flying-off deck forward which, with a length of 228 feet by 50 feet, was bigger than anything before and with a speed of thirty knots or more could stop to retrieve her seaplanes and then catch up with the rest of the fleet, something that had been lacking in previous seaplane carriers. Her hangar beneath the flying-off deck had room for four Short two-seater seaplanes and six Sopwith Pup aeroplanes. With no landing-on facility the Pups were strictly a 'use and ditch' solution but at least they would be able to get airborne in most conditions.

When Commander Dunning demonstrated that it was possible to land on the forward flight-deck of *Furious* in August 1917 it proved to be a turning point in aircraft carrier design. No longer did designers think in terms of seaplanes but they looked to the possibility of aircraft landing on the flight-deck after an approach from astern of the carrier. Seventeen battleships and light cruisers had been fitted with gear to let them handle balloons but it was soon realised that they were a mixed blessing. Whilst they certainly extended the distance that an observer could see it was quickly realised by the enemy that if there was a balloon in the air there had to be a ship beneath it and where there was one ship there were bound to be others.

Trials had been carried out with non-rigid airships and they had been found wanting. They were vulnerable to enemy fighters and lacked sufficient range and speed to allow them to co-operate with the Fleet at sea; later a role was found for them in the defence of convoys.

The rigid airships that were coming into service were still far from satisfactory; their range could not get them across the North Sea and their ceiling was limited to less than 3,000 feet. Even the German Zeppelins' vastly superior performance could not protect them from fighter attack, and enthusiasm in the Royal Navy for lighter-than-air craft waned, just as the performance of heavier-than-air craft was improving.

By mid-1917 the Navy was just beginning to get on top of the U boat problem and the RNAS was able to play a useful part. It was the advent of the flying boats that made this possible. They had a range that would allow them to patrol as far as a line from the Cherbourg peninsula to Cornwall, and a load-carrying capacity that ensured they could be armed well enough to deal with a U boat should they spot one. To the north and east of Britain seaplanes and flying boats patrolled an area enclosed by a line from Peterhead in the north to Rotterdam. The Irish Sea was included in this protected area with its northern limit being being defined by a line from the Isle of Mull to north-west Ireland. Airships were used to extend the patrolled area to a line from Brest to south-west Ireland. Within this

area, in the three months from July to September 1917, flying boats sank four U boats, a seaplane sank one and another was sunk in a combined effort by destroyers and ships with kite balloons aboard.

Blimps were too slow and too visible to be able to surprise U boats on the surface and would probably never qualify as U boat killers. However, they were very successful in hovering over the spot at which a U boat had submerged and forcing it to stay submerged long enough for the convoy to escape.

On 18 July 1918 seven Sopwith Camels were flown from *Furious* to attack the airship sheds at Tondern, yet again. One Camel developed engine trouble and returned to *Furious*. The remaining six aircraft reached their target and swept in low over the two sheds, dropping a total of twelve 50-lb bombs. Both sheds erupted in flames, destroying the two Zeppelins L54 and L60. On the way back one plane ran out of fuel and the pilot was drowned when he attempted to ditch. Three Camels landed in Denmark which was neutral and so the aircrews were interned. The remaining two aircraft made it back and landed close to the destroyer *Violent* and were picked up. This proved to be the only successful carrier-launched air raid of World War One.

Ashore in France and elsewhere the RNAS had made a valuable contribution to victory but this land-based role was largely one that, perhaps, should have been left to the Royal Flying Corps.

The war ended in November 1918 and it is fair to say that the RNAS at sea made little difference to its outcome, which in no way belittles the courage of those involved. The Service was in its infancy as was the equipment it was required to use. The really positive outcome of it all was that lessons for the future were learned by some but sadly not by all. In the years between the wars the RNAS was to be badly hampered by bureaucratic jealousy, ignorance and politicking by power-hungry people who seemed to care little for the Service or the future safety of the country.

CHAPTER FOUR

The Start of World War Two

The first months of World War Two became known as the 'Phoney War' because of the lack of activity on both sides, both on the ground and in the air. However there was nothing phoney about the activity at sea. U boats were active from the very start and British losses were high. The dangers posed by the German U boats in World War One were remembered by the Admiralty and to help counter this menace *Courageous* and *Hermes* were assigned to patrol the South-Western Approaches and *Ark Royal* the North-Western Approaches. Eleven days into the war *Ark Royal* was attacked with a torpedo west of the Hebridean Isles by U39, which came close to sinking her. *Ark Royal*'s destroyer escort counter-attacked and sank the U boat. Three days later *Courageous* was less fortunate. On 17 September 1939 she was struck by three torpedoes fired by U29 and 481 men were lost when she sank, along with the planes of two Swordfish Squadrons.

These two events made it only too clear that without adequate protection from support vessels, aircraft carriers, as currently operated, were sitting ducks. There is no question that from the start the enemy knew the value of aircraft and well understood the threat that carrier-borne planes posed for their U boat fleet. An aircraft carrier that is steaming on a straight course to allow aircraft to take off or to land on and is without adequate protection from other vessels must be a submarine captain's dream target! As a consequence the remaining carriers were withdrawn from this exposed anti-submarine work. Later in the war they were to be more than capable of taking care of themselves.

On 26 September 1939 the Fleet was making for Scapa Flow with three Dornier 18 flying boats shadowing its progress. Lieutenant B.S. McEwen RN in a Skua from *Ark Royal*'s 803 Squadron tackled them and shot one down; the first enemy

Heinkel 111, a German twin-engined bomber of WWII

aircraft to be shot down in World War Two. Although the remaining two Dorniers retired they had reported the position of the Fleet and at about 1400 that afternoon the attack came in the form of several Heinkel 111 bombers. Their principal target was the *Ark Royal,* a backhanded compliment if you like, to the threat posed to them by the aircraft carrier. One bomb that was heading for the bows of the carrier fell into the sea close by because of the rapid evasive action ordered by the captain of *Ark Royal*. This bomb, which could have caused so much damage, did no more than give the *Ark* a sound shaking. The German pilot, Adolphe Franke had other ideas and claimed to have sunk the carrier. This claim was supported by a report by a German reconnaissance aircraft that later spotted two British cruisers and believed them to be the two battleships that were sailing in company with *Ark Royal* when she was attacked. As there was no carrier with the 'battleships' it was assumed that she had sunk as a result of the bombing attack. This was the first time the Germans claimed to have sunk *Ark Royal* but it was not by any means to be the last! The German pilot was rewarded with promotion to the rank of *Oberleutnant* and awarded the Iron Cross. There is no record of which I am aware of his subsequent demotion nor of the requirement to return the Iron Cross when it was confirmed that he had not in fact sunk the ship!

Very early in the Second World War it became apparent that commerce raiders that had almost certainly taken up position well before the outbreak of war, were at work in the South Atlantic. *Ark Royal,* in company with the battlecruiser *Renown* and four destroyers, formed Force K, whose brief was to find and deal with the raiders and their supply ships. The heavyweight nature of this group was due to the knowledge that at least one German pocket battleship was likely to be part of this commerce raiding force.

The supply vessel *Altmark* was sighted in October but as she was incorrectly identified she managed to escape. She was later cornered in Norwegian waters and a considerable number of Allied merchant seamen were rescued from internment. A few weeks later SS *Uhenfels*, another supply ship, was spotted and soon afterwards was captured and taken as a prize by destroyers of the Royal Navy.

It became increasingly apparent that a powerful armed raider was at work in the South Atlantic but despite the best efforts of the crews of the *Ark*'s Skuas and Swordfish the raider escaped detection. We all accept that an ocean is a very large place but the sheer immensity of the oceans of the world escapes most people's understanding until it is experienced at first hand. Six million square miles of ocean were searched by nine squadrons of carrier-borne Swordfish in four months. To find the speck that is one specific ship in the South Atlantic is indeed like looking for the proverbial needle in a haystack and the aircrews may be forgiven for not finding the raider they sought. Nevertheless this lack of a sighting in such a vast area did at least indicate a much reduced area in which the raider was likely to be operating.

The raider was sinking Allied shipping at a disturbing rate, for example *Graf Spee* sank over 22,300 tons of shipping in six days and carried on operating in the well-frequented shipping lanes off Brazil to considerable cost in lives, ships and materiel. On 2 December 1939 *Graf Spee* captured *Doric Star* which was able to transmit the 'Raider, Raider, Raider' signal before she was boarded. The signal was picked up and with the aid of Direction Finding gear was used to indicate the area in which *Graf Spee* was operating.

Fuel does not last for ever and it was thought that the German commerce raider would soon need to replenish her store of fuel oil and the indications were that Uruguay would be the country and Montevideo, on the River Plate, the port where this would be attempted. The cruisers *Ajax, Achilles* and *Exeter* were despatched to cover the approaches to the River Plate arriving in the area on 12 December 1939

At dawn on 13 December smoke was sighted to the north by *Ajax*, and *Exeter* was ordered to investigate. At 0615 she signalled to the other vessels that she believed the smoke to be from a German battleship. She continued to shadow the battleship from the south, slowly closing the range. *Graf Spee* opened fire at a range of some ten miles, a distance far beyond the reach of the guns of the British vessels which had to endure her fire as they attempted to get close enough to use their own armament. When *Exeter* had reduced the range sufficiently she too opened fire. While this was going on *Ajax* and *Achilles* placed themselves to the east of *Graf Spee* to divide her attention and to divert some of her fire from *Exeter*.

Graf Spee's main armament consisted of two triple 11-inch gun turrets. *Exeter* had three twin 8-inch turrets and the smaller cruisers were armed with four twin 6-inch turrets. Clearly the six 8-inch guns carried by *Exeter* posed the greater danger for *Graf Spee* and she concentrated her fire on the heavy cruiser and soon scored a number of hits, quickly putting one gun turret out of action and damaging *Exeter*'s steering gear. Despite this damage she raced in at 32 knots in an attempt to use her torpedoes. This occupied *Graf Spee* sufficiently to allow the smaller cruisers to close the pocket battleship to a point where their guns could be of value and they began to exchange fire with *Graf*

Spee's 5.9-inch guns. *Exeter* paid dearly for her attempt to engage and to keep *Graf Spee*'s interest from the lighter vessels for long enough for them to get within effective striking distance. In spite of the damage she had suffered she was able to get close enough to attempt two torpedo attacks.

As the exchange of fire continued the damage sustained by *Exeter* was such that she was forced to withdraw. Her heavy gun turrets were knocked out of action, her steering gear was damaged and her speed was much reduced. *Ajax* and *Achilles* used the threat of a torpedo attack and their high speed to harry the *Graf Spee* and cause her to shift her gunfire again and again. This distraction gave the severely damaged *Exeter* the chance to put down a smoke screen which allowed the three ships to move out of range of *Graf Spee*'s big guns. *Ajax* had sustained some serious damage but she was able to continue to shadow the German ship in company with *Achilles* who had suffered much

A Fairey Sea Fox seaplane

less damage than her two companions. *Graf Spee*'s armour had protected her well against the lighter gunfire of the three British cruisers and her damage was of a relatively minor nature but the crew's morale was at a low ebb. *Exeter* was so badly damaged that she retired to the Falklands for repairs.

As soon as the signal that a German battleship had been found was received the cruiser *Cumberland* left the Falklands and made for the River Plate.

The British ships were normally equipped with spotting aircraft that could be launched by catapult. Unfortunately those of *Achilles* were ashore for servicing, and both of *Exeter*'s Walruses were badly damaged by gunfire before they could be launched, as was one of the Sea Foxes aboard *Ajax*. This left just the remaining Sea Fox aboard *Ajax* which was catapulted off to spot the fall of shot from the British vessels. As the turrets did not cease their firing whilst the catapulting operation took place the blast from her guns must have made the launch an even more interesting occasion than usual! Lieutenants Lewin and Kearney climbed to 3,000 feet where some cloud offered concealment if the need for it was felt. The Sea Fox continued to report the fall of shot from the British ships and at one point she closed in on *Graf Spee* to make a more detailed assessment of the damage inflicted on her. This close inspection was resented by the German battleship and the Sea Fox withdrew after being hit by anti-aircraft fire, but not before she had observed thirty or more hits on *Graf Spee*.

Graf Spee entered the River Plate and anchored off Montevideo which prompted a frenzied spate of diplomatic activity by both sides in an effort to resolve the future of the battleship to their advantage. Meanwhile *Ajax* and *Achilles* were joined offshore by the cruiser *Cumberland*.

Reconnaissance flights were made at regular intervals until on the late afternoon of 17 December the *Graf Spee* was seen to raise her anchors. Expecting the battle to be resumed the three British cruisers headed towards the River Plate, doubtless with the thought that it would make sense to be close enough, when battle was recommenced, to avoid being outranged by the battleship's superior armament.

Ajax's Sea Fox flew off and took up station off *Ajax*'s starboard bow ready to spot the fall of the cruisers' shot but as there was no sign of the German vessel emerging the plane was ordered to move closer to *Graf Spee* to observe and report. As darkness was beginning to fall several flashes were seen to appear on the darkened shape of the vessel, looking very much as if it were gunfire but it was quickly realised that they were scuttling charges and that the Germans were sinking their own vessel. At 2054 the Sea Fox signalled '*Spee* has blown herself up.'

Clearly many more than the few representatives of the FAA were responsible for the successful outcome of this engagement that became known as The Battle of the River Plate, but beyond a shadow of doubt the lone Fleet Air Arm plane played a vital part which was recognised by the award of the DSC to Lt Lewin and a Mention in Despatches to Lt Kearney, the first FAA awards of the war.

Doubtless the fact that the remainder of Force K, including the fleet carrier *Ark Royal*, was known to be about a day's sailing away from the River Plate played its part in the decision to scuttle rather than fight.

Ark Royal returned to Freetown, in West Africa, and continued her search operations in the South Atlantic. Early February 1940 saw her on her way home and joining in the search for six German merchant ships that were also trying to return home. Five of them were sunk by Swordfish from *Ark Royal* off the coast of Spain. U boats were lying in wait for her in the Bay of Biscay but she managed to give them the slip and berthed in Portsmouth on 15 February. Her refit took some five weeks and doubtless her ship's company were able to enjoy some well deserved leave.

With her refit completed *Ark Royal* left Portsmouth to sail to the eastern Med. on 20 March 1940. The intention was to work up her aircrews away from the alarms and excursions of Home Waters. Her Skuas had been left at Hatston in the Orkneys to help the resident squadron of Sea Gladiators defend the Home Fleet Anchorage at Scapa Flow.

At dawn on 9 April the 'Phoney War' came to an abrupt end with the invasion of Denmark and

The Norwegian Sea, the area where the 'Phoney war' came to an end

The History of the Fleet Air Arm

Norway. The very next day *Ark Royal* and *Glorious* were ordered to rejoin the Home Fleet 'at best possible speed'. The German invasion of these two countries, in which air power played a vital part, had found the Royal Navy without a single carrier in Home Waters.

The nearest aircraft carrier was *Furious*. She had just completed a major programme of repairs and refitting but was berthed at Greenock on the west coast of Scotland and because of the work that had been carried out on her all her planes were ashore. The Skuas from *Furious* were at Evanton, on the east coast of Scotland, and the urgency of her departure was such that she sailed without fighter cover, which seems an incredible chance to take. Her Swordfish squadrons were flown on from Campbeltown as she put to sea so at least she would have some reconnaissance, anti-submarine and offensive capacity.

Intelligence had been received to the effect that some German cruisers were in Bergen harbour and the only aircraft that could be mustered for an attack were in Scotland, one squadron at Hatston in the Orkneys and the other at Wick. The Skuas based at Wick flew up to join those at Hatston. The planes were bombed-up with 500-lb bombs and set out on the 600-mile round trip to Bergen. When they reached their target they found that the 6,000-ton German cruiser *Königsberg* was the only warship in the harbour.

The attacking aircraft climbed to 8,000 feet and dived steeply through furious anti-aircraft fire onto their target below. The attack was over in three minutes but it was a total success, delivering three direct hits and twelve near misses. A near miss in comparatively shallow water can often do a great deal of damage and indeed on this occasion one near miss exploded virtually beneath the vessel and blasted a great hole in its side. Quite quickly *Königsberg* caught fire and shortly afterwards her magazines exploded in a vast cloud of smoke and flame. One aircraft was lost in the engagement but in terms of warfare it was a small price to pay for the destruction of an enemy cruiser.

As soon as *Furious* arrived in Norwegian waters (11 April) she launched a torpedo attack against two German destroyers lying in Trondheim Fjord. This was a totally wasted effort as the vessels were in shoal water and all the torpedoes grounded before they reached their target. It is always easy to criticise with hindsight but in this case it does seem that a glance at the appropriate chart would have given information that could have ensured a very different outcome. A snowstorm thwarted a second attack and caused the loss of two aircraft and damage to a third when on its return it crashed on attempting to land.

On 13 April the battleship *Warspite* entered Ofot Fjord which leads to Narvik and Bjervik, in company with nine destroyers, and catapulted off one of her Swordfish. The conditions were less than perfect with a deck of cloud literally roofing in the fjord. Clearly the cloud would provide a retreat if the Swordfish was too hard pressed but the clouds were well stuffed with rock and not the sort of place in which one would choose to practise blind flying for longer than absolutely necessary. The Swordfish, carrying two 100-lb bombs and two 250-lb anti-submarine bombs, headed towards Narvik.

The first sighting made by the Swordfish was of an enemy destroyer. The Telegraphist Air Gunner aboard the Swordfish radioed the position of the destroyer back to *Warspite*. As soon as the German destroyer came under fire from a British destroyer it withdrew to a safer berth. Passing Narvik the Swordfish flew up Herjangs Fjord and the pilot, Petty Officer Rice, spotted U64 anchored close to the jetty at Bjervik. He dived to 300 feet to drop his bombs while Leading Telegraphist Air Gunner Pacey raked the conning tower with machine-gun fire to discourage the U boat's gun crew as his contribution to the proceedings. Fire was returned and some damage to the tail of the plane was incurred but Petty Officer Rice's first bomb scored a direct hit on the bow of the U boat which sank more or less at once. Petty Officer Rice was able to nurse his plane back to *Warspite* where she was safely taken inboard.

The carriers *Ark Royal* and *Glorious* had been recalled from the Mediterranean and by 24 April they were in Norwegian waters to give support to the British and Norwegian forces at Andalesnes and Namsos. *Furious* had received some bomb damage and as soon as she was relieved by *Ark Royal* and *Glorious* she returned to Scapa Flow for repairs.

In addition to her normal complement of aircraft *Glorious* carried eighteen obsolescent RAF Gladiators which it was thought would be more suitable than faster planes for working from the makeshift landing grounds that would be their lot when they were flown ashore. As soon as they were within striking distance these planes were flown off and made their way to Lake Lesjaskog, near Andalesnes, where a temporary airstrip had been prepared for them.

On 25 April Swordfish and Skuas were flown off to attack targets in the vicinity of Trondheim. The Skuas were to act as dive-bombers. After this operation *Glorious* was ordered to rejoin the Fleet which she did on 1 May.

Planes from *Ark Royal* continued to attack targets in this area until 28 April. One of these targets was Vaernes airfield which was attacked with considerable success. These attacks however were not without their cost. A number of aircraft were lost, several because they ran short of fuel before they could reach the safety of their ship. Fortunately most of the aircrews were rescued. A Skua was disabled by fire from a Heinkel 111 in the course of one of these patrols but its pilot, Capt. Partridge RM, was able to make a forced landing on a frozen lake. At this time some aircraft, and the Skua was one of them, had been fitted with IFF sets (Identification, Friend or Foe) which emitted a signal intended to reassure British forces that the aircraft approaching was friendly. For obvious reasons it was undesirable to allow one of these sets to fall into enemy hands and so Capt. Partridge and his observer set fire to the plane before making their way to Andalesenes. At Andalesenes they had the good fortune to be taken aboard HMS *Manchester* and to be given passage home where they eventually rejoined their squadron.

Ark Royal left Norway on 28 April and made her way to Scapa Flow where she refuelled and replaced gear that had been lost or damaged in the course of the recent actions. Ten of her aircraft were lost to accidents and three to enemy action. On 5 May she was back in the vicinity of Narvik where her aircraft were again in action in support of the Allied forces ashore in the area of Narvik. As before a number of aircraft were lost but most of the aircrew were saved. Sadly Lt Lucy, who had played an important part in the raid that had destroyed the *Königsberg*, was one of those who lost their lives.

Ark Royal was back in the area on 6 May and did her best to support the forces ashore but it was a losing battle. *Furious* and *Glorious* returned to the area on 9 May. Both vessels were packed with aircraft, many of which, it was intended, should be flown ashore to support the ground forces fighting there. *Glorious* flew off the Walruses of 701 Squadron that were to be based at Harstad where they were to carry out reconnaissance and communications duties. Twelve days later RAF Hurricanes were flown ashore, as were a number of Gladiators.

On 26 May *Furious* was back at Greenock disembarking her planes. Narvik was retaken on 28 May by Allied forces but it was clear that it was only a matter of time before the Royal Navy would find itself evacuating the forces that were ashore.

Meanwhile *Ark Royal* returned to Norwegian waters arriving on 2 June. Two days later aircraft from the *Ark* covered the first withdrawals from Narvik and on the 7th took on board the five Walruses from Harstad that were all that remained of the planes of 701 Squadron that had been flown ashore from *Glorious* less than a month before. At the same time *Glorious* accepted the surviving Hurricanes and Gladiators that had earlier been put ashore to operate from Bardufoss.

Clearly RAF fighters and ground support planes did not have sufficient range to operate so far from their bases in Britain and the major part of the fighting therefore fell to the FAA. It was a role for which the FAA had not been trained and because of the neglect to which it had been subjected between the wars it was poorly equipped for the task. They were up against an air force of a considerable size, well equipped and well trained for the task they had to undertake. To say that the one real success had been the sinking of *Königsberg* is

HMS Glorious, *sunk in the Norwegian Sea in the early days of WWII*

not to belittle the determined efforts of the FAA crews. Through no fault of their own they were on to a loser before they started.

Whilst *Glorious* was loading the aircraft that were to be taken back to the UK a number of German warships including *Scharnhorst* and *Gneisenau*, two very powerful modern battle cruisers, were heading for Harstad with the intention of attacking the Allied base that was situated there. This was a fleet that *Glorious* and her totally inadequate escort did not want to meet on their way back to the United Kingdom, as they would be absolutely out-gunned.

It seems that the captain of *Glorious* had little understanding of the value of aircraft as an integral part of the fleet. He was insistent that the five Swordfish should be sent ashore in support of the Army, thereby depriving the fleet of the anti-submarine protection and reconnaissance ability represented by the aircraft. It is very obvious that he was at odds with his air staff and had been quite seriously so for some time as his senior air officer had been sent home to await a court martial. Captain d'Oyly was anxious to get back to the UK to pursue the court martial of Commander Heath and asked the Flag Ship for permission to leave ahead of the main body of the Fleet. The official line has always been that *Glorious* was obliged to leave because of a shortage of fuel. This does not seem to be borne out by her log book nor does it tally with information recently uncovered by the relatives of many of those who died when *Glorious* was sunk. However, whatever the reason she left two hours ahead of the other ships with just two destroyers as an escort.

Back in Britain some of the civilians employed to listen to the German radio communications with a view to gleaning what intelligence they could, decided that the considerable increase in the amount of radio traffic indicated that *Scharnhorst* and *Gneisenau* were about to leave their berths in northern Norway. The assumption was that they would either enter the Atlantic or the Norwegian Sea. The radio boffins tracked the two German vessels and reported their progress repeatedly to the Admiralty. Regrettably they did not have sufficient clout at this stage and their warnings were ignored. No warning was sent to the British ships about to leave Norwegian waters.

It seems quite incredible now but Capt. d'Oyly had ordered the ship's complement of Swordfish to be struck down below for the passage home. Given the chance to carry out routine reconnaissance duties those planes would have explored the waters for a radius of sixty-five miles or more around the ship and would certainly have spotted the German ships and given *Glorious* the chance to run for it with every expectation of success. In the event when the aircraft carrier and her escort of two destroyers, *Ardent* and *Acasta*, first became aware of the German ships they were within range of the battle cruisers' main armament. Their fate was sealed. They stood no chance of survival.

To quote from *The Drama of the Scharnhorst*, by Fritz-Otto Busch:

'. . . the first covering salvo straddled the flight-deck which was packed tight with aircraft. Angry flashes flared into dazzling sheets of red flame and an enormous pall of smoke enveloped the luckless carrier.

The destroyers put up a magnificent fight . . . one of them laid down a smoke screen while the other went in to attack. But it didn't help them much . . . Direct hits battered the superstructure of the brave little ships; in spite of their hopeless situation they closed in again and again to fire their torpedoes at the German ships. Meanwhile

the crippled *Glorious* lay motionless beneath a massive cloud of smoke from which the flashes of explosions broke continuously . . .'

The battle raged for some two to three hours with the destroyers making repeated torpedo attacks which were at last rewarded with a direct hit on the after end of *Scharnhorst*. This did considerable damage, obliging her to put into Trondheim for repairs. The tenacity and courage of *Ardent* and *Acasta* did sufficient damage to both major warships to put them out of commission for almost six months.

All three British ships were sunk. Of the 1,560 men in the three ships about 650 died in the course of the action. Nine hundred men were left in the water clinging to wreckage and to Carley floats, the standard floatation gear for abandon ship situations in the Royal Navy during World War Two.

Despite the admiration expressed in Fritz-Otto Busch's book the Germans made little or no effort to pick up survivors. Three days later forty-one survivors were picked up by Norwegian and Dutch fishing boats. The rest, over eight hundred and fifty men, died.

There was in fact at least one Royal Navy ship within reach but it did not divert to the scene of the battle in the hope of picking up survivors. This was the cruiser *Devonshire* under the command of Vice-Admiral John Cunningham that was taking King Haakon of Norway to Britain.

It seems that there is some dispute about the receipt by *Devonshire* of a signal from *Glorious* detailing the engagement. One version holds that the signal was so garbled as to be unintelligible and another claims that no signal was received. In a recent Channel Four television account of the sinking it was claimed most emphatically by members of the Signals staff who were aboard *Devonshire* at the time that they had received a perfectly clear and informative signal and that the Signals log book was immediately taken from the Signals Office by higher authority and has not been seen since. It is also on record that a Telegraphist Air Gunner aboard *Glorious* who was in the cockpit of his Swordfish servicing his radio heard the signal transmitted and confirms that it was not garbled. The Admiralty first learned of the sinkings twenty-four hours later from the German radio.

The Captains of *Ardent* and *Acasta* were each awarded a posthumous Mention in Despatches and Vice-Admiral John Cunningham was awarded The Grand Cross and Star of St Olaf. The court martial of Commander Heath never took place but his career was blighted.

The only positive outcome of this sorry affair was a much improved attitude at the Admiralty towards the intelligence-gathering potential of listening to the enemy's radio transmissions, which was to everyone's advantage.

It was decided to attack *Scharnhorst* while she was incapacitated in Trondheim and to this end *Ark Royal* flew off fifteen Skuas manned by the most experienced aircrews she had aboard. Four RAF Beauforts were to attack nearby Vaernes airfield and six Blenheims were to act as a fighter escort. The raids were to be co-ordinated in an attempt to reduce the dangers of an attack by fighters from Vaernes. The planes had about forty miles to fly across enemy territory before they could reach their target in Trondheim Fjord. Surprise was to be essential but it was unfortunately lost when the RAF planes attacked too early and the Germans were alerted and waiting for the Skuas. They were met with a very heavy barrage of flak and a considerable number of German fighters. Eight of the fifteen Skuas were lost.

Very soon after this abortive and expensive raid the FAA's involvement in the Norwegian campaign came to an end and not long afterwards the evacuation of the Allied forces was carried out leaving the Norwegians to the tender mercy of the German occupying forces.

At the same time as the German invasion of Norway was taking place the German Army and Air Force were attacking the British and French troops in France with overwhelming force. It was

Junkers 87, Stuka, German dive-bomber WWII

not simply that the German forces were so much more powerful than the Allies but they were indulging in a form of warfare that was very different from that which had been anticipated by the Allies. The static warfare of the 1914/1918 war influenced much of British and French thinking but the Germans had largely discarded that concept and had developed what they called the *Blitzkrieg*, the Lightning War. They outflanked and overran static defence points and if such points proved to be difficult to eliminate they would happily bypass them by land or air. This was a war of movement and infiltration and they were not above using the confusion caused by masses of civilians fleeing before their onslaught. One of the Germans' innovations was the way they used their Junkers 87 dive-bombers.

Instead of flying straight and level and dropping their bombs when they believed they were in a position to hit their targets, pilots of the dive-bombers literally aimed the plane itself at the target in an exceedingly steep dive, dropping their bombs just before they pulled out of the dive. This allowed them to approach their target with very little warning and to bomb with devastating accuracy. Diving like this produced an incredibly loud and unnerving noise which was often added to by sirens that were mounted on the wings of the planes. Both the British and the United States navies had dive-bombers in service so they were not an unknown weapon but it was the sheer numbers used by the German air force as part of the savage *Blitzkrieg* that made them such an impressive weapon.

The Allies were driven back to the coast and some 338,000 British and other forces were evacuated through Dunkirk by a motley armada of vessels ranging from warships, coastal and fishing vessels to yachts. Swordfish and surface vessels

The evacuation of troops from the Dunkirk beaches

were busy attacking E boats and U boats and generally keeping enemy warships at a distance from the evacuation area while RAF planes were doing their utmost to keep German aircraft away from the beaches.

In the circumstances the air cover that was provided could only be called pitiful. It was no one's fault. It was a time of chaos and confusion and inadequate resources. I recall an FAA flying instructor telling me in the early forties that at the time of the Dunkirk evacuation he had just flown solo for the first time, which would have taken about ten flying hours. In common with the rest of his course he was sent off repeatedly in a Tiger Moth to Dunkirk to drop food and medical supplies to the troops on the beaches. These 'makey-learny' pilots would be given large parcels of gift-wrapped goodies which they carried on their laps and threw out when they were over the beaches. He said that navigation was fairly straightforward. On the outward leg they simply flew towards the massive cloud of smoke that hung over the scene and on the return trip an approximately reciprocal course was usually enough to get them back home again.

After Dunkirk it was obvious that Britain was next in line to receive the full and undivided attention of the German forces, in particular the German air force. To help the Royal Air Force in the forthcoming Battle of Britain fifty-eight Fleet Air Arm pilots were seconded on loan to the RAF, flying Spitfires and Hurricanes with RAF squadrons. Eighteen of them were killed in action.

CHAPTER FIVE

From the Capitulation of France to August 1942

When France negotiated her surrender to the Germans on 16 June 1940 she agreed to deliver her powerful fleet to them. This ran counter to her long-standing promise to have her fleet sail for British ports should she be forced to capitulate. She instructed the units of her fleet which were at sea or in ports outside France to refuse to join her erstwhile allies in what had now become, at least in part, a war to free France from the Germans. Even more astonishingly most of the French Fleet complied with this order. A very few French ships disobeyed and made their way to British bases to join the fight against the common enemy, but it is a sad fact that the majority did not.

The French Government also held 400 German aircrew as PoWs which she had long promised to send to Britain so that they could not fight again. She failed to do that and kept them as a bargaining counter, as if one could extract promises from Hitler and company and expect them to abide by those promises!

The French Fleet was large, modern and powerful and had it fallen into German hands it would have created a problem of major proportions for the Allies. Intense diplomatic activity had been going on from before the French capitulation to 2 July to try to prevent this happening, but to no avail.

There were just two courses of action open to the British. One was to simply accept that the French Fleet would probably join forces with Hitler at some time in the future and prove to be a major threat to our security. The other was to put the French ships out of action ourselves to remove that potential danger. In reality the French left us no choice: the French Fleet had to be neutralised.

An important part of the French Fleet was at anchor in the Algerian ports of Oran and Mers-el-Kébir. Two French battle cruisers, both superior to

Scharnhorst and *Gneisenau* were in Oran along with a battleship, a number of light cruisers, submarines, destroyers and numerous other vessels. A fleet that would have caused disastrous problems for Britain if it had fallen into Hitler's hands.

Before France fell her Navy had accepted responsibility for guarding various areas of the Mediterranean. With the fall of France the French Navy refused to undertake those duties and so, to cover this gap in our defences, the Admiralty had been forced to form a new battle group called Force H. The group initially consisted of three battleships, *Hood, Valiant* and *Resolution*, one aircraft carrier, *Ark Royal*, two cruisers and eleven destroyers, but ships were detached and others joined from time to time as circumstances dictated. In addition to the planes aboard *Ark Royal* the battleships and cruisers carried a number of Walruses. This powerful force was commanded by Admiral Somerville who had been instrumental in rescuing 100,000 French soldiers from the beaches of Dunkirk. He was ordered by Winston Churchill to prevent the French Fleet from being surrendered intact into German hands and told that he should use whatever force might be necessary to achieve this end. At daybreak on 3 June 1940 Force H left Gibraltar and headed for Oran.

Captain Holland, who had been the British naval attaché in Paris for some time was ordered to make one last attempt at negotiating an agreement. He was taken by the destroyer *Foxhound* to Oran where *Foxhound* was refused permission to enter the harbour. After some discussion Captain Holland was taken ashore by motor boat and attempted to see the French Admiral Gensoul who refused to meet him and their 'discussion' was conducted throughout the day by an exchange of notes.

Meanwhile Force H arrived off Oran two hours

Oran was the scene of the bombardment of the French Fleet

after Captain Holland's destroyer.

Captain Holland put a number of propositions to Admiral Gensoul.

1 Sail with us and fight the common enemy.
2 Sail with us to a British port with reduced crews who will then be repatriated. The ships will be returned to France at the end of the war or full compensation paid in lieu of if they are damaged or lost.
3 If you feel you must honour the terms of the Armistice and not allow your ships to be used against Germany or Italy sail with us with reduced crews to some port in the West Indies where they will be demilitarised or entrusted to the USA for the duration of the war.
4 Demilitarise your ships where they are.

The French prevaricated and played for time all day. It was known that Admiral Darlan had ordered the French warships that were at sea and in other ports to make for Oran. It was obvious that the French hoped to muster sufficient power in both surface ships and submarines, in the vicinity of Oran, to be able to frustrate Force H's intentions. It was equally clear to Admiral Somerville that his own ships could be put at considerable risk by the arrival of units of the French Navy. These time-wasting ploys of the French could not be allowed to continue and a time limit of six hours was set. Admiral Gensoul was given an unequivocal warning that if no satisfactory conclusion was reached by then Force H would sink the French ships in

Oran. Presumably it was this ultimatum that persuaded Admiral Gensoul to see Captain Holland at the last minute, but he had left it too late and the guns of Force H opened fire three minutes after the deadline had expired.

Force H engaged the French fleet for ten minutes in the course of which *Ark Royal*'s Swordfish spotted the fall of shot for the guns of the Fleet. This initial bombardment sank a battleship and two destroyers and damaged *Dunkerque* so that she had to be beached. Meanwhile five Swordfish laid mines at the entrance to the harbour at Mers-el-Kébir, the nearby military port. The bombardment of the ships in Oran was followed by an attack by Swordfish and Skuas from *Ark Royal* with bombs and torpedoes. These attacks were not particularly successful and five planes were lost to French fire.

At dusk, which was shortly after the action ended, *Strasbourg* with an escort of six destroyers suddenly left Oran harbour and made off to the east at full speed, successfully eluding the ships of Force H. *Ark Royal* launched six Swordfish armed with bombs in pursuit of the French vessels. When the Swordfish attacked, their bombs straddled *Strasbourg* but failed to score any direct hits. Two of the Swordfish ran out of fuel and had to ditch on the return passage but the crews were picked up by a British destroyer.

More Swordfish, armed with torpedoes this time, took off and found *Strasbourg* three miles off the North African coast making clouds of black smoke and steaming at 28 knots. The Swordfish dropped down to sea level under heavy and accurate anti-aircraft fire. Sunset was a short time away and so they waited until the sun was setting before they made their attack to gain the advantage of attacking with *Strasbourg* silhouetted against the setting sun whilst they were to some extent lost in the gloom of the dusk along the coast. This was the first torpedo attack that *Ark Royal*'s aircraft had made on a capital ship at sea and they dropped their torpedoes outside the destroyer screen believing that they could not penetrate it. The Swordfish appeared to score just one hit which did not stop the French battle cruiser and she disappeared into the dark of the night.

Further air attacks were made over the next several days on the vessels in Oran, some with greater success than had been achieved by the first attempt. Between the air raids the ships of Force H fired repeated salvos and eventually it was considered that sufficient serious damage had been done to the French Fleet to immobilise it and Force H withdrew.

In addition to the ships sunk in the initial bombardment a battle cruiser of the Strasbourg class was badly damaged and run ashore to avoid sinking, a Bretagne class battleship was sunk and another heavily damaged and two destroyers and a seaplane carrier were sunk.

For the FAA the whole sorry affair had demonstrated three things. *Dunkerque* had been incapacitated for a very long time by torpedoes launched by aircraft, something which the bombardment with the 15-inch shells of the capital ships had failed to do. This success was because the torpedoes struck the heavily armoured ship below the water-line opening up huge areas of the hull to allow the ingress of massive amounts of water.

The Swordfish that attacked *Dunkerque* took off in the dark, which allowed them to reach their target at first light, thus achieving that vital element, surprise. The ability of carrier-borne aircraft to operate sucessfully in the dark had long been a matter of debate. This successful attack put an end to the discussion.

Despite its lack of success the chase of and attack on the *Strasbourg* had demonstrated that aerial torpedoes could be used to attack fast moving ships at sea but techniques had to be greatly improved if they were to be successful.

Meanwhile, *Hermes* had been shadowing the recently commissioned French battleship *Richelieu* in the Atlantic for the best part of two weeks. *Richelieu* finally entered Dakar in Senegal, French West Africa, and showed no inclination to put to sea. As it seemed unlikely that *Hermes* would have a chance to attack *Richelieu* in the open sea she took up a position that would enable her torpedo aircraft to deliver a strike against the French battleship whilst she lay at anchor in the harbour.

At first light on 8 July 1940 *Hermes* flew off six Swordfish to attack *Richelieu*. One hit was made right aft on the battleship in difficult conditions and in the face of very heavy anti-aircraft fire. The attacking force believed they had done very little damage to the French battleship but they were wrong. The damage was extensive, in fact it was enough to keep her out of action for a long time, but this was not immediately apparent.

Because the damage to *Richelieu* appeared to be minimal it was decided to mount further attacks but before these could be organised the truth was learned and the raids were cancelled. As a result of the single torpedo strike *Richelieu*'s propeller shafts were twisted, the after end of the battleship was flooded extensively and the steering gear was badly damaged. All this incurred in a place where repair facilities were rather limited. After initial repairs were made she was capable of getting under way in an emergency but it was to be a year before *Richelieu* could be restored to a full battleworthy condition.

An event of this kind really does point up the offensive capability of naval aircraft. Here we have just six rather elderly planes crewed by between twelve and eighteen men who were able to seriously disable an almost brand-new, heavily armed battleship, crewed by about 1,500 men.

Following the unhappy engagements at Oran and Dakar, Force H sailed for the central Mediterranean. Close to Sardinia an Italian Cant 506 seaplane was brought down by a section of Skuas from the *Ark* on 9 July but not before the pilot had radioed back a report on the fleet's position. Later the same day Force H was attacked by

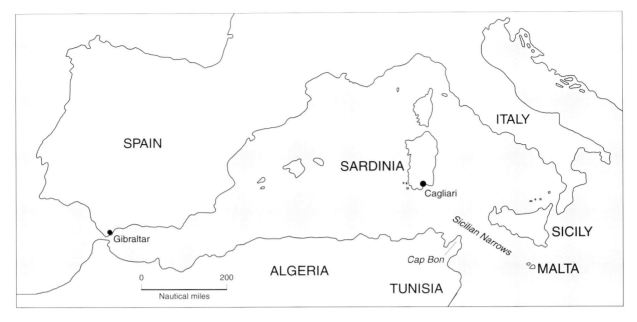

The western Mediterranean

three waves of Italian Savoia Marchetti 79s; a total of some forty bombers was used and they dropped more than 100 bombs. The attack was not pressed home and no damage was suffered by the British ships. Skuas were in the air during the raid and brought down two Marchettis and damaged two others.

It was usual for the SM. 79s to attack from a very high altitude; 12,000 to 15,000 feet which happily did not make for great accuracy in their bombing attacks, but unless the patrolling Skuas were at a similar altitude they had small chance of catching the Italians before they dropped their bombs.

Things improved when *Sheffield,* a cruiser with Force H, was fitted with an early version of an air warning radar set. This radar was invaluable as it gave advance warning of the approach of hostile aircraft, an indication of the size of the attacking force and the direction from which they were coming. *Sheffield* relayed this information to the *Ark* where it was used by the fighter direction team to control the patrolling aircraft. To maintain radio silence for as long as possible the *Sheffield* would pass the information by a flag hoist to the *Ark* from

whence instructions would go to the patrolling Skuas by high frequency radio in a simple code form.

With so much of the Mediterranean in unfriendly hands Malta became an important base for the Navy. It was clear that the greatest danger was to be from air attack and more fighters were going to be needed to defend Malta. The first reinforcements to be sent to Malta in the summer of 1940 were twelve RAF Hurricanes carried aboard *Argus.* With their wings removed to facilitate stowage the Hurricanes were loaded aboard the carrier at Abbotsinch, Glasgow and then *Argus* and her heavy escort, made their way into the Mediterranean.

When *Argus* and her escort were well inside the Med. the Hurricanes were reassembled and ranged on deck ready to be flown off. At their pre-flight briefing the pilots realised that they were intended to fly off at a distance from Malta that exceeded the range of their planes: needless to say this idea was not popular with them! Their protest was equally unpopular but eventually common sense prevailed and they were not required to take off for a further twenty-four hours. In the course of that twenty-four hours Italian aircraft mounted an attack on *Argus* and her escort, fortunately without damage to any of the vessels in the group but I doubt if it did anything to improve the popularity of the Hurricane pilots!

At dawn on the appointed day the pilots boarded their planes and made ready to leave. The Hurricanes were to be led by a Skua which took off first with barely enough room on the crowded flight-deck to get airborne. By a combination of good luck and even better airmanship the Skua staggered into the air, narrowly avoiding a wet and early demise in the drink just ahead of *Argus*. The Hurricanes found no problems with take-off and with the Skua to show the way they settled down to the long flight to Malta in two Vee formations. In the event all went well and the Sunderland flying boat that followed them as a rescue plane had no call on its services.

In November 1940 another similar operation was staged to put a further twelve planes onto Malta but unfortunately it was not as successful as the first attempt. Unbelievably it seems that the same briefing officer ordered the planes to fly off at about the same spot as it was initially intended to fly off the earlier group of Hurricanes. Although the RAF aircrew were all experienced Battle of Britain pilots they did not question the decision and took off as ordered. One Skua and four Hurricanes reached Malta using the dust in the bottom of their petrol tanks for fuel. One Skua landed in Sicily and of the remainder just one Hurricane pilot was picked up by the Sunderland that was escorting them; the remainder were lost with their planes, a terrible waste of desperately needed men and aircraft that should never have been allowed to happen.

HMS Illustrious, *a welcome addition to the Mediterranean Fleet*

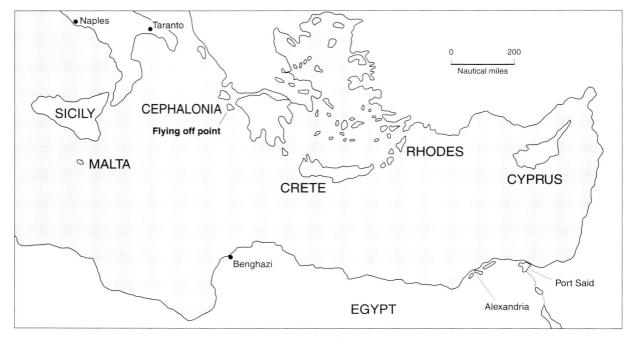

The eastern Mediterranean

The offensive power of the Mediterranean Fleet was greatly enhanced on 2 September 1940 when the fleet was joined by the new Fleet Carrier *Illustrious*. She had been built with heavy deck armour which was to prove its worth. In addition she carried the latest radar equipment. Her complement of planes consisted of two squadrons of Swordfish and one of Fulmars.

The Fulmar was a two-seater fighter with eight forward-firing wing guns. With its Rolls-Royce Merlin engine it could make about 220 knots which was a useful speed in those days.

Illustrious wasted no time in getting into action. Two days after her arrival, her aircraft, in company with Swordfish from *Eagle*, attacked airfields on Rhodes and then on 17 September fifteen of her Swordfish attacked Benghazi, sinking two destroyers and damaging a number of other vessels. On 14 October 1940 Léros was attacked.

Between 2 August and 9 September 1940 Cagliari, a port in the large bay at the south of Sardinia, suffered four raids from FAA planes.

These were a combination of mine-laying in the approaches to the port and the destruction of shoreside military and air force facilities along with a number of parked aircraft.

Although they lacked the high profile of some other actions these raids on Cagliari achieved a large measure of success for the loss of only two Swordfish. One Stringbag and its crew were lost in an accident on take-off and the other fell to anti-aircraft fire at the target.

After the operations at Cagliari were completed *Ark Royal* in company with other ships of Force H was destined to take part in the ill-fated attempt to take Dakar. Vichy French forces held Dakar and it was thought, quite wrongly, that they would co-operate with the Free French under the command of General de Gaulle. The first step was for the *Ark* to embark two French Caudron Luciol training planes at Freetown, about 500 miles south-east of Dakar. These were to be used to land Free French emissaries, who were hoping to organise an unopposed amphibious landing, on the local airfield at Dakar. The collaborationist Vichy French would have none of this and hostilities commenced on 24 September.

Although *Richelieu* had been badly damaged in

the earlier raid by planes from *Hermes*, most of her armament was intact and she used it to good effect, scoring several hits on *Barham* with heavy-calibre shells and causing damage by near misses to other vessels. *Resolution* was struck by a torpedo and her damage was such that she had to withdraw. The Vichy French aircraft were superior to anything *Ark Royal* could put into the air against them and nine Swordfish were lost before the attempt to take Dakar was abandoned. When all the forces were withdrawn from Dakar *Ark Royal* was sent back to England for a refit in the course of which her obsolete Skuas were replaced by Fulmars.

At this time the Italian Fleet was anchored in the harbour at Taranto on Italy's south-east coast and its mere presence was tying up a large number of British warships that could be put to better use. No responsible commander can afford to ignore the fact that a powerful force is at hand even if it is only lying at anchor in a harbour and vessels must be kept available to deal with any sortie that may be attempted. To reduce this threat it was planned to attack the Italian Fleet with aircraft from *Illustrious* and *Eagle*.

The start of this operation was dogged by a series of mishaps. It was originally intended to attack the ships lying at Taranto on 21 October 1940, Trafalgar Day, an auspicious day in the Navy's calendar. The initial scheme required thirty Swordfish from *Illustrious* and *Eagle* to attack in two waves of fifteen aircraft. Unfortunately *Illustrious* suffered a fire in her hangar and the raid had to be postponed until 30 October. When all was made ready it was realised that there would be no moon on the thirtieth to illuminate the target. The strike was put back to 11 November. The final problem arose because *Eagle* found that she had taken on contaminated fuel from a supply tanker. Three of her Swordfish had been lost because of this problem. This put *Eagle* out of the operation and as a consequence five of her Swordfish were transferred to *Illustrious*. The strike force had now been whittled down to twenty-one aircraft.

At last on 6 November everything was in order and the Fleet sailed from Alexandria towards Taranto.

The RAF flew a photographic reconnaisance flight over Taranto Harbour on the 10th which showed that the Italian Fleet, which included five battleships, was still at anchor.

The next day found *Illustrious* and her escort within 170 miles of Taranto some 40 miles west of Kabbo Point on Cephalonia and a strike force of twelve Swordfish were flown off at 2100, half of them armed with bombs and the remainder with torpedoes. Two aircraft of the bombing force also carried flares. The nine remaining Swordfish took off shortly afterwards. All the planes taking part had been fitted with long-range fuel tanks which increased their range to 400 miles, and to save weight the Telegraphist/Air Gunners were left behind.

En route a torpedo-carrying plane and three of the bombing group became separated from the main force in cloud but carried on independently to the target.

The flare-carrying plane in the first group to arrive at Taranto dropped its flares to the east of the harbour and then joined with the other flare-carrying plane in a dive-bombing attack which soon set the oil tanks ablaze.

The next three aircraft to arrive flew over San Pietro Island and headed for the group of Italian battleships. Commander Williamson who led this group scored a direct hit with his torpedo on the *Conti di Cavour* just before he was shot down by anti-aircraft fire.

A direct hit with a torpedo can cause devastating damage, often blasting a hole in the side of a vessel through which two or even three double-decker buses could be driven side by side. This hit was no exception, measuring some 27 feet across. The official report refers to the fact that 'this caused the Italian battleship to list badly' – presumably to no one's surprise! Reconnaissance the next morning showed the *Conti di Cavour* to be beached with her decks well below the surface of the water. The two remaining aircraft of this sub-flight continued their attack despite both the intense anti-aircraft fire they encountered and the balloon barrage through which they had to weave their way to reach their targets, and attacked the battleship *Andrea Doria* but with only limited success. The next sub-flight came in from the north and two of

its three torpedoes found their marks on the new battleship *Littorio*, these two strikes blowing large holes in both the starboard bow and the port quarter and she quickly started to settle.

Next on the scene was a sub-flight of three Swordfish armed with bombs. They had some difficulty in identifying their targets; the lead plane dived on two cruisers from 1,500 feet and a Swordfish that followed close behind dropped its

Taranto harbour after the successful Fleet Air Arm attack. The clouds of oil escaping from the damaged ships give some indication of the extent of the damage inflicted

bombs across a trot of four destroyers. The third bomber in this group failed to find its target in the *Mar Piccolo* and rather than waste his bomb load the pilot planted them on a seaplane hangar.

Half an hour after the first strike force had left *Illustrious* a further group of aircraft was flown off and headed for Taranto. Of these nine Swordfish four were armed with bombs and as before two of these planes also carried flares, the remainder being armed with torpedoes. En route to the target the auxiliary fuel tank was coming adrift from one plane from *Illustrious*, causing the loss of a great deal of petrol and, having insufficient to get to the target and back, the plane returned to *Illustrious*.

Just before midnight the two flare-carrying planes of the second group illuminated the target and the planes carrying torpedoes went into action. The *Littorio*, which was sinking, was struck yet again and the battleship *Caio Duilio* took a torpedo amidships which resulted in both forward magazines being flooded. Next morning the *Caio Duilio* was seen to be beached and it appeared that vessels were lashed alongside *Littorio* in an effort to keep her from sinking. Despite this her bows were well down and her decks were partly awash.

A plane that had been delayed by a taxying accident arrived fifteen minutes after the last aircraft had left the scene and pressed on with its solo attack on a cruiser. This required the pilot to dive through the balloon barrage in the dark and at the same time to face the combined barrage of the Italian Fleet. The courage required to press on with an attack in such circumstances beggars belief. Happily Lt Clifford and his observer escaped unscathed and returned to *Illustrious* at about 0230.

Next morning reconnaissance photographs showed that the *Mar Piccolo* was covered in oil and debris with vessels in various stages of destruction scattered around. The oil depot was smouldering happily and the seaplane hangars were totally destroyed.

Taranto was a great victory, so much damage to the enemy at so little cost. For the loss of two Swordfish and two aircrew the raid on Taranto did more damage to the Italian Fleet than was inflicted on the German Navy at the Battle of Jutland at the cost of 6,000 British casualties. Not only was a considerable part of the Italian Fleet destroyed or severely damaged but the remnants of the Italian Fleet were compelled to withdraw to Naples where they were too far from the routes used by British convoys to pose the threat they had been as an intact fleet at Taranto. This freed two British battleships and their attendant vessels for action in other spheres of activity. An additional bonus was the blow to the morale suffered by the Italian Navy as was to be illustrated in later encounters.

The Japanese took on board the lessons of Taranto and tailored their navy accordingly which led directly to their devastating attack on Pearl Harbor. The Americans also learned the lesson but they had to experience the attack on Pearl Harbor before they built a navy that depended largely on a huge carrier fleet to drive the Japanese from the Pacific.

Argus had arrived at Gibraltar with more aircraft that were to be delivered to Malta and joined with Force H which was scheduled to escort her to within flying distance of the island. On 10 November *Ark Royal*, as part of Force H, left Gibraltar for what was to be the last time. Two days later the planes were flown off from *Argus* and Force H turned back to Gibraltar.

The next day the *Ark* exercised fourteen of her Swordfish and as the last of them was landing on there was a loud explosion somewhere about midships on the starboard side. A single torpedo had struck *Ark Royal* just below the bridge.

Unfortunately she was doing 18 knots when the torpedo struck and the great volume of water that would be scooped inboard through that vast hole was to be the end of her. Within three minutes she had a twelve-degree list.

Although she was only thirty miles from Gibraltar and strenuous efforts were made all night to tow her, at 0613 that morning she rolled over and sank. Of the 1,540 members of the ship's company just one life was lost and that occurred in the explosion. Some of her aircraft, Swordfish and Fulmars, were able to reach Gibraltar safely.

At the beginning of December 1940 General Wavell was in charge of the British Forces in the Western Desert and drove the Italians from Egypt. Quite soon they were in headlong retreat westwards. Planes from *Eagle* and *Illustrious* flew strikes against Italian transports at Bardia and

HMS Ark Royal, *torpedoed in 1940*

Italian shipping was attacked wherever it was found, even as far afield as Tunisia, in support of the Army ashore.

The Germans reacted to the Italian defeats by sending large numbers of aircraft to Sicily with the intention, in part at least, of neutralising Malta.

Force H, operating from the western end of the Mediterranean, was escorting a convoy bound for Malta and Greece and on 7 January 1941 *Illustrious, Warspite* and *Valiant*, with their usual escort of smaller vessels, left Alexandria to take over responsibility for the convoy from Force H. In the course of the forenoon of 10 January the handover of the convoy was made and the Mediterranean Fleet headed with its charges towards the Grand Harbour at Valletta with Fulmars from the carrier patrolling overhead.

Shortly after 1000 a number of Italian aircraft arrived. The Fulmars went into the attack and shot down two of the enemy aircraft and drove off the rest but this left them short of ammunition. The next wave of attacking aircraft were Junkers 87s and there were no Fulmars in the air to meet them. The Fulmars that had not landed on were in pursuit of two SM. 79s that were racing for Sicily.

For some reason the flagship delayed for some minutes before it gave permission for the carrier to fly off the remaining Fulmars and bombs were dropping as the last of the planes took off. The Fulmars had no hope of getting to the Ju 87s in time to tackle them before they dropped their bombs. The Stukas were bombing from 12,000 feet and the Fulmars' rate of climb was about 1,200 feet a minute. Unless they had sufficient warning of the approach of the enemy planes there was no way they could reach them in time to effect the issue.

The German planes did considerable damage to

Illustrious. Despite the heavy anti-aircraft fire that was put up by the Fleet the *Luftwaffe* hit the after deck of *Illustrious* repeatedly. Two of their heavy bombs hit the lift, others made it hell for the engine room crew who somehow kept the engines working throughout. The ship was close to being out of control for three hours with several fires blazing away. The Italians made another ineffectual attack at this time.

The German planes returned at 1600 but the Fulmars which had refuelled at Malta were back too and they drove off all except one of the enemy who unfortunately was able to drop one more 1,000-lb bomb on the after deck of *Illustrious*, which caused the fires to flare up and intensify yet again.

Illustrious was only forty miles from Malta but it

This picture of HMS Eagle *shows the above water section of the ram that extends well forward under water*

was to be some six hours before she was able to berth there. The fires continued to blaze throughout the night and it was not until the next forenoon that they were extinguished. Casualties were heavy, particularly among the aircrews.

Once *Illustrious* had arrived Malta represented help and some additional degree of safety but that safety was far from total. In three major raids on *Illustrious* whilst she was in Malta, mostly by German aircraft, it was estimated that the enemy used a total of over 400 planes. To oppose this aerial armada Malta had just three serviceable Hurricanes and a single Gloucester Gladiator.

They did what they could whilst *Illustrious* and others fought off the hordes of enemy aircraft with a well practised barrage of anti-aircraft fire.

It took thirteen days to make *Illustrious* fit to go to sea again and air attacks were made repeatedly during that time. It took two days for her to reach Alexandria, where a further six weeks of work was undertaken to ensure her seaworthiness for the long haul to America and the promise of major repairs in the peace of a shipyard beyond the reach of the *Luftwaffe*.

On 3 March *Illustrious* sailed down the Suez Canal and into the Red Sea. From there she went to South Africa and then on to the West Indies before docking in the huge US Naval Dockyard in Norfolk, Virginia. That voyage from Suez to the States must have seemed like a well deserved holiday cruise after her recent experiences. Such was the damage she had suffered that it was to be

A Fairey Albacore, an update on the Swordfish, complete with windows and central heating!

six and a half months before the repairs were completed.

Eagle had been worked hard and by the beginning of 1941 she was badly in need of a refit but with *Illustrious* out of action she could not be spared until she was relieved by the new fleet carrier *Formidable* and this was not to be until 10 March.

A Sunderland flying boat based on Malta reported on 27 March that she had spotted a number of Italian warships about eighty miles south of Sicily heading east. This suggested that the Italians intended attacking shipping that passed between North Africa and the Greek ports to the north.

The Mediterranean Fleet left Alex. without delay and sailed to intercept the enemy warships. By 0720 the next day one of *Formidable*'s Albacores reported the position of four enemy cruisers and seven destroyers now to the south-west of Crete, steering south-east towards the British ships. At about 0900 the Italian Fleet was seen to turn to the west and *Orion* and other ships of the Light Forces under Vice-Admiral Pridham-Wippell turned to follow them. Two hours later the Italian battleship was spotted and it became clear that the change of course by the Italian cruisers was an attempt to lead the Royal Naval Light Forces into an encounter with the heavy guns of *Vittorio Veneto* from which they would have suffered severely. The British ships turned away towards the south.

Formidable flew off a strike of six Albacores at 1000 with two Fulmars as a fighter escort. Before they had left the carrier they had been briefed to attack the Italian cruisers.

Having flown about 100 miles the aircraft sighted the Italian flagship *Vittorio Veneto* with her escort of destroyers. The Albacores attacked, diving through heavy anti-aircraft fire. The attack produced no visible results nor were there any casualties amongst the attackers. While the Albacores were attacking *Vittorio Veneto* the Fulmars fought off two Junkers 88s that appeared, destroying one of them in the process. Thirty minutes later three Swordfish from Malame airfield in Crete attacked *Vittorio Veneto* but again there appeared to be no damage to the battleship.

While these attacks were in progress *Formidable* was in the throes of arming another strike force of two Swordfish and three Albacores with torpedoes. As before two Fulmars were attached to give fighter cover. This small force left at 1350 and an hour and a half later they came up on the enemy vessels, south of Cape Matapan. The torpedo-bombers attacked from out of the sun and scored at least one hit, which had the effect of slowing the enemy battleship down to eight knots. *Vittorio Veneto* was later able to make temporary repairs to this damage, which allowed her to make her escape. Clearly she had been losing oil rather heavily as the British battle fleet picked up her oil slick and followed it for some fifteen miles.

A further strike force took off from *Formidable* at dusk. This time there were six Albacores and two Swordfish which were joined en route by two Swordfish from Maleme. The attack lasted for fifteen minutes, each aircraft going in independently through an intense anti-aircraft barrage. As well as the barrage the enemy ships put up a smoke screen which obviously did nothing to help. The 10,000-ton cruiser *Pola* took a direct hit from a torpedo which stopped her engines and created a power failure. *Zara* and *Fiume*, *Pola*'s two sister ships, stopped to assist her. This allowed the Fleet to catch up with the Italian vessels and subject them to a heavy bombardment which sank the three sister ships and their destroyer escort. At first light, aircraft were searching for *Vittorio Veneto* but all they found were survivors in boats and rafts from the Italian vessels that had been sunk. The planes led the Fleet to the survivors but a halt had to be called to the rescue work as the ships were attacked by German bombers.

In addition to the damage incurred by the Italian flagship three cruisers and two destroyers were sunk. This, the Battle of Cape Matapan, so reduced the strength of the Italian Fleet that it was no longer a serious threat to ships involved in operations concerned with Greece. Later, when troops had to be rescued from Crete the operation would have been impossible if the Italian Fleet had been in a condition to interfere with it.

In mid-April 1941 *Argus* arrived once more at Gibraltar with twenty-six Hurricanes for the defence of Malta; the aircraft she had brought were transferred to *Illustrious*. Three days after leaving Gibraltar, escorted by Force H, *Illustrious* flew the Hurricanes off in company with a Fulmar whose task was to act as navigator for the single-seater planes. This operation was a complete success and it was repeated in the middle of May and a further nine operations of this kind were made in 1941. The new fleet carrier *Victorious* as well as *Illustrious*, *Furious* and *Argus* were all involved in these operations.

Formidable saw more action on 21 April; this time nine of her Albacores were used to spot the fall of shot for the bombardment by RN battleships of the harbour of Tripoli and the enemy shipping that was making use of its facilities. A couple of weeks later her aircraft were helping to escort a much needed convoy to Malta. In the course of this task seven enemy aircraft were shot down by her fighters.

The middle of May found *Formidable* back in Alexandria where she stayed until 25 May when she sailed as a part of the Mediterranean Fleet. The day after leaving Alexandria, aircraft from *Formidable* bombed and strafed the airfield at Scarpanto. The strike force had the good fortune to come in undetected until they announced themselves.

In the afternoon of the same day a number of Junkers 87s and 88s flew in from North Africa and attacked *Formidable*. There were two Fulmars patrolling above the ships and they immediately attacked the Junkers, shooting down four of them. Despite this some of the German planes managed to deliver their bomb loads and *Formidable* took two direct hits on deck, one forward and the other aft. Hull damage was also sustained from near misses. Despite the damage, and it was considerable, she was able to move under her own power and reached the safety of Alexandria the next day.

The damage *Formidable* had sustained was more than the local facilities could deal with so she was patched up and on 24 July she followed in the footsteps of *Illustrious*, this time to the yard at Portsmouth, Virginia, USA, arriving on 25 August 1941.

Her repairs took until the December of the same year and she sailed on the 7th, just a short time after *Illustrious* had sailed from Norfolk, Virginia. From 7 Dec 1941 there was to be no armoured carrier serving in Mediterranean waters for the next three years. The Indian and Pacific Oceans had prior call on their services.

The lack of carriers in the Mediterranean made Malta ever more important. She had the great virtue that no matter what was thrown at her she would not sink. We in Britain should not forget the debt we owe to the people of Malta. They took an immense amount of punishment but their steadfastness never wavered.

An FAA squadron of Swordfish was based there from the end of June 1940 onwards. When they

arrived they were almost immediately briefed for an attack on an oil refinery at Augusta in Sicily. Another similar raid was carried out on 14 August and two aircraft failed to return from this strike. These planes were used for the mundane bread and butter jobs for which little recognition is given. They protected Allied convoys, attacked enemy shipping and anything else that needed attacking or subduing. Often, when they returned to their base they would find that an air raid was in progress and they would have to stand off until things had quietened down sufficiently to allow them to land in safety.

When one realises that we are talking of near-routine raids and not one-off examples the figures strike home hard. For example, early in March 1941 something like one hundred enemy bombers attacked Malta in a single raid and this was not at all unusual. In an area as small as Malta that would mean an unenviable concentration of attacking aircraft.

Fleet Air Arm aircraft based on Gibraltar played a similarly unsung part. Much of their task was to deny the enemy passage of the Straits of Gibraltar. In December 1941 four of the nine aircraft in the squadron were fitted with Air-to-Surface Vessel Radar (ASV) and every night two-hour long patrols were carried out continuously from 1900 to 0900 the following morning.

The radar sets enabled the crews to carry out several attacks on U boats. In a three week period it is known that at least five U boats were damaged and the first confirmed sinking of a U boat was made on the night of 21/22 December. Other planes carried out similar patrols throughout the hours of daylight.

This tiny force virtually denied the passage of the Straits of Gibraltar to U boats from mid-December to the early spring of 1942.

The Fleet Air Arm was involved in a multitude of unspectacular actions throughout the Mediterranean and North Africa, each one eroding the enemy's capability to wage war against the Allies. Small groups saw action in Greece, Malta, Crete and the North African desert as a matter of daily routine. When a carrier was in harbour it was usual to send aircraft into the desert to lend their weight to the fray. Often before army activity at a particular point in North Africa, a number of Swordfish would take it in turns to fly above the German troops, dropping a bomb every hour or so simply to ruin their sleep. Others like the Swordfish squadrons based on Cyprus conducted anti-submarine patrols and were especially active against the Vichy French vessels that were working for the Germans in the region.

It is a pity that these events are too small to include in an account of this kind but it must be remembered that every oil dump that was destroyed, every enemy ship, however small, that was sunk, every enemy aircraft that was destroyed, either on the ground or in the air, and every installation that was damaged or destroyed was just one more step towards eventual victory. Sadly it must also be said that you were just as dead if you were killed on one of these less glamorous operations as you were if it happened on one of the more momentous occasions.

The Italians put up such a poor show in Greece that the Germans felt impelled to join in the fray and early in April 1941 they committed both ground and air forces to the fight. These measures were so successful that the Allied forces had to be evacuated by sea to Crete.

Meanwhile Hitler had decided that Crete had to be captured and committed 22,000 troops to the task, most of whom were to be delivered by air. On 20 May the battle for Crete started. It was not long before the Allied forces were in full retreat in the face of overwhelming enemy forces.

There had been a small FAA group operating from Crete and they fought not only with their own planes but also with a number that had been left behind when the RAF had retreated. They fought until there were no planes left with which to fight and then joined the trek towards the evacuation points.

When it became apparent that the ground forces would need to be rescued from Crete, some of Admiral Cunningham's staff strongly advised him to abandon the troops ashore rather than expose his ships to the full weight of the *Luftwaffe* with no aircraft to help defend the fleet. Such action ran counter to Cunningham's nature and he

rejected their advice. The Navy proceeded to rescue more than half of the men who were ashore. The cost was high, the cruisers *Fiji, Gloucester* and *York* were sunk as were the destroyers *Greyhound, Kelly, Kashmir, Juno, Imperial* and *Hereward*; the cruiser *Ajax* and five other ships were damaged but the Navy's honour was intact.

If the Italian Fleet had been a fighting force the Navy would have suffered even greater losses but fortunately the activities of the FAA at Matapan and Taranto and elsewhere had ensured the unwillingness or inability of the Italian Fleet to get involved.

Malta continued to be under siege and more and more aircraft were needed for her defence. In the four months from March to July 1942, 275 Spitfires were delivered. *Eagle* figured prominently in all these delivery trips. None of them was easy but despite that the success rate was very high: only six aircraft failed to reach Malta in this period. On a number of occasions *Eagle* was accompanied by *Argus* or the USS *Wasp*.

Month by month the weight of bombs being dropped on Malta was increased until in the four weeks of April the *Luftwaffe* dropped a total of 6,700 tons of bombs on this tiny island, much of it on the Naval Dockyard, which was for all practical purposes put out of action. At times the defending fighters were reduced to a mere half dozen serviceable planes. The island was no longer a viable place for surface ships or submarines to use as an operational base.

The Germans sent substantial numbers of planes back to the Russian Front thinking they had neutralised Malta, which allowed the defenders a measure of respite. However the battle went on even if its intensity was diminished and by the end of April the Germans had lost 40 planes out of a total of 131. This was an improvement but the Axis air force still had command of the central Mediterranean and Malta was effectively blockaded. It was imperative that a supply convoy should get through to her if she was to continue to hold out.

The plan was to despatch a convoy from either end of the Mediterranean at the same time in an effort to divide the forces that could be pitted

Malta convoy under attack

against them. The convoy of eleven merchant ships that was to sail from Alexandria was to be escorted by eight cruisers and twenty-six destroyers. As no carrier was available to escort the convoy it would be given air cover by FAA and RAF planes based in Egypt for the first part of its passage, and planes from Malta would afford the convoy some measure of protection once it was within reach; for the stretch in between there would be no air cover.

The convoy of six ships from Gibraltar was to be escorted by *Eagle* and *Argus*, which between them carried twenty-four fighters and eighteen Swordfish; in addition the escort included a battleship, four cruisers and seventeen destroyers. These ships would escort the merchantmen to the northern end of the Sicilian Narrows where one of

the cruisers and nine destroyers would stay with them for the rest of the way.

Both convoys set out at the same time and the first day or two were relatively free of problems.

On 14 June the convoy from Gibraltar was subjected to a number of attacks by both German and Italian planes from Sardinia and Sicily. The heaviest raid was made by ten high-level bombers, twenty-eight torpedo planes and twenty fighters. The brunt of the attacks was borne by *Eagle* and *Argus* but happily they both escaped unscathed.

The Italian cruisers *Montecuccoli* and *Savoia* in company with five destroyers left Palermo, on the northern coast of Sicily, to attack the convoy. They were beaten off by the convoy escorts with the loss of the destroyer *Bedouin* and some serious damage to *Partridge*.

Seven FAA planes were lost but the Sea Hurricanes and Fulmars destroyed thirteen of the enemy aircraft and damaged a number of others. Despite the major effort put out by the Axis air forces, the aircraft from the two small carriers had managed to keep the damage to one merchantman sunk and the cruiser *Liverpool* damaged badly enough to have to return to Gibraltar.

After dark that evening, off Cap Bon, the main part of the escort turned back to Gibraltar, leaving the convoy to negotiate the Sicilian Narrows in the care of one cruiser and nine destroyers, with Beaufighters from Malta taking over from the carrier-borne planes. The attacks continued during the next day and three more merchant ships were lost to enemy air attack. Just two merchantmen made it to Malta but they unloaded 25,000 tons of much needed supplies.

It is a measure of the desperate state of Malta's supply situation that this was treated almost as if it were a victory.

Meanwhile the convoy from the other end of the Mediterranean had been making progress

The Ohio *reaches harbour in a sinking condition*

towards Malta, gradually moving away from the air cover from North Africa. One merchant ship had suffered some damage from enemy air attacks and another that could not maintain her place in the convoy was sent back. In the course of 14 June the convoy was attacked by sixty to seventy dive-bombers no fewer than seven times. During these attacks the enemy planes sank one merchant ship in the convoy and another that failed to keep up with the convoy was set upon by forty dive-bombers and sunk.

Italian E boats (fast motor torpedo- or motor gun-boats) had attacked the convoy repeatedly and succeeded in sinking a destroyer and damaging one of the escorting cruisers.

Two merchant ships and two destroyers had been lost when news was received that two Italian battleships, four cruisers and twelve destroyers had ventured out from Taranto and were heading for the convoy. The only ships Rear Admiral Vian had with which to protect the convoy were light cruisers and destroyers, which were totally outgunned by the Italian battleships. Without the protection of an aircraft carrier they had been under continuous air attack and had expended two thirds of their anti-aircraft ammunition. It was therefore reluctantly decided to order the convoy to return to port.

On the way back to Alexandria two more destroyers were lost to air attack and a cruiser was sunk by a U boat. Altogether a very expensive operation; a cruiser, five destroyers and six merchant ships sunk; two merchant ships, three cruisers and two destroyers damaged. Of the seventeen merchantmen that set out only two reached Alexandria.

Without the strong support given by the RAF the west-bound convoy would have suffered even more badly than it did, as was shown when the convoy sailed beyond the protection of the land-based aircraft.

The convoy that left Gibraltar fared better than the convoy from Alexandria and that was due, at least in part, to the inclusion of two small and elderly aircraft carriers in the escort group.

Of the 275 Spitfires delivered to Malta between March and July 1942, by early August there were just 80 serviceable ones left. With the need for more planes and supplies of all kinds it was decided to form another east-bound convoy of fourteen fast merchantmen. This time it was to have massive naval support. In addition to two battleships, three cruisers and the anti-aircraft cruiser *Cairo*, and a great many destroyers, there were to be the aircraft carriers *Eagle, Furious, Indomitable* and *Victorious*. Eight submarines were positioned to intercept any enemy surface vessels that might venture out. A formidable force indeed, but perhaps an indication of the seriousness of the situation and the anticipated opposition.

The convoy entered the Mediterranean on the night of 9/10 August 1942. The following day, the 11th, *Eagle* was struck by four torpedoes from a U boat and sank in less than eight minutes. Her crew numbered 1,160 of which 760 were lost.

Later that day a group of thirty-six German bombers attacked the convoy but failed to register any hits. At about noon the following day some eighty aircraft arrived, apparently from Sicily. They were driven off after causing limited damage to *Victorious* with a bomb that failed to explode and a near miss that did some damage to the merchant ship *Deucalion*. Later that afternoon she was hit by a torpedo launched by a German aircraft and went down. A submarine attack followed the latest air attack but the convoy escaped unscathed. *Ithuriel* rammed and sank an Italian submarine. Further enemy air strikes followed and *Indomitable*'s flight-deck was struck by four bombs which damaged her armoured flight-deck so badly that she was put out of action and required major repairs that were carried out over a period of several months in a US dockyard. Without their armoured decks both *Victorious* and *Indomitable* would have been destroyed.

An Italian submarine penetrated the screen and torpedoed the cruiser *Nigeria,* the anti-aircraft cruiser *Cairo* and the tanker *Ohio* which, although badly damaged, stayed afloat. An air attack at dusk slightly damaged *Kenya* and sank two merchantmen. At about midnight off Cap Bon the convoy was assailed by a number of E boats. Their attack was successful: they sank five more merchant ships and the *Manchester* was so badly

HMS Indomitable *and* Eagle *from the deck of* Victorious *escorting a Malta convoy, August 1942*

damaged that she had to be scuttled. At first light the next day the convoy was within 100 miles of enemy airfields and the air attacks were to be continuous from here on. The merchant ship *Dorset* disappeared under a torrent of bombs and a ship called *Waimaramu*, carrying petrol and ammunition, blew up.

Royal Air Force fighters from Malta had by now joined the escort and they helped to cover the arrival of three supply ships. The *Brisbane Star* had been damaged but she limped into Grand Harbour the next day. *Ohio* was under tow at two knots for the last forty miles which must have been sheer hell, as by now she would have been the sole target for so many of the available enemy aircraft.

On 15 August she entered Grand Harbour to the well deserved cheers of both the assembled ships and the Maltese.

Thirteen FAA fighters from the escort were lost but thirty of the attacking planes were brought down. Lt Cork DSC, flying a Sea Hurricane, shot down five of them on 12 August.

Of the fourteen merchant ships that set out only five reached Malta and two of those were in a sinking condition. The RN lost an aircraft carrier and two cruisers and four more of HM Ships were damaged, two quite severely. Food shortages had brought Malta to the brink of surrender. Fortunately the 55,000 tons of supplies that those ships brought to Malta at such cost was enough to save the island.

A total of 718 aircraft reached Malta by the various ferrying attempts between August 1940 and October 1942. Spitfires accounted for 385 of these and a further 361 were Hurricanes. In addition there were eleven Albacores and seven Swordfish. Forty-six planes failed to reach Malta, thirty-four were lost en route and twelve had for various reasons to return to their parent ships.

CHAPTER SIX

Operation Torch to Operation Dragoon

When France capitulated in 1940 the country was divided into two parts, the northern part being administered directly by the Germans and the southern part by the Germans through a puppet French government that became known as the Vichy government. This puppet government was also responsible for the French-held areas of North Africa, namely Morocco and Algiers. It was generally pro-German and obstructed the Allied effort whenever the chance presented itself.

By autumn 1942 the tide had turned in North Africa and the British were driving the German forces under the command of General Rommel steadily westwards towards the Vichy French-held territory in North West Africa. Malta was more secure than she had ever been since the Italians entered the war and the armed forces based there were able to go onto the offensive, their target the shipping that was supplying the Axis forces in North Africa. There were two FAA squadrons of Swordfish and Albacore operating from Malta working closely with the RAF. More than thirty enemy ships were sunk by these two squadrons and a further fifty damaged.

The improving circumstances in the Mediterranean encouraged the Allies to look for more ways of discomforting the Axis forces, especially those in North Africa. The Eighth Army had broken out of Egypt at El Alamein and was driving the German Forces westwards at an ever increasing pace. If Allied forces could be established ashore in the Vichy French-held areas of Morocco and Algeria, attacking the *Afrika Korps* on two fronts became a distinct possibility.

America had entered the war against Japan in December 1941 when Japan had attacked her at Pearl Harbor. Shortly after this attack Germany declared war on the United States and America started sending air and ground forces to Britain.

By late 1942 the American Army and Army Air Force in Britain had built up into a sizeable force and it was decided to use them as part of the group that was intended to invade the Vichy-held areas of North West Africa.

In an operation named 'Torch' the Americans were given the task of invading Casablanca on the Atlantic coast leaving the British forces to tackle both Algiers and Oran on the Mediterranean shores. The date of the three landings was to be 8 November 1942. The invasion areas were too far off for the RAF or the US Army Air Force (USAAF) to give effective fighter cover and ground support to the troops and so this became the responsibility of the FAA and a contingent of American planes.

It was clear that the Vichy French Government was ill-disposed towards Britain and in the hope that they would find the American forces more acceptable all the aircraft involved were marked with the US star and the words Royal Navy on the after end of the fuselage were changed to 'US Navy'.

The invasion force left Britain in fifteen separate convoys, hoping to give the impression that they were routine Mediterranean convoys. The carriers left for Gibraltar at different times in the period between 22 and 30 October to avoid the possibility of German reconnaissance planes spotting an armada of aircraft carriers all heading in the same direction . . . a sure indication of a big operation about to take place

The Fleet Carriers were *Argus, Formidable, Furious* and *Victoria* and these were accompanied by three Escort Carriers *Avenger, Biter* and *Dasher*. Between them they carried more than 160 planes comprising Albacores, Fulmars, Martlets, Seafires and Sea Hurricanes. *Argus* and *Avenger* were to be part of the force attacking Algiers and the remaining aircraft carriers were intended to cover the landings at Oran. Both British task forces were to be supported by Force H.

The Americans provided their own naval support for the landings at Casablanca which included 136 carrier-borne aircraft.

Planes of the RAF and USAAF were waiting on Gibraltar to fly in once airfields in North Africa were in the hands of our ground forces.

The ships destined for Oran and Algiers made their way through the Straits of Gibraltar on 6 November. Anti-submarine patrols were mounted by RAF Sunderlands and Hudsons and fighter cover was flown by the FAA. In the course of the day just one plane was spotted, a high-flying French aircraft. The convoys and their escort vessels maintained an easterly course to give the impression of convoys carrying materiel for the British forces in the Med. until at a prearranged time that night they turned south to their respective destinations on the North African coast.

Surprise was complete, the deception programme having worked perfectly. The first men went ashore at 0100 and encountered little or no opposition. The Escort Carriers were lying offshore waiting to fly off fighter and anti-submarine patrols at first light. At 0530 two Albacores were in the air followed fifteen minutes later by four Martlets from *Victorious.* The Martlets headed for the military airfield at Blida. When they arrived they shot up the airfield and attacked two French planes that were taking off and then reported that there was little opposition to their activities.

Next, four carriers flew off forty-two aircraft to attack three Vichy French airfields which they did with a fair degree of success. Eight Albacores and a Fulmar destroyed five hangars and forty-seven planes at La Senia and their escort of Sea Hurricanes shot down five of the Vichy French Dewoitines that attempted to attack the strike aircraft. Four Albacores were lost in this engagement.

Any loss is always a matter for regret but time and time again the FAA were able to inflict losses on enemy ships, planes and installations quite out of proportion to the number of FAA aircraft involved. In this case for the cost of four Albacores and their crews the enemy lost fifty-two aircraft and five hangars.

Two RN destroyers were attempting to force a way through the boom across the entrance to the harbour at Algiers and came under heavy fire from a naval fort at Jethe'e du Nord. Six Albacores were called in and bombed the fort until it was silenced.

A little later Fort du Perre to the west of Algiers was holding up the advance of a commando group. Another Albacore strike took out the fort and allowed the commandos to continue on their way. The Albacores then went on to eliminate Fort Matifou.

Victorious flew off four Martlets to act as a fighter patrol over Blida airfield. When they arrived they encountered little or no enemy action although the AA guns were clearly manned. In the fields around the airfield farm hands appeared to be waving a welcome. The leader of the four Martlets, Lt B. Nation, radioed back to his ship that the French appeared to be willing to surrender. Back on board the report was treated with some scepticism and he was told to check that he really was over Blida airfield. It must have been one of the more satisfying moments of his life to be able to radio back that the name was inscribed in large letters in the middle of the airfield. Lt Nation was eventually given permission to land 'if he thought it safe so to do'.

Nothing loath he landed, taxied across to the admin. area, drew his service pistol and accepted the surrender of the airfield from a rather elderly French General. Fortunately it wasn't long before a commando group arrived and took over from him allowing him to rejoin the three Martlets that had been flying overhead and to resume their patrol.

On the second day a fresh landing was made at Bougie Beach just east of Algiers with Seafires giving air cover and support and further west FAA planes were busy doing the same for the fresh landings made at Oran.

Matters ashore had gone so well that by 9 November carrier operations in support of the ground forces were much reduced. This was just as well because German and Italian planes were now attacking Force H, and the merchant shipping involved in the landings and the carriers' fighters were needed to defend them.

By now the USAAF had flown in a number of Spitfires from Gibraltar to operate from captured airfields and the need for FAA aircraft was diminishing, so the carriers prepared to withdraw. *Argus* remained at sea giving air cover to the shipping in the area. As it was getting dark fifteen Ju 88s appeared and before the protecting fighters could intervene *Argus* was struck aft by a bomb which destroyed four of her fighters but fortunately did no other significant damage. It must have been her lucky day because later that night a U boat fired two torpedoes at her: one missed astern and the other passed harmlessly beneath her. By 10 November things had gone so well that *Avenger* actually put into Algiers for repairs. As soon as the forces ashore were well settled in, the ships that had brought them to North Africa and their escorts began to withdraw. Once *Avenger* had completed her repairs she joined the other escort vessels and in the course of the withdrawal she was hit by a torpedo from a German U boat. She blew up leaving just seventeen survivors. Her total destruction is put down to the fact that she was one of the earliest escort carriers built in the USA at a time when their fire precautions and the safety of their fuel delivery arrangements were less demanding than perhaps they should have been.

There was still a high level of submarine activity in the area and a patrol of Albacores from *Furious* found and torpedoed a U boat that had been damaged earlier by planes from Tafaroui.

The successful Torch landings grew into the Tunisian Front which advanced eastwards whilst the Eighth Army was pushing the *Afrika Korps* further and further westwards, creating the pincer movement that was the prime purpose of the landings. Eventually, in late April to early May 1943, the retreat became a rout with much of the remaining Axis forces attempting to get back to Europe from Tunisia ...particularly from Khelibia and the Axis attempt at staging a Dunkirk from there soon became known as 'The Khelibia Regatta' with light naval forces and FAA planes indulging in a turkey shoot.

Once North Africa was safely in the hands of the Allies the planners were looking towards a return

to Europe and Sicily was to be the stepping stone to that end. No time was wasted and Operation Husky, the invasion of Sicily was mounted on 10 July 1943.

Force H, plus *Formidable* and *Indomitable*, was given the task of ensuring that the Italian Navy was kept at a suitable distance from the operation and to this end it was positioned about 180 miles east of Malta. In the right hands the Italian Fleet should have been a force to be reckoned with, as it was still in possession of six battleships, seven cruisers and forty-eight destroyers. In the event the morale of the Italian Navy was so low that it made no attempt to defend its own shores.

The FAA played a small, but costly part in this operation. On the night of 15/16 July *Indomitable* was approached by a Ju 88. This single enemy plane hit the carrier's port side with its torpedo seriously damaging an engine room. The stricken ship made her way to Grand Harbour, Malta, in the company of *Formidable*, where temporary repair work was carried out over the next ten days. Her next stop was Gibraltar where she put all her aircraft ashore and departed for the Norfolk Dockyard in Virginia, USA to complete her repairs in less fraught circumstances. She was to be out of action for best part of a year.

Things went well for the troops ashore in Sicily and quite soon they were fighting their way up mainland Italy. It was felt that things could be speeded up if the well-equipped port of Naples were to fall into Allied hands. To this end plans were made for an amphibious assault twenty-five miles south-east of Naples at Salerno Bay, to be known as Operation Avalanche.

By now the Allied Forces in the Mediterranean had nearly 4,000 aircraft at their disposal, but most of them were based so far away that their use at Salerno was not a practical proposition, so air defence fell to the lot of the FAA yet again. Rear Admiral Vian, with his flag in the cruiser *Euryalus*, was to lead the carrier force which was designated Force V. Escort Carriers *Attacker, Battler, Hunter, Stalker* and *Unicorn* were to be used for the close support of the troops ashore. Between them they would carry rather more than a hundred Seafires. Force H was to undertake the same role as it had for the landings on Sicily – keep the Italian Fleet well away from the scene of the action. Force H was joined by the two Fleet Carriers *Formidable* and *Illustrious;* their task was to be to give air cover to Force H and to back up the Escort Carriers if necessary.

In the small hours of 9 September both Force H and Force V were in position. Force H had suffered an ineffectual torpedo attack on the night of the 8th but Force V was apparently undetected until the carriers started flying operations at sunrise on 9 September. In the event the only action required of Force H was to escort the surrendered Italian Fleet to Malta. The two Fleet Carriers stayed to add their strength to that of Force V, and it was to be needed. The landings were going badly.

Unbeknown to the planners a *Panzer* division was resting and re-equipping close by and it was creating considerable difficulties for the assault forces. Such was the strength of the defending forces that it was touch and go whether the beachheads could be held.

It had been anticipated that Montecorvino airfield would be captured by the end of the first day and Spitfires and P-40s would then be flown in to take over from the ship-based fighters. This was not to happen for another two and a half days by which time an improvised airstrip had been levelled at Paestum in the American sector.

Those three and a half days provided forty-two hours of daylight and in that time the FAA Seafires flew 713 sorties. With a likely period of about 90 minutes to each sortie the total flying time approached 1,100 hours. The Escort Carriers started with a total of 100 Seafires and they received more from *Illustrious* and *Formidable* before they withdrew. When the airstrip at Paestum was ready to receive aircraft there were just twenty-six Seafires fit to be flown ashore. It was to be 15 September before the situation ashore was stable

A Supermarine Seafire, the naval version of the Spitfire

enough to allow the remaining Seafires to withdraw.

The use of one kind of aircraft in an operation like this was intended to simplify matters as far as spares, repairs and maintenance was concerned. The idea was good but the Seafire was the wrong plane. The Spitfire was never designed to go to sea. Adding an arrester hook and calling it a Seafire did not change that fact. The propeller on a Seafire was quite long and had a distressing tendency to hit the steel flight-deck if the landing was less than perfect. The undercarriage was narrow and fragile and frequently collapsed and its tyres were prone to burst when subjected to a heavy landing. They were doubtless good enough for landings ashore but in the more robust conditions encountered aboard a carrier's flight-deck they were far from adequate. The Escort Carriers' top speed was such that it needed to steam into a reasonable wind to help generate enough airflow over the flight-deck to enable a Seafire to land safely. If this was lacking, and the wind can be fickle in the Med., then the Seafire was prone to a high rate of accidents. The Fleet Carriers, with their greater speed through the water, were a safer bet for Seafire landings on days when there was little wind.

Operation Dragoon is the name that was finally given to the invasion of southern France. It started life as Operation Anvil but was postponed to allow the Normandy landings to become established before embarking on another major operation. When it was reinstated its name was changed to 'Dragoon'. Allied forces came ashore on the Riviera beaches close to Frejus, which lies between Cannes and St Tropez, on 15 August 1944. As at Salerno land-based aircraft were too far away to be able to give adequate support to the landings and so once more it fell to the lot of the FAA to give air cover and support to the invading

forces until a sufficient number of airfields were captured or constructed to allow the RAF to operate ashore. Seven RN Assault and Fighter Escort Carriers were to be used and these were assembled in the Mediterranean well in advance of D-Day in order to give the aircrews time to conduct working-up exercises to ready them for the real thing. The Escort Carriers were *Attacker*, *Hunter*, *Stalker*, *Khedive*, *Emperor*, *Pursuer*, *Searcher* and two USN Escort Carriers (CVEs – Carrier, Heavier-than-Air, Escort Vessels) *Kasaan Bay* and *Tulagi*. The joint force was commanded by Rear Admiral Troubridge RN, who flew his flag in the cruiser *Royalist*, specially fitted out for the command and control of a carrier force. The nine carriers carried a total of 224 fighters with a reserve of nearly ninety planes. Their task was to provide fighter cover and ground support for the troops ashore. The task force arrived off the Riviera beaches in the small hours of the morning of 15 August. Just before dawn the carriers started to fly-off the first of their strike forces. The landings went as planned, meeting only limited opposition, the Normandy landings having drawn off considerable numbers of German troops and aircraft. Quite quickly the role of the carrier-based fighters changed, and the emphasis moved from defence to offence. Without the *Luftwaffe* to contend with the fighters were free to roam far and wide attacking German defence positions, road, railway and canal targets as they chose. Things had gone so well in the first eleven days that the German forces had retreated beyond the reach of the Seafires and on 29 August 1944 the last of the carriers was withdrawn to Maddalena on the north-east corner of Sardinia.

Considering the scope and size of the operation the losses were light. In all, sixty aircraft were lost, thirty-five to flak and twenty-five to accidents of one kind or another.

CHAPTER SEVEN

The Sinking of Bismarck

At the outbreak of war in 1939 the Germans were working on the construction of a new battleship, *Bismarck.* She was a heavily armed vessel of some 50,000 tons and could make 30 knots with ease. Her decks were armour plated with nearly five inches of toughened steel. By the spring of 1941 work on her was finished and her sea trials were completed. She was ready for action.

Prinz Eugen was a newly built heavy cruiser of nearly 20,000 tons, capable of making 32 knots. These two formidable vessels with their heavy armament presented a serious threat to British shipping in the Atlantic, should they ever break out from the Baltic.

On 18 May 1941 both vessels left the German-occupied Polish port of Gdynia and, in company, made their way westwards across the Baltic Sea. Two days later a Swedish naval vessel spotted them accompanied by several destroyers heading west in the Skagerrak, the channel between the northern end of Denmark and the south-western end of Norway. Although Sweden was neutral this information quickly found its way to British representatives who immediately informed the Admiralty. The next day a Coastal Command Spitfire photographed both vessels anchored in Kors Fjord, near Bergen. The fact that they were willing to expose themselves to increased danger caused by moving so much closer to powerful British forces in this way confirmed the Admiralty's belief that they were ready to indulge in some form of offensive activity.

On the following day, 22 May, the crew of an RN Maryland volunteered to carry out a search of Bergen and the nearby Kors Fjord for the two ships; the pilot was Lt Goddard; Cdr Rotherham was the observer and Telegraphist Air Gunner Milne completed the crew. They took off from Hatston in the Orkneys, at the very north-eastern tip of Scotland, into extremely low cloud and laid a course for Kors Fjord. As they approached the Norwegian coast the cloud ceiling began to lift until they ran into clear weather, a mixed blessing in the circumstances.

The two ships had last been seen in Kors Fjord and this was where the Maryland crew first looked for them. There was no sign of their quarry so they turned their attention to Bergen Fjord, enduring very heavy flak in the process, but they drew another blank so a report was radioed back to Britain stating that *Bismarck* and *Prinz Eugen* appeared to have put to sea. The fear was that if they could break out into the Atlantic they would probably concentrate on adding to the destruction of the Atlantic convoys that had been suffering so much at the hands of the German U boat fleet.

Early 1941 was a tough time for Britain. She and the Commonwealth stood alone and ill-prepared against the great strength of the German armed forces, which were led by men who seemed intent on dominating the world in the most brutal way. Britain was under attack day and night by enemy aircraft and many of her major cities were daily suffering raids that were laying waste vast areas and killing and maiming huge numbers of people.

America was willing to sell us arms and food but we had to get them across the three thousand or so miles of the wide Atlantic Ocean and it was here that our merchant seamen were suffering well-nigh unbearable losses. The RN was stretched to its limits trying to protect the unarmed merchant ships from the unrelenting attacks of the German submarines and the last thing they needed was to have a fast, modern, enemy battleship and a powerful heavy cruiser on the rampage in the same area.

The Home Fleet was anchored at Scapa Flow, the Orkney Naval Base that guarded the Northern

A Blackburn-built Fairey Swordfish – a plane that achieved undying fame in WWII

Approaches to Britain. Two heavy cruisers, *Suffolk* and *Norfolk* were ordered to patrol the area between Iceland and Greenland known as the Denmark Strait, and the two cruisers *Birmingham* and *Manchester* were instructed to keep an eye on the Iceland–Faroes Gap. Both areas had ice to their north with floes in their southern parts and both were renowned for the poor visibility and bitterly cold weather that was the daily lot of seamen who ventured into that area.

Naturally the Germans flew regular reconnaissance flights over Scapa and the flight on 20 May reported that *King George V, Hood* and *The Prince of Wales* (battleships), *Victorious* (a Fleet Carrier), *Repulse* (a battle-cruiser) and six cruisers were at anchor.

On 22 May the German reconnaissance flight noted that all four big ships were still at anchor. This information was inaccurate inasmuch as Admiral Sir John Tovey had ordered *Hood* and *The Prince of Wales* to sea in the early hours of that day. *King George V* and *Victorious* followed within twenty-four hours. *Victorious* was, at this stage, a new Fleet Carrier and she was loaded with RAF Hurricanes which she was about to transport to the Mediterranean and put ashore at Malta. The

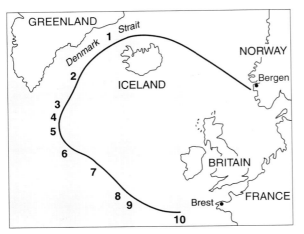

May 22nd. *Bismarck* and *Prinz Eugen* leave Bergen
1. May 23rd. *Suffolk* and *Norfolk* find the two German ships
2. May 24th. Action joined. *Hood* sunk
3. Later that day Swordfish attack *Bismarck* causing some damage.
4. May 25th. *Suffolk* and *Norfolk* lose contact with the German ships for 31 hours
5. May 26th. A Catalina finds the enemy capital ships
6. Swordfish resume shadowing. *Bismarck* appears to be making for Brest
7. Torpedo strike of 15 Swordfish flown off from *Ark Royal*. In the foul weather they mistake the *Sheffield* for the *Bismarck* and attack her ... without damaging her
8. Later the same day a second strike of 15 Swordfish find *Bismarck* and seriously damage her steering gear
9. Remainder of the Home Fleet catch up with *Bismarck* and pound her with heavy gunfire all night
10. May 27th. *Bismarck* sinks

only FAA planes she had aboard were six Fulmars and nine Swordfish which were intended to act in the defence of *Victorious* in the course of the passage to Malta. These Swordfish had no recent practice in torpedo attack work. However there was a squadron of Albacores based in the Orkneys that was trained and worked up to handle torpedo attacks. Unfortunately they came under the control of the Air Officer Commanding Coastal Command and he refused to release them in time to be taken aboard *Victorious*.

On 23 May the heavy cruisers *Suffolk* and *Norfolk* spotted both the *Bismarck* and the *Prinz Eugen* working their way south-westwards in the Denmark Strait and sent a signal reporting the position of the enemy vessels. As soon as Vice-Admiral Holland received this information he had *Hood* and *The Prince of Wales* turn onto an interception course.

In the small hours of 24 May the wind had come in strongly from the north and had dispersed much of the fog. *Suffolk* and *Norfolk* continued to shadow the two enemy vessels, use being made of the Walrus from *Norfolk* which had to contend with poor weather and intermittent snow showers.

Prinz Eugen had been fitted with long-range radar which picked up *Hood* and *The Prince of Wales* in plenty of time to allow the Germans to prepare themselves for the forthcoming encounter.

Action was joined at 0600. A brief eight minutes later *Hood* was a blazing inferno. Her back was broken and within minutes she disappeared below the sea taking all but three of her 1,420 crew with her.

Just precisely what happened will probably never be known but clearly one or more heavy shells fell squarely onto *Hood*'s deck. Whether these penetrated her lightly armoured deck and simply exploded below decks, or, perhaps first struck the 21-inch torpedoes in the four torpedo tubes that were mounted on the upper deck and caused them to explode to add to the carnage, there is no way of knowing. It might just explain the immensity of the explosion and the fire that followed.

At the time I was in a destroyer a great many miles from the scene of the disaster but even today I can still feel the stunned silence that enveloped the ship when the news was piped to us.

In the course of this brief engagement *The Prince of Wales* had suffered a number of direct hits that had caused serious damage. Her gun turrets were jammed and there was considerable incidental damage, leaving her no choice but to withdraw. Why *Prinz Eugen* allowed her to escape instead of harrying her to her death is difficult to understand.

Bismarck did not escape unscathed. Shells from *The Prince of Wales* holed her in two places. A fuel tank and lines had been broken and this reduced *Bismarck*'s speed. The damage was such that it was realised that a proper repair could not be undertaken at sea and so it was decided that she should make for St-Nazaire in German-occupied France. Meanwhile *Prinz Eugen* was to carry on alone with

The last moments of HMS Hood

the commerce raiding.

The Prince of Wales joined *Norfolk* and *Suffolk* and the three ships continued to shadow the *Bismarck* at extreme radar range.

Admiral Tovey had mustered every possible vessel of the Home Fleet and sent them to find and destroy *Bismarck*. Amongst this fleet was the aircraft carrier *Victorious* with her recently embarked Fulmars and Swordfish. At 2100 she was within striking distance of the German vessels and flew off all nine of her Swordfish armed with torpedoes. Their orders were to damage *Bismarck* sufficiently to slow her down and thus allow the heavy units of the fleet to bring her to action again.

Conditions were bad, with squalls and snow-storms all the way to the target and one can believe that the crews of the open cockpit Swordfish suffered at the hands of the arctic weather in the course of the 250-mile round trip.

Bismarck was picked up on airborne radar at a distance of sixteen miles. The cloud cover thickened as they approached but despite this the attacking planes were spotted at a range of some six miles. Surprise was lost and the Swordfish had to endure an intense barrage of anti-aircraft fire as they approached their target. Four miles from *Bismarck* Lt-Cdr Esmonde's plane was hit and the starboard lower aileron was damaged. The control difficulties created by this damage caused Esmonde to change his plans and he attacked the battleship's port bow whilst he was still in a good position.

It seems that in the general turmoil and confusion Lt Gick lost contact with his sub-flight. Hugging the water to escape the worst of the flak he found a good striking position and launched his torpedo in a single-handed attack. It proved to be the only torpedo to strike the target. Whilst this torpedo hit was more spectacular than effective, striking the ship's armoured belt, combined with the violent evasive manoeuvres forced upon *Bismarck* by the attacking forces, it exacerbated the damage caused earlier by *The Prince of Wales* to the point where fuel losses now became a serious problem. All nine Swordfish returned safely to *Victorious* from this engagement, but not without a measure of difficulty for some.

The foul weather caused *Suffolk* and *Norfolk* to lose contact with *Bismarck* some three hours after the torpedo strike and she remained out of contact for the next thirty-one hours.

In place of the planned dawn attack the Swordfish started searching for her again in what was fast becoming the norm – exceedingly bad weather. Two Swordfish failed to return from this sortie but fortunately the crews were picked up. One crew was adrift in their dinghy for nine days before they were found by a trawler fifty miles to the east of the southern tip of Greenland. The other crew ditched close to an abandoned lifeboat they had spotted and managed to board her. They found that she was well provisioned with food and water which kept them going for the next seven days when they too were picked up off the east coast of Greenland.

By now *Bismarck* had lost so much fuel that it was anticipated that she would attempt to reach Brest and ships were deployed to intercept her. *Ark Royal* as part of Force H was one of these ships.

The next contact with the enemy battleship was made at 1030 on 26 May when a Coastal Command Catalina found *Bismarck* apparently making for Brest. The Catalina was driven off by a furious anti-aircraft barrage and had to retire damaged

but the position had been reported and contact was renewed by a Swordfish from *Ark Royal* three-quarters of an hour later. In a very short time another Swordfish from the *Ark* spotted *Bismarck* and the two planes remained in contact until they were relieved by two more. In this way the shadowing continued until late that night.

Two pieces of luck were now to come to the aid of the Royal Navy. Incredibly the captain of *Bismarck* sent a long coded signal to a base in Europe with a call sign that was unmistakably that of *Bismarck*. This gave British direction-finders a first-class fix on *Bismarck*. Shortly after this a coded message from a senior *Luftwaffe* officer was intercepted by the code-breaking establishment at Bletchley Park. It was quickly decoded and found to be a request for the destination of the *Bismarck*; it seems the officer had a nephew serving on *Bismarck* and was concerned for his well-being! Even more astonishing a reply was sent giving him (and incidently the Royal Navy) the information. Armed with these two juicy plums of intelligence the Navy was in a position to concentrate its efforts in precisely the right area.

Without this good fortune it is quite possible that *Bismarck* would have reached Brest and the safety she so desperately sought. A large part of the Home Fleet had been forced to turn back to their base as they were fast running short of fuel and the *Bismarck* was rapidly approaching shelter.

By the afternoon of the 26th the weather had deteriorated to what can only be described as 'terrible'. Into these appalling conditions fifteen Swordfish armed with torpedoes were flown off from *Ark Royal* and made their way towards the last known position of *Bismarck*. Half the time the fifteen planes were flying blind and when a ship was picked up on their radar they attacked. Why on earth they were not warned that *Sheffield* was in the area we shall probably never know. Unfortunately the Swordfish found her and eleven of them launched their torpedoes at her. Somehow *Sheffield*'s captain managed to evade them all. The Swordfish can surely be forgiven for this attempt to sink one of their own vessels in the dreadful weather conditions in which they were flying. All praise to the captain of *Sheffield* for his skill in eluding the torpedoes and not adding to the tragedy of *Hood*.

Later that day a second strike of fifteen aircraft was flown off by *Ark Royal* into weather that had shown no sign of improving. Icing conditions were bad at the height at which the Swordfish were flying and the engines of several planes iced up and cut out, only restarting when they had glided down to warmer air at approximately 7,000 feet. Despite the foul conditions at about 2030 all the planes found their target and attacked through thick cloud and intense flak. At least two, and maybe more, torpedoes found their mark and one in particular sealed *Bismarck*'s fate. This torpedo struck right aft and so badly damaged both propellers and rudder that she was unable to maintain a steady course. The remaining vessels of the Home Fleet caught up with *Bismarck* and she was subjected to such a truly heavy pounding from their guns throughout the night that it required

just one torpedo from *Dorsetshire* to sink her the following morning.

It was a close-run thing: *Bismarck* was within less than 500 miles of Brest when she was finally sunk; at 25 knots that is less than twenty hours' sailing.

Some accounts suggest that *Bismarck* was scuttled but this seems to be very unlikely. By this time she was so badly damaged that the cruiser *Dorsetshire* was sent in to sink her, which she did with one torpedo. Within seconds of this torpedo striking her port side *Bismarck* was seen to roll over to port and sink, from which it must surely be reasonable to assume that *Dorsetshire*'s torpedo delivered the *coup de grâce*.

The loss of life was even greater than when *Hood* went down, some 2,000 men being lost. *Dorsetshire* rescued 110 survivors and would have picked up many more but was forced to leave almost three hundred Germans to their fate when a submarine was detected close enough to be a danger to her.

CHAPTER EIGHT

The Channel Dash of Scharnhorst *and* Gneisenau

Towards the end of March the German battleships *Scharnhorst* and *Gneisenau* returned to Brest after a successful period of commerce raiding in the course of which they had sunk some 116,000 tons of Allied shipping. After the loss of *Bismarck* they were joined by *Prinz Eugen*.

The Royal Air Force dropped an immense weight of bombs in the vicinity of the three capital ships, causing them some damage but not enough to put them out of action. *Scharnhorst* had a remarkable escape from total destruction at this time. She had been moved to a port to the south of Brest called La Pallice where she completed certain repairs that then had to be tested at sea. Whilst she was undergoing these trials she was attacked by British aircraft, one of which succeeded in dropping five bombs, two small and three large armour-piercing bombs, that hit her from stem to stern. The two smaller bombs exploded inboard but caused only limited damage. The three heavy armour-piercing bombs penetrated the upper deck but failed to explode; if they had *Scharnhorst* would surely have been finished. As it was they created enough damage to cause *Scharnhorst* to take in a considerable amount of water and adopt a decided list. It seems incredible but these bombs caused no casualties. Her crew were able to get their ship back to Brest where repairs were carried out and completed early in 1942.

It was clear to the Admiralty that these vessels would either put to sea to resume their commerce raiding or, more likely, attempt to reach a more secure base, preferably one which still posed a threat to British interests. The latter choice was the most attractive one for the German High Command. The chance of German vessels meeting up with Allied warships in the Atlantic had increased considerably since their last foray into the area. If they could reach a safe northern haven they would be a potential threat to the Arctic convoys that were now sailing with supplies of war materiel to Russia and afford a strike force should the Allies attempt to land in Norway.

Fleet Air Arm 825 Squadron, which had played an important part in the sinking of *Bismarck*, was reformed in January 1942 at Lee-on-Solent, still under the command of Lt-Cdr Esmonde. Esmonde was to receive a well merited DSO for his leadership in the attacks on *Bismarck*. On 4 February 825 Squadron moved to the RAF station at Manston in Kent in anticipation of the enemy ships making a run for it up-Channel. The British believed that the Germans would plan their dash up-Channel so that the ships would pass through the Dover Straits at night. The Germans had other ideas. Their plan was to leave at night to conceal the fact of their departure for as long as possible. This would mean they would pass through the Straits of Dover in daylight but they had assembled a massive force of aircraft to protect the fleet at this point.

The German planners decided that the night of 11 February was the ideal time to leave and as that day approached the weather situation also favoured the attempt. A number of mostly fortuitous events combined to keep the information of the departure of the German vessels from the Admiralty.

Just as the fleet was about to depart the RAF staged a heavy raid which delayed its departure. *Sea Lion*, a submarine that had the harbour of Brest under observation, had to retire to recharge her batteries thirty minutes before the German Fleet's delayed departure and so failed to see them leave.

If the RAF had not bombed Brest at that time *Sea Lion* would have seen and reported the sailing of the German fleet.

Three RAF Hudsons were on patrol over the area, watching for signs of the German ships' departure. Two of the Hudsons developed radar problems and had to return to their base. One radar set was quickly repaired but unfortunately take-off was delayed because the plane got stuck in the mud and did not arrive off Brest until some time after the fleet had sailed. The remaining Hudson was recalled before the departure of the German ships because fog was developing at its airfield.

First thing the next morning the RAF flew two routine weather flights over the Channel. The pilots of these four planes were forbidden to break radio silence so when they spotted the the German fleet of fifty to sixty ships ranging from the three battleships down to minesweepers and E boats, three pilots maintained radio silence. The fourth pilot attempted to pass the information back to his base but failed to raise anyone on the English side of the Channel. It seems that he had more luck with the Germans as they logged his calls and prepared

for action. A further hour was to pass before the British authorities were aware of the situation.

Sixteen and a half hours after the ships had left Brest the order was given to activate the contingency plan called 'Fuller'. This top secret plan was in the safe at the RAF station at Biggin Hill and the man responsible for its safe keeping was on leave and had taken the keys to the safe with him!

It was not until 1055 of that forenoon that Lt-Cdr Esmonde was informed, by which time the heavily escorted ships were well on their way up-Channel accompanied by an umbrella of fighters with many more on call at airfields along the French coast. By 1220 a minute strike force of six Swordfish, commanded by Lt-Cdr Esmonde was in the air heading for a rendezvous with an equally small fighter force of ten Spitfires to give them some protection from the fighter patrols over the German Fleet and the masses of land-based German aircraft that could be called upon at a moment's notice.

Scharnhorst *and* Gneisenau *on their dash up the Channel*

Almost from the start German fighters attacked the force with heavy cannon fire.

Approaching at just fifty feet above the sea Esmonde's plane lost part of one wing to a cannon shell which caused control difficulties but he pressed on with the attack only to be shot down by an Fw 190 soon afterwards.

The second Swordfish of this sub-flight was piloted by Sub-Lt Rose, who, although he had been hit in the back by a shell splinter and his fuel tank, which had been struck by cannon fire, was leaking badly, managed to drop his torpedo at a range of about 1,200 yards. Having made his attack Rose climbed away to a height of some 1,200 feet but the loss of petrol was so great that it quickly became clear that he had no hope of reaching the English coast and so he ditched. He and his observer Sub-Lt Lee were picked up by Motor Torpedo Boats. Leading Airman L. Johnson, the Telegraphist Air Gunner, had been killed during the approach to the target.

The remaining aircraft of Esmonde's sub-flight, piloted by Sub-Lt Kingsmill, was able to drop its torpedo before they too were shot down. On their run in, TAG D. Bunce managed to shoot down an enemy fighter plane.

The three Swordfish that made up the second sub-flight were piloted by Lt J. Thompson and Sub-Lts P. Bligh and L. Wood. These three planes strove to reach their targets but were shot down in a hail of fire with the loss of all crew members.

It is difficult to believe that those who sent the attacking aircraft on such a forlorn mission could have expected anything but total disaster. Such a tiny force with no hope of surprise stood no chance against the overwhelming might of three very heavily armed, modern battleships with their vast escort and massive air cover. The use of seasoned and proven aircrew ensured that the attack would be pressed home to the point of catastrophic losses. The heroism of the aircrews was never in doubt – but what a terrible waste. Of the Swordfish crews there were just five survivors and only one was not wounded. The crew members were:

Sub-Lt W. Beynon	Sub-Lt Parkinson
Sub-Lt P. Bligh	Sub-Lt B. Rose
Leading Airman D. Bunce	Sub-Lt R. Samples
Leading Airman W. Clinton	Leading Airman Smith
Lt-Cdr E. Esmonde	Lt Thompson
Sub-Lt Fuller Wright	Leading Airman E. Topping
Leading Airman Johnson	Lt W. Williams
Sub-Lt C. Kingsmill	Leading Airman Wheeler
Sub-Lt E. Lee	Sub-Lt Wood

Lt-Cdr Esmonde was posthumously awarded a Victoria Cross, four officers received DSOs and an Airgunner a CMG, the remainder, all of whom died, were mentioned in despatches.

CHAPTER NINE

CAM Ships, MAC Ships and Escort Carriers

CAM Ships

German long-range bombers were operating from airfields on the west and south-west coasts of France and to the north from Norway and attacking Allied shipping in the Atlantic with increasing success.

The planes used were Heinkel 111s, Junkers 88s and the four-engined Focke-Wulf 200s, (Condors): the greatest numbers were Condors. These bombers would carry out their own attacks on shipping but, much worse, they would call up U boats and give them the position, course and speed of the convoy they had found.

Clearly the only real defence would be aircraft that could get up there and attack the German planes, preferably with enough success to make the technique uneconomical for the enemy; ideally

---

Focke-Wulf Fw 200, the Condor, a German plane used for maritime reconnaissance and attack

A CAM ship launching a Hawker Sea Hurricane

this would require an aircraft carrier with every convoy. Equally clearly aircraft carriers were not available in sufficient numbers to be used in this way.

The Admiralty's immediate stop-gap answer was to have catapults fitted to the fo'c'sles of a number of merchant ships from which aircraft could be launched. These vessels were called Catapult Aircraft Merchantships (CAM ships). This was strictly a one-off solution inasmuch as there was usually nowhere to land other than in the sea when the mission was completed. Having ditched or parachuted into the sea, if it was the pilot's lucky day he would be picked up by one of the convoy's vessels. The plane, of course, was a write-off.

Initially this was a small-scale experiment using just five ships, four naval vessels and a merchant ship, the first of which sailed with its convoy at the end of May 1941. Some Fulmars and some elderly Hurricanes were converted for catapulting and the crews were given a course of instruction in the none too gentle art of coaxing a plane to leap into the air from a standing position.

It was intended that the ships should operate out of Belfast. Fortunately there was an airfield close by and the planes were flown there, where their wings were removed to make it possible to tow the planes through the streets to the docks, where they were reassembled and loaded aboard their parent vessels.

When all was ready and the ships were about to go operational one of the four naval vessels, *Patia,* was sunk off the mouth of the Tyne. The first of the remaining CAM ships sailed at the end of May 1941.

Pegasus (originally named *Ark Royal*) saw service in the World War One as a seaplane tender but was later converted to become the RN's catapult training ship. Early in the summer of 1941 she was pressed into service as an RN catapult ship to work alongside the CAM ships that were escorting Atlantic convoys.

Serving as a pilot in a CAM ship must have been a frustrating career. Most of their launches ended without the satisfaction of shooting enemy planes down but they did frequently chase them off and on occasions inflicted damage to the intruding aircraft. However, the deterrent effect of these actions did help to reduce the U boat attacks and must undoubtedly have been of value. Certainly it seems that the powers that be thought enough of the results to enlarge the scheme.

The RAF was brought into the picture and in May 1941 when they set up a Merchant Ship Fighter Unit at Speke, support groups were established as far away as Archangel and Nova Scotia. When the RAF unit was fully operational it had sixty Hurricanes to service the thirty-four merchant ships that had been fitted with catapults. By May 1942 the FAA had withdrawn from the CAM ship operation, leaving the RAF in sole charge of the Merchant Shipping Fighter Unit which continued to operate until it was disbanded on 7 September 1943.

MAC Ships

As the war progressed so the need for a more effective form of air support in mid-Atlantic became ever more urgent. German long-range bombers were still operating from airfields on the west and south-west coasts of Europe and Scandinavia as were their reconnaissance planes. The number of U boats operating in the North Atlantic was growing all the time. The ability of these aircraft to direct large packs of U boats onto a convoy was becoming increasingly costly for Allied shipping.

Discussions were held with the USN from which came the brilliant idea that it should be possible to convert a fast merchantman; tankers or grain ships were the favourite vessels, to serve both as a merchant ship and an aircraft carrier. The conversion allowed 80 per cent or more of the original cargo-carrying capacity to be retained. The acronym given to these Merchant Aircraft Carriers by the Admiralty was MAC ship. These vessels were never taken into the RN and always flew the Red Ensign. As a result the aircrew were required to sign on as deck hands in the Merchant Navy, giving them the right to wear the coveted silver badge of that Service on their naval uniform as well as the wings of their own service. One suspects that this privilege caused a few dyed-in-the-(navy blue)-wool eyebrows to twitch on first acquaintance!

The aircraft from the MAC ships were armed with rockets and depth-charges and they never hesitated to attack when the opportunity presented itself. Although no kills were claimed it is highly likely that damage was done on numerous occasions; certainly the appearance of a plane was enough in itself to cause a U boat to dive, although later on in the war U boats did attempt to sit on the surface and exchange fire with attacking aircraft.

When MAC ships were introduced U boats were hunting in packs and it was not unusual for a dozen or so of them to gather around a convoy and attack from a variety of directions, thereby swamping the defences. The MAC ships put an end to that tactic simply by keeping the U boats at such a distance that they could not reach the convoys. It was not necessary to sink the U boats. It was enough to drive them below the surface where they had to use their electric propulsion units, thus reducing their speed and their endurance.

The measure of the success of these vessels is that for the remainder of the war no successful U boat attack was made against a convoy that included a MAC ship amongst its defences.

If the crews of these aircraft were not often shot at, there were hazards enough to satisfy most people. Take-off and landing were frequently performed in the dark and not necessarily with the mother ship steaming into the wind but in really difficult conditions the carrier might drop astern of the convoy to help an aircraft land on.

North Atlantic weather is not renowned for its consideration towards those who choose to tangle with it, especially in the winter months. To ditch in icy cold water with equally cold winds blowing gave little chance of survival for those who were not quickly picked up. Survival suits as we know them today did not exist.

The Atlantic is a breeding ground for some pretty fearsome storms with gale force winds common and even more violent winds not unusual. The stronger the wind the greater the height of the seas. The greater the seas that were running the more erratic would be the motion of the flight-deck for the returning aircraft. It was normal for Swordfish to patrol either ahead of or to one side of the convoy, almost never astern of it. If a Swordfish found itself lagging behind the main body of the convoy and the wind piped up, as it is wont to in the North Atlantic, the Swordfish's low flying speed could mean that it had no hope of regaining the deck of its parent ship. At least one Swordfish is known to

have been lost in this manner.

Fog can be a major problem in extensive areas of the Atlantic and to grope your way back to the minute deck that you call home in thick weather with a diminishing supply of fuel, can be a nail-biting pastime. It must be remembered that the fantastic satellite navigation systems that we take for granted today were unthought of then. Navigation in those days was done by guess and by God with the aid of a 2B lead pencil.

When you had found your favourite ship it was still necessary to put down safely onto its deck and if the ocean was in a good mood you were in luck, your tiny landing field was probably not rising, falling and rolling more than twelve feet or so in any one direction as you approached it. If the sea was having an off-day things could be rather more difficult. It is little wonder that a good landing was defined by FAA pilots as 'one from which you

HMS Striker, *a typical Escort Carrier, her merchant ship origins are obvious*

could walk away'!

In September 1943 Sub-Lt Singleton took off from _Empire MacAlpine_ only to see his ship disappear into dense fog. The decision to attempt to land back onto the invisible ship was made and this was done by using the ship-borne radar and the radar in the aircraft. Somehow he put his plane down safely onto the minute deck of the MAC ship in what must rate as one of the most remarkable landings in the history of the Service.

Escort Carriers

From the MAC ship it was but a small step to the Escort Carrier, a merchant ship conversion that was devoted solely to the housing and operation of aircraft, in short a mini aircraft carrier.

The first Escort Carrier to enter the fray was the remodelled German freighter _Hanover_ of 5,537 tons that had been captured by HMS _Dunedin_ in February 1940. Converted in a shipyard in Britain she was given a full-length flight-deck which on a ship of five and a half thousand tons just had to be small, but it was adequate. There was no island. In place of the more usual six arrester wires she was given just two and a crash barrier to catch those who missed the arrester wires. _Hanover_'s size ruled out the possibility of a hangar, which must have made things difficult for the maintenance crews at times.

Her conversion was completed and she was commissioned as HMS _Audacity_ on 20 July 1941 when she received six Martlets and by the beginning of September she had finished 'working up'.

On 14 September _Audacity_ sailed from the Clyde for her first taste of escort duty, her task to help protect a convoy bound for Gibraltar. Just two days out her planes were in action attacking a U boat with machine-gun fire forcing it to submerge, so frustrating an attack on the convoy. Three days later they were in action again against another U boat with the same result.

The next action that _Audacity_'s planes were involved in was against a Focke-Wulf 200 that was attacking the Rescue Ship _Walmer Castle_. Two Martlets homed in on the big German plane, coming under heavy fire as they pressed home their

HMS Nairana, _an escort carrier in typical North Atlantic weather_

attack. The first Martlet fired a short burst from each of her guns, severing the tail of the German aircraft which promptly plunged into the sea, killing all aboard her.

Audacity's career was a short but highly successful one. Her fighter squadron shot down five Fw 200s and drove off four more, three of them with significant damage. More important, the actions of *Audacity's* aircraft repeatedly kept the U boats too far from the convoys for them to become a serious threat. This achievement is not so readily quantifiable as were her successes against enemy aircraft but the very fact that Admiral Dönitz ordered his U boat pack to concentrate on sinking *Audacity* must underline her worth in those four short months of service. On 21 December 1941 she was struck by two torpedoes fired by a U boat and sank.

While *Audacity* was proving the viability of the Escort Carrier idea the Americans were converting five more merchant ships to this role. These ships were named *Archer, Avenger, Biter, Charger* and *Dasher*. By this time the USN was training BFAA pilots and *Charger* was retained to aid in this programme. The other three were passed to the RN as part of the Lend-Lease scheme.

The Americans designated these ships as 'CVE' which was short for 'Carrier, Heavier-than-Air, Escort Vessels'. This, perhaps, may seem a little odd until one learns that the USN operated a number of blimps on anti-submarine duties in the Atlantic after they entered the war in December 1941. Having most of the world's supply of natural helium in North America they were able to use lighter-than-air craft without the potential danger of explosion that accompanies the use of hydrogen to inflate them. However that may be, the ships soon became generally known to both navies as 'Escort Carriers'.

All five of these American-built Escort Carriers were equipped with diesel engines which proved to be a constant source of mechanical problems throughout the lives of the ships.

Archer, the first merchantman to be converted to an Escort Carrier by the Americans, was commissioned on 17 December 1941 and started active service in March 1942. In addition to her engine

problems she was destined to have more than her share of bad luck.

Three of *Archer's* aircraft were lost to accidents onboard: one went over the side, another missed both arrester wires and hit the crash barrier, which did the plane no good at all and the third caught fire in the hangar. Fortunately the sprinkler system and the crew's efforts were able to confine the blaze to just one plane.

Later a 250-lb bomb exploded whilst being handled aboard *Archer*, killing nine and injuring ten armourers.

As if these problems were not enough a Swordfish from *Archer* was shot down while flying over an American ferry station on Ascension Island in an attempt to drop a message to them about a raider that was on the loose in the South Atlantic. What on earth the trigger-happy American gunner thought he was firing at in the South Atlantic a thousand miles from anywhere is difficult to fathom!

Despite her misfortunes and deficiencies *Archer* did what was asked of her and in her quiet way chalked up a number of successful operations. Unfortunately her mechanical troubles persisted and after ferrying twenty-five P-40s to the American forces in Morocco as part of the North African landings, she was taken out of service in August 1943.

Avenger was lost on 15 November 1941 when she was torpedoed on her way home from the 'Torch' landings where her return had been delayed by the inevitable engine problems. These vessels carried the petrol for their aircraft in their double bottom and this was ignited when the torpedo struck *Avenger*. There were twelve survivors.

At this time the American standards applicable to fuel safety arrangements were not as stringent as those in force in the RN and on 27 March 1943 *Dasher,* exercising off the Island of Arran, blew up with the loss of more than 300 men.

The enquiry that followed concluded that a cigarette end ignited petrol from a leaky petrol valve. The fuel systems on the remaining American-built Escort Carriers and all new Escort Carriers received from the USA were overhauled and brought up to the standard generally in operation in the RN. It is to be hoped that the smoking regulations were enforced with a little more enthusiasm too.

A number of Escort Carriers were built in British yards but it made far better sense to have the USA, with its greater capacity and yards free from the problems of air attack, build these ships. In all, America provided thirty-eight Escort Carriers on Lend-Lease.

The troublesome diesel engines in the earlier American-built Escort Carriers were replaced by steam turbines in the remainder of the class and they proved to be much more reliable.

The work of the Escort Carriers covered most of the tasks expected of carriers generally. About twenty or so spent the major part of their time escorting convoys in and around the North Atlantic. At some stage it occurred to the U boat commanders that it might be more profitable to stay on the surface and fight back rather than submerge and be subjected to a depth-charge attack. To this end they added to their close-range anti-aircraft armament. This prompted a change of tactics by the aircraft from the carriers. Each Swordfish was accompanied by two fighters, usually Hellcats. When a U boat was discovered on the surface the fighters would attack from either side

to deter the gun crews and then the Swordfish would go in and attack with rocket projectiles. These projectiles were designed to penetrate the hull of the submarine and then explode when they were inside.

Most Escort Carriers were used to ferry aircraft at one time or another but seven of them spent most of their time transporting American-built aircraft to FAA establishments in the UK. Others were used for reconnaissance, fighter and assault purposes and many of the Escort Carriers were modified to enable them to carry out these specific duties more effectively. They provided air cover for the landings at Salerno and for the invasion of southern France, and were used in support of Russian convoys. Later they participated in the actions that took place in the Indian and Pacific Oceans.

The comparatively low landing speed of the Swordfish and its good-natured, rugged construction made it the obvious choice of plane for these ships and three or four were often to be found in Escort Carriers but Martlets, Seafires and Sea Hurricanes were also used. However if the wind was light the seventeen knots or so top speed of the average Escort Carrier could cause landing and take-off problems for the faster planes.

CHAPTER TEN

The Russian Convoys

Once Russia had entered the war in June 1941 it became obvious that we had to give as much material support as possible and this resulted in regular convoys carrying war materiel from the US and the UK to the Russian arctic ports of Archangel, Murmansk and the Kola Inlet. The thankless task of organising and escorting these convoys fell to the RN with minimal help from the Russians. Even on basic things like weather reports and forecasts, what little information that was supplied was usually either not applicable or quite misleading.

The first convoys were gathered together in the Icelandic port of Hvalfjord. Later their starting point was changed to Reykjavik and then in September 1942 it was changed again, this time to Loch Ewe in Scotland and later to the Clyde. Until

---

The seas on which the convoys fought their way to Russia

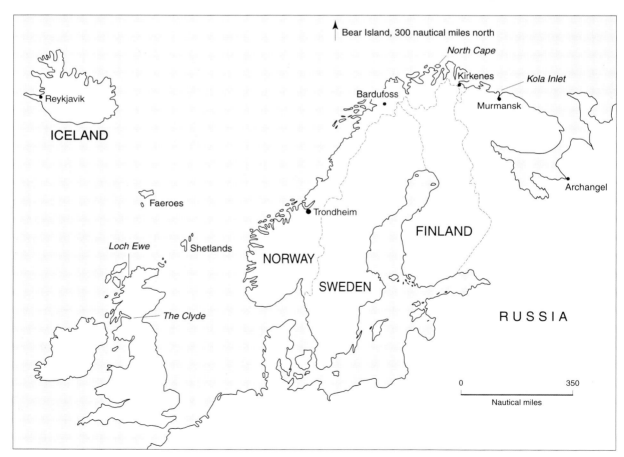

An open cockpit Swordfish about to take off on convoy protection duties

the end of 1942 their destination was either Murmansk or Archangel but after the end of '42 they were all routed to the Kola Inlet.

In mid-January 1942 the German battleship _Tirpitz_, along with the pocket battleship _Lutzow_, two cruisers and an adequate destroyer screen had been moved from Germany to Trondheim as a precaution against the possibility of an assault by the Allies on German-occupied Norway and in February _Prinz Eugen_ and _Scheer_ joined her. This added up to a powerful force posing a real threat to shipping in the North Atlantic and to the Russian convoys.

Numerous attempts had been made by the RN and the RAF to put these vessels out of action but without any real success. The steep-sided fjords gave a very large measure of protection to vessels anchored within them.

On the night of 22 February 1942 it was learned

that _Lutzow_ was heading for Kiel. _Victorious_ flew off seventeen Albacores with orders to find and attack her. It seems they missed her because she was enveloped in heavy snow as they passed over her position. Even if they had been aware of her presence below them there would have been no hope of making an attack in such extreme weather conditions.

Very early in March 1942 convoy PQ12 set out for Russia: fortunately the Admiralty had included the Fleet Carrier _Victorious_ amongst the escort vessels. On 7 March reports were received that _Tirpitz_ had emerged from Trondheim Fjord and was believed to be heading to intercept the convoy with a number of Condors assisting her in her

Seen beside the Condor (opposite), the Walrus (top) and the Albacore (below) look like aircraft from a bygone age

search for the convoy. Albacores and Walruses flew reconnaissance flights in an attempt to find the enemy battleship.

At 0630 on the second day of the search six Albacores were flown off to continue looking for _Tirpitz_. A short time after 0730 twelve more Albacores armed with torpedoes were flown off to be on hand should _Tirpitz_ be found by the reconnaissance group.

At 0815 _Tirpitz_ was found and her position, course and speed were passed to the strike force of twelve Albacores which at once began to climb to get above the deck of cloud, at the same time setting a course that would allow them to intercept the enemy vessel. Once the strike force was on its way a plane that was equipped with Air-to-Surface Vessel radar picked up _Tirpitz_ and reported her progress until at 0840 she was sighted by the strike force from some distance off.

Below the cloud base of 4,000 feet the weather had cleared to the point where there was excellent visibility. When the planes were about fifteen miles from _Tirpitz_ they descended through the cloud and attacked in sub-flights of three aircraft from different angles. From the moment they

broke through the cloud and dived to their attack they came under very heavy anti-aircraft fire. Despite the fact that the attack was pressed home with some determination, _Tirpitz_ twisted and turned and appeared to successfully comb the torpedo tracks, although there was so much smoke about that it was difficult for the aircrews to be certain. For a successful attack on such a fast and manoeuvrable vessel twelve planes were too few. With a sufficient number of planes _Tirpitz_ would have been unable to avoid all the torpedoes that would have been launched against her. Two planes were lost to enemy fire after completing their attack. Within two hours _Tirpitz_ was safely tucked away again in Vestfjord.

On the face of it it was an abortive raid but the net result was that on Hitler's orders she was never again to be exposed to attack by FAA planes on the open sea, which considerably limited her activities. She did make one foray in an effort to attack the scattered ships of convoy PQ17, but beat a hasty retreat when she learned that _Victorious_ was part of the Home Fleet, even though the Home Fleet and _Victorious_ were not part of the escort of this convoy.

Considering how close the convoys had to sail to German-held territory the casualties in the early convoys had been remarkably small, just one ship lost out of more than a hundred, but in March 1942 things began to change for the worse. Casualties from U boat and air attacks began to increase quite steadily for the next three or four months, culminating in the loss of twenty-four of the thirty-seven vessels that left Reykjavik in the convoy designated PQ17.

The only air cover available for most of these convoys was provided by the few Walruses that could be catapulted from the accompanying cruiser escorts and they were no match for the considerable numbers of enemy aircraft and U boats that were ranged against them.

By May 1942 the Germans had based over 260 aircraft at Banak, Bardufoss and Kirkenes. Nearly 200 of these planes were either dive-bombers or torpedo-bombers.

PQ16 sailed for Russia on 21 May, consisting of thirty-five Merchant ships and an anti-submarine escort. One of the merchantmen was fitted as a CAM ship with a single Hurricane aboard. The convoy was attacked for five long days. It was estimated that at least 1,000 sorties were flown against the convoy by the *Luftwaffe*. The single Hurricane was catapulted off *Empire Lawrence* and shot down one enemy aircraft and damaged another before it had to ditch. Six ships were sunk by air attack and one was lost to a U boat. That no more ships were lost to the onslaught by the German planes must be a tribute to the quality of the anti-aircraft fire of the escorting vessels.

Towards the end of June the ill-fated convoy PQ17 was formed in Iceland. There were thirty-seven ships and an escort similar to that which accompanied PQ16. It sailed from Reykjavik and on 1 July and was sighted by a U boat to the north-east of Iceland. The U boat called up some aircraft but they were fought off successfully. After this attack fog hid the convoy from further harm for a couple of days. To the east of Bear Island the fog dispersed and PQ17 was attacked from the air again, this time losing three ships. The convoy was well on its way and had sustained just three losses, altogether things were going well.

Unbeknown to the convoy, *Tirpitz, Hipper* and *Scheer* with six destroyers were on the move. They had left Trondheim and were heading for Altenfjord to be in a position to attack PQ17 as it drew closer. Air reconnaissance had spotted this movement and the information had been passed to the Admiralty, who believed that the convoy was about to be attacked and gave the order for it to scatter. What the Admiralty did not know was that the sortie by the German ships had been called off and they had returned to Alten Fjord. Once the convoy was dispersed the individual ships had no defence and were picked off piecemeal by U boats and German aircraft. Of the original thirty-seven, eleven ships reached their destination: the rest were lost.

Ever since this incident it has been a source of discussion, sometimes quite heated. Was the Admiralty's decision right or wrong?

In my opinion, with the limited knowledge available to the Admiralty at the time there was no right decision possible. Whatever was decided could have been disastrously wrong. It is easy with hindsight to say the convoy should have remained together and with the knowledge we now have it is obvious that it would have been the best course to take. Without the knowledge that the German ships were not going to attack the convoy, the Admiralty's choices were to allow the convoy to stay together and provide a once-in-a lifetime target for the German fleet's guns from which no merchantman or escort vessel would have escaped, or, order it to scatter and give some of the vessels a chance of survival, even though it was apparent that there were large numbers of U boats and at least 250 enemy planes waiting for their opportunity to attack. In the event eleven merchant ships survived, as did the escort vessels. What is totally unreasonable is the very occasional accusation of cowardice and desertion on the part of the escort vessels by some of the more bitter critics.

The escalation of losses culminating in the loss of 65 per cent of the ships in PQ17 brought it home to the organisers of the Russian convoys that air cover had to be provided on a much more realistic scale. It was to be another three months before another convoy to Russia was attempted.

Iceland was abandoned as the mustering point for these convoys and instead they were formed-up in Loch Ewe. Air cover was provided for the next convoy by the presence of an Escort Carrier. On 2 September 1942 PQ18 left Loch Ewe bound for Russia. The convoy consisted of forty merchant ships and about the same number of escort vessels, a mixture of destroyers, corvettes, minesweepers, anti-aircraft ships, oilers and rescue vessels. A week later, when the convoy was off Iceland, it was joined by the Escort Carrier _Avenger_; she carried three Swordfish and twelve elderly Sea Hurricanes with six more dismantled Hurricanes stowed in the hangar as a reserve. The Germans had at least 200 aircraft, a battleship, two cruisers, five destroyers and a dozen U boats available.

Heartened by their success with PQ17 the _Luftwaffe_ was waiting for the appearance of the next convoy, hoping to deal out the same degree of punishment to it. They launched their first attack on 12 September. The first enemy planes to appear were Blohm and Voss 138s whose task was to report on the position of the convoy and to shadow its progress. Sea Hurricanes were sent up to deal with them but in the course of chasing them off they left the convoy without air cover, allowing it to be attacked by torpedo-carrying He 111s which sank eight of the merchant vessels.

The next two days saw repeated attacks by the _Luftwaffe_ but the defenders had learned their lesson and stayed close to the convoy. Whilst the engagement lasted the Sea Hurricanes were in action continuously, landing on only to refuel and replenish their supply of ammunition. Four Hurricanes were lost, one to enemy action and three to what has become euphemistically known as 'friendly fire' from the merchant ships: three of the pilots were rescued from the sea by the escort vessels. In the course of the three days' action the Sea Hurricanes claimed to have shot down five enemy planes and inflicted damage on twenty-one more. Anti-aircraft fire from the escort vessels doubtless contributed to the total number of German aircraft brought down but German records suggest the FAA figures to be far too modest. They state the number of their planes lost in the

attacks on PQ18 was forty-one and presumably they should know.

The _Luftwaffe_'s losses were such that they largely abandoned this form of attack and as a rule, after the passage of PQ18, they left the U boats to deal with future convoys.

There were no further losses to the ships of the convoy PQ18 by air attack until it was split into two parts and the part of the convoy destined for Archangel lost the air cover afforded by the planes from _Avenger_. Two ships of the detached part of the convoy were lost to aerial torpedoes but during the attack a single Sea Hurricane that was launched from a Catapult Armed Merchant ship destroyed two of the attacking He 115 torpedo-bombers and prevented any further attacks.

Whilst the Sea Hurricanes dealt with the air attacks _Avenger_'s three Swordfish were busy dropping depth-charges on no fewer than sixteen U boats. What damage was done to them is not known but the fact that sixteen U boats were attacked with depth-charges was obviously a major contribution to the well-being of the ships of the convoy. One U boat was pinpointed by Swordfish and with the help of one of the escorting destroyers it was sunk.

Ironically, having established the effectiveness of an aircraft carrier as part of the convoy's escort there were to be no more carriers available for Russian convoy duties from September 1942 until the middle of February 1943. Carriers that were available for duty at sea were required to support the landings in North Africa.

On 15 February 1943 _Dasher_ left Loch Ewe as part of the escort for Russian convoy JW53. After just two days _Dasher_ had to return to Loch Ewe severely damaged by the foul weather she had encountered, leaving the convoy to sail on without air cover and happily also without losses. It was to be another year before an Escort Carrier became available for the protection of these convoys.

On 20 February 1944 a convoy of forty-three ships left Loch Ewe for Russia. They were joined the following day by the Escort Carrier _Chaser_, with six Wildcats and eleven Swordfish armed with rockets on board. The rest of the escort comprised two cruisers and seventeen destroyers.

There were fourteen U boats lying in wait for the convoy and the Swordfish made repeated attacks against them. No sinkings were claimed but the very fact that the submarines were kept out of reach of the ships in the convoy was success enough.

The return convoy left Kola Inlet on 2 March and the U boats were lying in wait for it. This time the crews of the Swordfish were to have the satisfaction of being instrumental in the sinking of three of the German submarines. On each occasion the Swordfish attacked the subs and left them sufficiently damaged to await the *coup de grâce* from surface escort vessels.

The next Russian convoy left Loch Ewe on 27 March 1944 with the luxury of two escort carriers, *Activity* and *Tracker*. Between them the two carriers had on board three Swordfish, twelve Avengers and fourteen Wildcats.

Five days out from Loch Ewe a U boat was sunk in a joint attack by an Avenger and *Beagle*. Two days later another U boat was sunk by Swordfish

and Avengers and before the convoy reached home three more U boats had been attacked and six shadowing aircraft had been shot down. It seems that the officer commanding the U boat forces in Norwegian waters had attempted to organise an ambush of the convoy with a number of U boats. This was foiled by the fighters from *Activity* and *Tracker* destroying six enemy shadowers in two days, thereby depriving the Germans of the accurate position reports that were central to their planning processes. Not a single ship was lost.

The following convoy escorted by *Activity* and *Fencer* was at least as successful. One shadowing aircraft was shot down, three U boats sunk and eight others attacked.

A convoy left the Clyde for Russia on 3 February 1945 with escort carriers *Campania* and *Nairana* in attendance (not to be confused with the World

Freeing the anchor gear of ice

War One carriers of the same name), both vessels carrying Swordfish and Wildcats. Three days out a Junkers 88 that was shadowing the convoy was shot down by a Wildcat from *Campania*. The following morning an attack by twelve Junkers 88 torpedo-bombers was staged. One was shot down by anti-aircraft fire from a Corvette in the escort group and the rest were driven off by the Wildcats from *Nairana*.

A week later Junkers 88 torpedo-bombers were back attacking the convoy from several different directions in an effort to confuse the defenders. Fortunately *Campania* had been fitted with a new design of radar before she left the UK and it was well able to cope with the situation, giving more than adequate warning of the approach of the hostile aircraft. Forewarned the fighters were able to get into position in good time to tackle the enemy aircraft and the ships were able to take evasive action. The Wildcats had a hard time of it but eventually drove off the enemy aircraft without loss to themselves, but the fierceness of the encounter can be judged by the fact that when it was all over 813 Squadron had just one serviceable aircraft left!

When the convoy had unloaded they still had the return passage to make. In the early stages U boats attacked with some measure of success until the weather in the form of force twelve winds (hurricane force) scattered the convoy. In the forenoon of 20 February the winds had abated sufficiently for the convoy to start to reform. Before this was completed twenty-five Ju 88s were detected by radar and a force of Wildcats was scrambled to tackle them. Three Ju 88s were shot down, two more were claimed as probable and one as a possible. Fortunately the early warning provided by *Campania*'s new radar gave the ships time to take evasive action and the defending aircraft the chance to position themselves to advantage. A considerable number of torpedoes were dropped by the enemy planes but thanks to the measures the early warning made possible there were no casualties in the convoy.

The final Russian convoy sailed shortly after VE Day. Although peace had been agreed the Navy was taking no chances on some fanatical U boat captain having a last fling and gave the convoy two aircraft carriers in addition to other escort vessels to see them safely to their destination. Apart from the routine problems associated with sailing in arctic waters it was trouble free.

Tirpitz

At the beginning of 1943 *Tirpitz* lay in Altenfjord and it was planned to use Swordfish from the Escort Carrier *Dasher* to attack her. Unfortunately before the raid could be mounted *Dasher* suffered an aviation gasoline explosion which destroyed her, with great loss of life.

Twelve months later Operation Tungsten was

Tirpitz

Aircrew boarding a Fairey Barracuda

being planned. This was to be a bigger affair alto-gether with more modern planes than hitherto. Two squadrons of Barracuda embarked in the *Victorious* and two more in *Furious.* One wing of Corsairs was taken aboard *Victorious* and two squadrons of Seafires went to *Furious.* The Escort Carriers *Emperor, Fencer, Pursuer* and *Searcher* took onboard an impressive number of Hellcats and Wildcats and a squadron of Swordfish joined Fencer for anti-submarine duties. Well over 120 planes were to be used. The escort was to be the Home Fleet's Second Battle Squadron made up of *Duke of York, Anson, Sheffield, Jamaica* and *Royalist* with a screen of twelve destroyers.

By the 3 April 1944 the Fleet was assembled and at about 0430 the first of the Barracudas took off from both of the larger carriers. Shortly after the Barracudas had left the huge fighter escort took off

from the various aircraft carriers. As the strike force approached Altenfjord *Tirpitz* was about to leave her berth for the first time in six months. Earlier she had suffered a midget submarine attack and it had taken all that time to make her seaworthy. The surprise was total. Hellcats and Wildcats came over the surrounding hills and dived onto the German battleship with their multi-ple machine-guns blazing. The surprise had been such that *Tirpitz* had no time to put up a smoke screen and the fighters took full advantage of the uninterrupted visibility. Other Hellcats and Wildcats turned their attention to the anti-aircraft emplacements ashore. Ten thousand feet above the attacking planes a protective fleet of Corsairs wheeled ready to tackle any German fighters that might appear.

As soon as the Hellcats and Wildcats were out of the way the first Barracudas went in to attack, scoring six direct hits with their bombs. The second wave of Barracudas arrived shortly after the first had departed and proceeded to gain eight more direct hits despite the fact that *Tirpitz* had by now started to put up a smoke screen.

Fourteen direct hits and a number of probables compelled the planners to call off the raid planned for the next day. The FAA lost just two Barracudas. *Tirpitz* was out of action for three months as a result of this raid.

Although this strike was so successful in inflicting damage on *Tirpitz* she was not destroyed and would again become a potential danger to Allied shipping as soon as she was repaired. Further raids were planned but had to be called off because of foul weather. Some were actually initiated but with reports of thick cloud over Altenfjord there was no point in proceeding and the aircraft were recalled.

It was not until mid-summer that conditions improved enough to make another air strike possible. *Formidable*, *Furious* and *Indefatigable* were the carriers chosen to take the aircraft within striking distance of *Tirpitz*. Fighter protection was to be given by Corsairs, Hellcats, Seafires and Fireflies that had just come into service with the FAA and three Swordfish were earmarked for anti-submarine work. Operation Goodwood was mounted on 22, 24 and 29 August 1944.

The Germans were not to be so easily surprised this time. They had erected an observation post high on one of the nearby mountains to give early warning of the approach of hostile aircraft. Forty-four Barracudas were escorted by forty-eight fighters and as soon as they were sighted by the German observation post the word was passed to *Tirpitz* and she developed a dense smoke screen which totally frustrated the attacking force's efforts. The forty-four planes could claim just one near miss.

Two days later a further raid was launched on *Tirpitz* by thirty-three Barracudas armed with 1,600-lb armour-piercing bombs; Corsairs and Hellcats were along too and they were bombed-up with smaller bombs. The attacking force came at *Tirpitz* from various directions to reduce the anti-aircraft fire in any one sector and despite the smoke screen put up by the German ship they scored two direct hits, one by a 500-lb bomb which did a limited amount of damage, and another by one of the 1,600-lb armour-piercing bombs. The armour-piercing bomb penetrated the armoured deck but failed to explode; if it had it is doubtful that *Tirpitz* could have survived.

It is difficult to think of anything more frustrating than to make the effort entailed in mounting operations of this kind only to have them nullified by the weapon failing to detonate when it is delivered. With all the scientific and engineering skills available to the powers that be during a war like World War Two, one would have thought that it would be possible to overcome what appears to be a comparatively minor technical problem, yet it happened again and again.

The FAA tried again on 29 August but the result was no better. The combination of the early warning and an effective smoke screen was more than the FAA weaponry could overcome.

A total of 242 sorties were flown over the three days of this operation and because of the efficiency of the smoke screen only two hits were obtained. The FAA lost eleven planes in these attacks. Apart from the limited damage done to *Tirpitz* the only other successes were the destruction of seven seaplanes, two Bv 138s, and four very small merchantmen. Not only did the air strikes fail to achieve anything worthwhile commensurate with the effort expended but *Nabob*, an Escort Carrier, was struck by an acoustic torpedo launched by U 354. Badly damaged, her crew kept her afloat and got her back to Britain but she was not to be in action again. The frigate *Bickerton* that was hunting the U boat that had torpedoed *Nabob* was herself struck and this time the damage was such that she could not be saved and was scuttled off North Cape. Three days later U 354 was sunk by a Swordfish from *Vindex* off Bear Island.

Royal Air Force Lancasters using 12,000-pound 'Tallboy bombs' eventually sank *Tirpitz* at Tromsø on 12 November 1944.

The Norwegian Sea

Most of Norway's western coast is fringed by strings of islands with deep water between them and the mainland coast. The Leads, the channels between the islands and Norway, were ideal for the sheltered movement of German-controlled shipping. In The Leads, both on the convoluted coastline and the islands, there are numerous anchorages where vessels could lie up safe from bad weather and hopefully from the prying eyes of British reconnaissance planes. To discourage the offensive activities of the British planes many of the anchorages were heavily defended by anti-aircraft weaponry.

Throughout the German occupation of Norway FAA aircraft harried shipping using The Leads. They were mostly small ships but much used for transport of essential supplies for the occupying forces ashore. In addition to attacking this shipping directly the FAA planes laid mines either overtly or covertly. If the Germans were aware that mines had been laid the channel was denied to them until it was swept, and the ships had to sail in the Norwegian Sea outside the protection of the islands, where they could be more easily attacked by air, surface or submarine forces. If the mines were laid secretly then ships were likely to be sunk by the detonation of the mines as they actuated them and again shipping would be denied the use of the sheltered waters until they had been swept.

It is difficult to gather figures but at a conservative estimate at least 120,000 tons of enemy-controlled shipping was destroyed by these measures but I suspect that the true total must be a great deal higher than that. Certainly until the Fleet Carriers left for the Pacific at the end of 1944 the planes of the FAA had been responsible for the destruction of more enemy shipping in the Norwegian Sea than any other branch of the armed forces.

CHAPTER ELEVEN

The War Against Japan

In 1937 Japan invaded China and treated the people of those areas they had occupied with great brutality. They claimed they were establishing 'The Greater East Asia Co-prosperity Sphere', which convinced no one, least of all the Chinese. Step by step they proceeded to extend their 'Sphere of Co-prosperity' until in the summer of 1941 they invaded Indo-China. The United States of America decided to act. They imposed an oil embargo on Japan which brought further Japanese expansion to a stop. America said it was prepared to lift the embargo if Japan evacuated China and refrained from further aggression. Naturally Japan did not care for this suggestion and was prepared to go to war to free itself of the problem. The Japanese were aware of the immense resources at America's command but felt that the elimination of the United States Navy from the equation would keep America out of the Pacific and began

The Japanese attack on the US Fleet at Pearl Harbor

to plan to achieve that end. At that time Japan had a fleet that was at least the equivalent of the combined British, Commonwealth, Dutch and US naval forces that were in the western Pacific.

The Japanese Navy had a number of large aircraft carriers and the planes of its Army and Navy Air Forces outnumbered the combined aircraft in the Pacific of all the countries likely to oppose them. Some 750 planes were carried in their aircraft carriers and there was a similar number ashore for them to call on if need be. They had been greatly impressed by the success of the FAA at Taranto and laid their plans with this in mind.

By refuelling their carriers at sea the Japanese could deliver at least 500 planes to within striking distance of a considerable part of the American Fleet in Pearl Harbor, Hawaii. The USN had about 600 planes in the Pacific but they were based at a number of locations and were certainly not on full war alert as were the Japanese by this time. To ensure complete surprise they decided to attack without the warning of a declaration of war.

To aid this deception Japanese diplomats were engaged in discussions in America with their counterparts in the US government when the Japanese Navy struck. The attack on Pearl Harbor on 7 December 1941 achieved total surprise. It would seem that given the circumstances the United States displayed an astounding degree of naïvety. Defences were not manned, ready use ammunition was not available to most of the anti-aircraft guns and so on. In a matter of hours, for the cost of twenty-nine aircraft a large part of the American Pacific Fleet was destroyed.

After the first shock it was realised that bad as things were they could have been even worse. Some shoreside installations and the destroyer and submarine groups at Pearl Harbor had escaped serious damage. Three large aircraft carriers and their escorts were in other parts of the Pacific and so they were unharmed. There was in fact a substantial nucleus around which to rebuild the fleet but more important than this was the lesson the USN had learned – the aircraft carrier had usurped the position held by the battleship for so long.

With a large part of the American Fleet out of the

way Japan felt free to extend the area of her activities. Burma, Malaya, Indo-China, Siam, Singapore, Formosa, the Philippines, Java and many other places were quickly occupied by the Japanese and any form of resistance was put down with the utmost savagery.

With the fall of Java and Singapore the Japanese were in a position to enter the Indian Ocean and threaten the supply of oil from the Persian Gulf, which could have been a disaster for Britain, who desperately needed this oil in its fight against Germany. With the loss of Singapore as a naval base it was decided that Colombo on the west coast of Ceylon – known now as Sri Lanka – and Trincomalee on the north-east coast should become home to the newly constituted Eastern Fleet.

The Fleet consisted of five outmoded World War One battleships, three aircraft carriers, seven cruisers and sixteen destroyers, on the face of it a formidable force. Four of these five battleships were slow, with maximum speeds well below twenty-five knots. Their major armament was 15-inch guns in turrets fore and aft and a number of smaller guns that fired through large apertures on either side of the ship, much as in Nelson's day! The apertures were covered with canvas screens in an effort to keep the sea in its rightful place but in fact so much water came inboard through these screens that many of the mess decks played host to four inches of sea water, and a great deal more if the weather was really bad. Contrary to mess deck rumours I never did see fish swimming on the mess decks. At sea level on either side the ship had the doubtful protection of huge anti-torpedo bulges but no serious armour and the crowning glory was an enormous ram on the stem just below water level. 'Oh daddy how did you win the war?'

Of the five ancient battleships only *Warspite* had been brought up to date. She now had an armoured deck which the others lacked, and could make twenty-five knots. The Japanese opposition in the area had four battleships of equal vintage but they had at least been modernised. Ancient or modern the battleship had had its day and it was air power at sea that really mattered and here the Japanese had a considerable superiority. As had

been so strongly demonstrated at Pearl Harbor and elsewhere sea power without adequate air power was an absolute nonstarter.

Ashore in Ceylon the RAF and FAA had about ninety planes and afloat the RN had the same number. Against these 180 planes the Japanese fleet could muster 300, but the disparity did not stop there. The Japanese fleet had about 100 Zero fighters with a top speed of about 350 knots, pitted against which the Fleet Air Arm afloat had thirty-three fighters, a mixed collection of Fulmars, Martlets and Sea Hurricanes. Generally the performance of the Fulmars and Martlets was

Fairey Fulmars in flight, a successful eight-gun carrier fighter plane

decidedly poorer than that of the Zeros: only the Sea Hurricanes were a match for them and the Fleet Air Arm had just nine of them.

The remaining fifty-seven aircraft aboard the British carriers were the outdated Swordfish and Albacore torpedo, bomber, reconnaissance and anti-submarine planes with a top speed of 160 knots and a range of about 500 miles. Their opposite number was the Japanese Kate torpedo bomber, top speed over 220 knots and a range of over 1,000 miles, twice that of the FAA strike aircraft. What is more they carried a 21-inch torpedo against the 18-inch torpedo carried by the Albacores and Swordfish. The Japanese aircraft carriers could also muster about 100 dive-bombers that could carry 1,000 pounds of bombs for 1,000 miles.

The British aircraft carriers had the advantage of radar which enabled them to use their fighters more efficiently and the Albacores and Swordfish were accustomed to operating at night, which the Japanese were not. This allowed them to make night attacks with little opposition. Unfortunately their Japanese counterparts had twice their range and in the event of a night attack by British planes, come daylight their parent ship could still be well within the range of the Japanese attack planes and fighters, and would suffer accordingly. Generally Admiral Somerville's hands were tied by the need to stay within reach of the protection offered by the aircraft ashore in Ceylon.

Admiral Somerville could not engage in actions that held the possibility of the loss of an important part of the Eastern Fleet: lose Ceylon to the Japanese and there were ports on the west coast of India that could provide a base for his fleet but lose the fleet, and the Japanese would be able to dominate the Indian Ocean and Arabian Sea to the total detriment of the British forces in the Middle East, India and places like Burma where British and Commonwealth troops were heavily engaged fighting the Japanese.

Intelligence that had been received indicated that the Japanese would be likely to attack Colombo or Trincomalee and to do this they would approach Ceylon from the south-east and fly off their aircraft at first light. Admiral Somerville planned to station his fleet to the southeast of Ceylon and wait for the Japanese to come within range of his strike aircraft so that they could make a night torpedo attack. When the attack was completed the fleet would retreat towards Ceylon to take advantage of the protection offered by the fighters based ashore.

There were six Catalina flying boats in Ceylon and these were to carry out reconnaissance flights with a view to spotting and reporting the approach of the Japanese fleet.

On the basis of Intelligence assessments Admiral Somerville put his fleet on station on 31 March 1942 and stayed there for three days, moving towards the Japanese line of approach under the cover of darkness in the hope of making a night attack and retiring to the cover of shore-based aircraft before daylight. It seemed as if the intelligence was wrong so Admiral Somerville took his fleet into the Maldive Islands, about 350 miles to the west of Ceylon, to replenish their fuel and water supplies, which were getting low. In fact the intelligence was not wrong, but the timing was a little adrift.

As the fleet arrived at Addu Atoll in the Maldives a patrolling Catalina reported the approach of the Japanese fleet. It was about 360 miles from Ceylon. There was no way the Eastern Fleet could intercept the Japanese; they were too far away. More than ninety bombers and dive-bombers escorted by thirty-six fighters attacked Colombo Harbour which was badly damaged. Because the raid had been anticipated the harbour had been cleared of most of the ships that had been lying there but *Tenedos*, a destroyer, and an armed merchant cruiser were sunk and a submarine depot ship, *Lucia*, incurred some damage. Forty-two British fighters opposed the Japanese attack. The Japanese lost seven fighters and the British lost twenty-seven aircraft, a loss they could ill afford. Six of them were Swordfish from a shore base: they had been armed with torpedoes and sent to attack the Japanese ships, a forlorn task with little or no hope of success or even survival.

At the time of the attack on Colombo the heavy cruisers *Cornwall* and *Dorsetshire* had been detached from the main part of the Eastern Fleet and were ordered to rejoin the main body of the Fleet. They had the misfortune to be spotted by a Japanese reconnaissance seaplane. As soon as the information was received the enemy carriers flew off a strike force of fifty-three aircraft which attacked and sank both cruisers. In view of this loss and the striking range of the enemy aircraft, twice that of the FAA's planes, it was decided to withdraw the old 'R' class battleships that were so

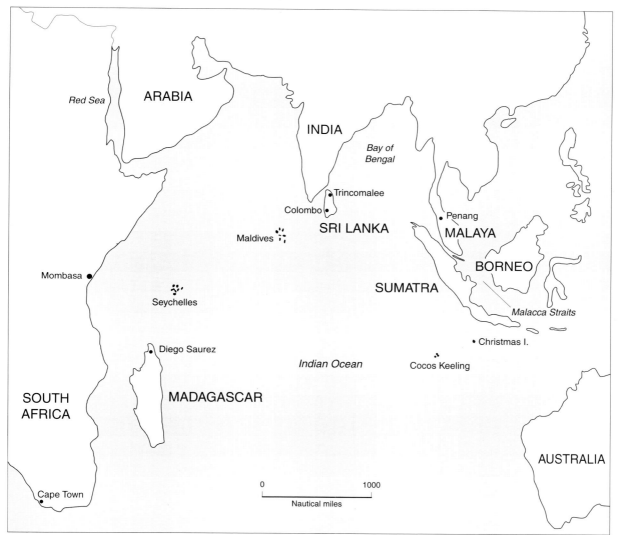

The Royal Navy's early engagements in the war in the Far East took place in the Indian Ocean

vulnerable without adequate air support, to Mombasa in East Africa.

Shortly after the raid on Colombo the Japanese fleet launched an air attack on Trincomalee, a naval base on the north-east coast of Ceylon, with similar results to their raid on Colombo.

The elderly British aircraft carrier *Hermes* with no aircraft embarked was escorted by the Australian destroyer *Vampire* and two fleet auxiliaries when they were spotted by a Japanese aircraft sixty-five miles south of Trincomalee. In no time at all they were attacked and overwhelmed by ninety Japanese planes and all four ships were sunk.

Once they had recovered their planes after this attack the Japanese First Air Fleet returned to Japan via the Malacca Straits to prepare for their next major operation, the invasion of the island of Midway in the North Pacific Ocean. In the short period they had been in the Indian Ocean the First Air Fleet had sunk 100,000 tons of shipping and brought traffic in the Bay of Bengal to a standstill. If Admiral Nagumo had stayed a little longer he would very likely have discovered just how weak the opposition was and that might well have led to a very different outcome.

A Japanese occupation of the Vichy French island of Madagascar on the western side of the Indian Ocean could have posed serious problems for Britain and her allies. Japanese forces occupying Madagascar would have been in a position to dominate the sea lanes to the Red Sea and therefore the Suez Canal and also the route around the Cape of Good Hope. The Vichy French had proved to be completely uncooperative to the point of outright hostility in other areas so there was no reason to believe they would be helpful in this situation. Indeed there was a strong suspicion that the French would be happy to allow the Japanese to establish bases on the island rather than allow the Allies access.

The decision was taken to invade and occupy Madagascar. The harbour of Diego Suarez at the northern end of the island was the obvious place to capture and plans were laid accordingly. A fleet was put together at Gibraltar which included the aircraft carrier *Illustrious,* and was designated Force F. The Fleet sailed south on 1 April 1942 under the command of Vice-Admiral Syfret. *Indomitable* was detached from the Eastern Fleet with instructions to join Force F. *Formidable* remained with Admiral Somerville's Force which was to be stationed about 250 miles east of Diego Suarez as a guard against the possibility of interference by the Japanese.

On 3 May *Indomitable* joined with Force F and two days later the amphibious assault went in over the beaches in the vicinity of the port. The two aircraft carriers provided the essential air support. Planes from *Illustrious* attacked shipping and any form of opposition by naval forces. The first strike force from *Illustrious* consisted of eighteen Swordfish armed with bombs, torpedoes and depth-charges. They sank *Bougainville,* an armed merchant cruiser, the submarine *Bevezire*s and an armed trawler. The sloop *D'Entrecasteaux* was dive-bombed and driven ashore. Meanwhile

aircraft from *Indomitable* bombed and strafed the nearby airfield. The next day a Swordfish destroyed the submarine *Le Heros*. These raids put an end to naval opposition and reduced enemy air activity to a minimum. In these two days the French destroyed four British aircraft. In the same period FAA planes brought down four Morane-Saulniers and two Potez and claimed eleven 'probables'. With the Vichy French naval losses added to the list the result was a very favourable one for the FAA.

With the air opposition subdued and the naval opposition eliminated the aircraft could now turn their full attention to helping the ground forces. Fleet Air Arm planes attacked enemy strongpoints that were causing trouble, carried out reconaissance flights and spotted the fall of shot for the naval gunners. Three Swordfish even dropped dummy parachutists in an operation designed to draw off some of the enemy forces to the south-west of Diego Suarez.

Enemy resistance in northern Madagascar came to an end early on 7 May. The Japanese failed to come to the aid of their allies because they were heavily engaged elsewhere. The Madagascar operation coincided with the Battle of the Coral Sea which inflicted the first serious defeat on the Japanese forces by the Allies.

With Diego Suarez in British hands the carriers retired to Mombasa to carry out routine maintenance and then *Indomitable* and *Illustrious* conducted a sweep across the Indian Ocean to Ceylon. When this was completed in July 1942 *Indomitable* was ordered to sail for the Mediterranean, where her aircraft were desperately needed.

Meanwhile *Illustrious* and *Formidable* carried out another sweep of the Indian Ocean without making contact with the enemy. On 28 July the two carriers had returned to Ceylon but two days later they were back at sea again, this time making a sweep of the Bay of Bengal. It was hoped that their presence in the Bay of Bengal would attract the interest of the Japanese and at least keep some of them away from the impending assault on Guadalcanal in the Solomon Islands.

The Fleet inadvertently achieved its primary purpose on 2 August when a 'Mavis' flying boat sighted and reported their position. Later the same day Hellcats attacked and destroyed another Japanese shadower.

Indomitable had been badly damaged almost as soon as she arrived in European waters so on 24 August *Formidable* sailed from Mombasa to take her place. This left *Illustrious* as the only Allied carrier in the Indian Ocean.

By the end of 1942 the USN had lost four of its carriers with another extensively damaged; the Japanese had lost six of theirs and they were being pressed so hard by the US Pacific Fleet that they ceased to operate in the Indian Ocean. Desperate for carriers to keep up the pressure on the Japanese, the USN asked that *Illustrious* should help, if only with diversionary attacks. Not only was *Illustrious* the only British carrier in the Indian Ocean but her complement of aircraft was so badly depleted that serious help was just not possible.

While the Eastern Fleet was doing what it could with very limited resources in the Indian Ocean, the Americans mustered what aircraft carriers they could and started operations against the Japanese who were established on many islands in the central and western Pacific. In the early stages the damage suffered by the Japanese at the hands of the planes of the USN was mostly of a minor nature but the experience they were obtaining was to be invaluable. In addition they were establising two important facts. One was that American carrier-borne aircraft were a match for the enemy planes in most respects and the other was that the safety of modern aircraft carriers was now no longer totally dependent on the support of a battle fleet.

On 4 June 1942 the Japanese committed four aircraft carriers to the Battle of Midway and lost all of them to the USN carriers *Enterprise, Hornet* and *Yorktown*. The American Navy lost the *Yorktown*.

As he approached Midway Admiral Yamamoto was unaware of the presence of the American carriers; his reconnaissance planes had failed to spot them. The commander of the US Task Force was better served and knew that the Japanese carriers were heading for Midway and struck at the very moment the Japanese carriers were ranging their aircraft on deck in preparation for an attack on the

US forces at Midway. Planes from *Enterprise* and *Hornet* arrived over the Japanese task force undetected and dive-bombed the three carriers when they were at their most vulnerable. They were so badly damaged that all three carriers sank before the day was out. Later the same day the remaining Japanese carrier launched a strike force against the American ships and severely damaged *Yorktown*. Planes from *Enterprise* and *Hornet* were flown off, and bombed and sank the *Hiryu*, the Japanese carrier that had escaped destruction that forenoon. With their air superiority lost the enemy fleet had no choice but to leave the area as fast as it could; by the next day, 5 June, the Japanese fleet was in full retreat.

From Papua New Guinea, so close to Australia, to the Carolines, many miles to the north and Midway Island, just a stone's throw from Pearl Harbor in Pacific terms, the grim battle for the Japanese-occupied islands was fought throughout the latter half of 1942 and on into 1943 by the Australians and the Americans.

Meanwhile the British and Australian ground forces fought a desperate battle for Burma and other nearby territories. This was a major effort that has received little recognition compared with the publicity given to the American battles in the Pacific.

During 1943 the United States began to rebuild its fleet. In not much more than a year they took into commission eight Essex class Fleet Carriers, each with a complement of ninety planes, nine Light Fleet Carriers, each with thirty-five aircraft, and thirty-five Escort Carriers. By mid-1943 they had almost 17,000 aircraft in the Pacific. This represented not only an increase in numbers but also an improvement in performance; their new aircraft were generally superior to those of their opponents. At the same time the Japanese were also working desperately to increase their carrier capacity.

At the request of the Americans at the end of 1942 *Victorious* was detached from the Home Fleet and sailed to Norfolk, Virginia for a limited refit before entering the Pacific.

The planes *Victorious* had aboard when she left the Norfolk Navy Yard at the end of January 1943 were Grumman Avengers and Martlets. She made her way into the Pacific via the Panama Canal working up her air and flight-deck crews as she went. A deck landing accident that led to a fire made it necessary to divert to Pearl Harbor for repairs and it was 8 May before she could leave. Nine days later she joined the American carrier *Saratoga* and other USN fleet units at Noumea, New Caledonia. There followed a series of joint exercises in the course of which it became apparent that the air defence organisation aboard *Victorious* was such that she was the obvious choice for the position of fighter carrier. The *Saratoga* took on the responsibility for the strike aircraft for the invasion of New Georgia. This entailed a temporary exchange of aircraft between the two carriers.

The task force left Noumea on 27 June and returned on 25 July 1943. The fighter aircraft had flown more than 600 sorties from *Victorious* but met little opposition. Now that the airfields on New Georgia were in American hands the need for an additional carrier in the Pacific was no longer so pressing and *Victorious* made her way back to the UK for a major overhaul.

With the Salerno landings in Italy secure it was possible to send a carrier to the Indian Ocean where U boats were fast becoming a problem. The Escort Carrier *Battler* joined Admiral Somerville's fleet in October 1943 and began work as part of a close escort group defending convoys in the Indian Ocean. The Axis U boats responded by leaving the protected convoys alone and sought out ships that had been routed independently. Admiral Somerville decided to seek out and destroy the submarine supply ships.

The Japanese and German submarines were based on Penang with the supply ships *Charlotte Schliemann* and *Brake* stationed in the area of the Seychelle Islands. *Charlotte Schliemann* was sighted by a Catalina and sunk by the destroyer *Relentless* and two weeks later, on 12 March, a Swordfish from *Battler* found and attacked *Brake* and led the destroyer *Rocket* to her to complete her destruction. The U boats were now forced to return to Penang every time they needed to replenish their fuel and stores, thereby greatly reducing

the time they could stay on patrol and the sinking of Allied shipping fell off accordingly.

Early in 1944 *Battler* was joined by the Escort Carriers *Ameer, Atheling, Begum* and *Shah*. An aggressive sweep in the region of the Seychelles in August of that year was carried out by *Begum* and *Shah* and Avengers from the carriers found U 198. They attacked and damaged the submarine, which obliged her to stay on the surface and two frigates were called up to help finish her off.

As ever with convoy escort work the real measure of its success is the lack of casualties, not the number of U boats sunk and, as elsewhere, no ship was lost whilst under the protection of aircraft from the Escort Carriers.

Very early in 1944 the main Japanese Battle Fleet had been driven out of their forward base in the Caroline Islands by the US carrier-borne aircraft and had moved into Singapore where there were excellent dockyard facilities within easy distance of their main sources of fuel supply in the East Indies. The move caused some concern that they might be contemplating a move into the Indian Ocean.

The British Eastern Fleet, which had recently been reinforced, now had one large carrier (*Illustrious*) and three battleships with which to oppose the Japanese Battle Fleet, which had three large aircraft carriers and five battleships. Late in March three Japanese heavy cruisers ventured into the Indian Ocean and sank two merchantmen close to the Cocos Keeling Islands. *Illustrious* with other vessels from the Eastern Fleet carried out a search for the Japanese cruisers but failed to find them.

It was intended to build up the Eastern Fleet, particularly the air arm, and in preparation for this installations ashore in Ceylon underwent a considerable degree of expansion. At the time of *Illustrious'* arrival the shoreside facilities could support some 400 aircraft.

The American Admiral Nimitz asked the British Pacific Fleet to attack the extensive oil refineries and fuel storage tanks on Sumatra.

With *Illustrious* and a number of Escort Carriers available it was decided to attack Sabang, a harbour at the northern end of Sumatra. The USS

Saratoga joined with the ships of five other navies and a fleet of twenty-seven ships sailed for Sabang. The strike group reached the point at which the aircraft would be flown off early on 19 April 1944. Flying operations started at 0515; *Illustrious* flew off seventeen Barracudas and thirteen Corsairs. *Saratoga* launched eleven Avengers, eighteen Dauntlesses and twenty-four Hellcats. The attack was beautifully co-ordinated: the Avengers and the Barracudas hit the target within one minute of each other, surprise being complete. The only opposition was from anti-aircraft fire which was late starting and both ragged and unco-ordinated. Harbour installations, oil storage tanks and a radar station were destroyed. There was very little shipping in the harbour but one small ship was sunk and another was damaged and ran aground, presumably to avoid sinking. The Corsairs and Hellcats attacked aircraft on the ground at a near-by airfield and at another on an island close by, destroying a total of twenty-four aircraft. Two Barracudas had the misfortune to have their bombs hang up on the first attempt to release them and went round again, this time successfully.

The early attacks on the airfields ensured that no Japanese aircraft took off whilst the raid was in progress but as the Fleet was withdrawing three torpedo aircraft took to the air. Before they could do any harm they were shot down by the Hellcats of the Combat Air Patrol.

The only casualty on the Allied side was a Hellcat but its pilot was picked up by a British submarine that was stationed there for just that purpose. Every effort was always made to recover Allied aircrew who were shot down. If they were taken prisoner they could expect to be tortured by the Japanese to extract the last bit of information and then to be beheaded. The Japanese were quite ruthless in this respect. An account is on record of an Allied ship being sunk by a Japanese warship which picked up seventy-three survivors from the water and then beheaded them one by one.

Once the fleet was back in Ceylon the *Saratoga* received orders to return to the States for a refit.

At Surabaya in Java there was an important refinery and a large store of aviation spirit and since *Saratoga* would be passing to the south of

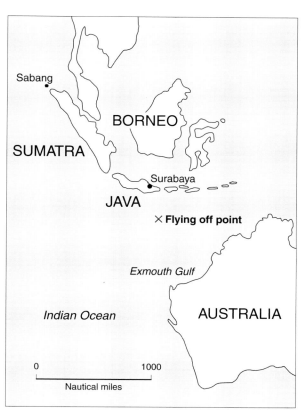

Sumatra, the heart of Japanese oil production

Java on her way home it was decided to take the opportunity to attack this installation. The British Eastern Fleet, with *Saratoga* in company sailed for Exmouth Gulf on the west coast of Australia to refuel before turning north to Java.

On 17 May 1944 the fleet was in a position about 180 miles south of Surabaya, which was to be the flying-off point for the strike force of aircraft. Forty-five Dauntless and Avenger torpedo-bombers and a fighter escort of forty Corsairs and Hellcats were flown off and headed for Java. Once over the target the force divided into two groups: one attacked the harbour and dockyard and the other tackled the oil refinery. Despite the fact that surprise was achieved the results were disappointing.

It was not until the aircrews were being

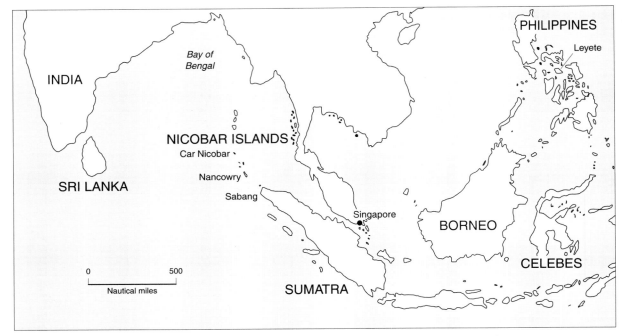

The Bay of Bengal and the East Indies

debriefed that the poor results became apparent. Admiral Somerville was aboard one of the battleships and by the time the aircraft had been recovered, aircrews debriefed, the information collated and passed to the C-in-C the fleet was too far from Java for a second strike to be a practical proposition. After the immediate withdrawal *Saratoga* and her escort of three destroyers parted from the Eastern Fleet and returned to Pearl Harbor. The British fleet headed for Trincomalee.

A number of lesser forays were made over the next few months and early in June 1944 *Illustrious* and other vessels carried out a diversionary operation into the Bay of Bengal at the request of the Americans. United States forces were about to invade the Marianas and felt that it would help their cause if the common enemy on the fringe of their operations was kept busy. It was intended that *Atheling*, an Escort Carrier, should accompany *Illustrious* to provide fighter patrols with her Seafires and Wildcats: unfortunately the difference in speed of some twelve knots between *Illustrious* and *Atheling* caused problems and *Atheling* was left behind. Planes from *Illustrious* destroyed a number of aircraft on the ground and a few small coastal vessels were dive-bombed and

sunk but that was the limit of the success of these raids.

Bad weather over the targets and poor intelligence combined to reduce the effectiveness of this and other raids at this time. The weather in the region of Southern India and the adjacent Asian areas is governed by the monsoon seasons. At this period moisture laden air would be coming off the Indian Ocean, creating the wet season of the monsoon as soon as it reached land. This usually meant a deep deck of cloud, often reaching down to sea level, creating poor visibility over many of the targets.

Reconnaissance of enemy bases was always difficult for the Eastern Fleet. Distances were such that reconnaisance could only be carried out by carrier-borne aircraft, thereby alerting the enemy to the presence of a carrier group and destroying all hope of surprise.

This operation was to be the last time in World War Two that carrier operations relied on just one aircraft carrier for the use of returning planes. The number of planes flown off by a carrier on an

A Vought Corsair Mk II about to take off from the flight-deck of HMS Venerable. *A lend-lease plane that played an important part in the Pacific war*

operational sortie had increased considerably from the earlier days of carrier work. Swamping the enemy's defences with all possible aircraft had paid dividends. That was the plus side but when fifty or sixty planes returned from a sortie, all low on fuel and some damaged or with wounded aircrew aboard, delays in receiving them could not be tolerated. Clearing the effects of a bad landing by one of the returning aircraft could take time enough to put the remaining planes in jeopardy if there was not a 'spare deck' on hand to receive them. If the problem arose with one of the first planes to land-on, most of a carrier's complement of aircraft could be in serious trouble. For this reason the spare deck philosophy became standard practice.

Victorious and *Indomitable* arrived to reinforce the Eastern Fleet in July 1944, which allowed *Illustrious* to sail to South Africa for a refit that was to take two months. Whilst *Illustrious* was away *Victorious* and *Indomitable* joined with three battleships, seven cruisers and two destroyers to bombard Sabang at the northern end of Sumatra. This was to be a bombardment by the Fleet rather than an air strike but the carriers were to provide planes to spot the fall of shot and to give air cover to the Fleet. Both carriers put all but nine of their Barracudas ashore and in their place each took onboard forty or more Corsairs.

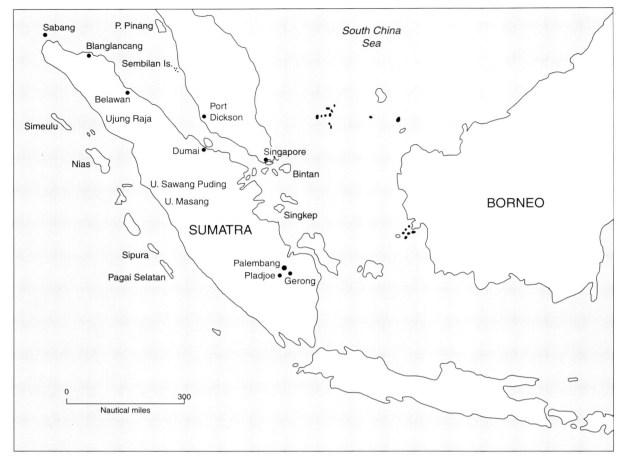

The bombardment was carried out on 25 July with considerable success using aircraft from both carriers to spot the fall of shot, to carry out photographic reconnaissance and to provide Combat Air Patrols over the Fleet throughout the operation. Only two small enemy ships were present and both were sunk. Severe damage was inflicted on the port installations and the oil storage plant, which was the prime purpose of the attack.

It was not until the Fleet was withdrawing that a few enemy aircraft put in an appearance. The Corsairs on Combat Air Patrol went into action and shot down four Japanese planes without loss to themselves.

At this stage of the far eastern war the Japanese were still relying on the Mitsubishi Zero as their fighter. This plane had served them well but was now being outclassed by the more modern Allied

Palembang, Pladjoe and Gerong, where FAA planes scored a major victory

planes. They had replaced their dive-bomber 'Val' with 'Judy' and their torpedo plane 'Kate' had given way to 'Jill'. Both aircraft were faster than their predecessors but far slower than the Hellcat fighters that were in use by the Allied fleets. Neither did they have self sealing fuel tanks as did the more modern Allied planes. However they still had one advantage: their range was far greater even than the newer aircraft in use by the Allies.

The Japanese Air Fleet had suffered great losses and this was reflected in the quality of many of their replacement pilots who, unlike the earlier Japanese pilots, lacked experience and ability by Allied standards.

Towards the end of August 1944 _Indomitable_ and _Victorious_ joined forces to attack two more targets in Sumatra. One was the largest cement works in South East Asia situated at Indaroeng and the other was the harbour of Emmahaven, its port installations and any shipping that might be found there. The raid on the cement works was a success but the strike at Emmahaven achieved very little. These two strikes were followed by a raid on an important rail centre at Sigli in the extreme north of Sumatra which achieved a moderate amount of damage but not enough to satisfy Admiral Fraser, who had taken over from Admiral Somerville. As a result the aircrews were required to undertake an extensive weapons training programme. In view of the near total lack of up to date reconnaissance information available to the aircrews involved in these raids their limited success was perhaps not entirely their fault.

The Americans asked the Eastern Fleet to carry out another diversionary attack in mid-October 1944. This time it was to be on the Nicobar Islands, some 800 miles to the east of Ceylon, to coincide with their invasion of Leyte in the Philippines. The Fleet was composed of _Indomitable_ and _Victorious_, a battle cruiser, four cruisers and ten destroyers. Airfields on Car Nicobar Island, the coastal defences, the harbour installations and any shipping that was present at Nancowry and Sabang in the north of Sumatra were to be the targets on 17 and 19 October.

On 17 October Corsairs from _Victorious_ made low-level attacks on two airfields and their anti-aircraft defences while Barracudas attacked and sank a small ship and inflicted some damage on nearby barracks. When this was over and the planes were recovered by their carriers, the ships with them started a bombardment of the coastal defences whilst Hellcats flew overhead and spotted for the fleet. On this day there was no opposition from enemy aircraft but two Corsairs and a Barracuda were lost to anti-aircraft fire.

Sabang was to be the next target and the fleet moved off to be in a position to launch an air attack on the installations there. The weather was poor: it was still the monsoon season, and whilst the ships were under way it worsened to a point where it

would not have been profitable to launch an attack on Sabang. Instead, on the 19th planes were in the air over the Nicobars again looking for coastal vessels to attack and indeed anything that offered itself as a target. The Japanese had flown in some aircraft and a number of them attacked the Corsairs and Hellcats that were in the air. Two Corsairs and a Hellcat were lost in this engagement but the British planes accounted for seven of the enemy. All in all it was not a very profitable operation.

After this operation the carriers put their Barracudas ashore and embarked Avengers in their place. For the aircrews the next two months were taken up with getting to know their new aircraft which had very different characteristics and requirements from the old Barracuda and there was a lot to learn.

Meanwhile _Illustrious_ and _Indefatigable_ rejoined the Eastern Fleet. With four modern Fleet Carriers the Eastern Fleet now had a total of 230 up-to-date aircraft at its disposal. With the reinforcement of the Fleet came a change of C-in-C, Sir Philip Vian, who had been in charge of the escort carriers at Salerno, was to replace Admiral Fraser.

Rear Admiral Vian's first operation was frustrated by bad weather. The target was to be the refinery at Pangkalan Brandan in Sumatra. The island of Sumatra was home to a number of oil refineries on which Japan relied very heavily. Between them they supplied three-quarters of Japan's aviation spirit.

The strike force consisted of twenty-eight Avengers with a like number of Corsairs and Hellcats to act as escort; each of the Avengers was armed with four 500-pound bombs. They were flown off in bad weather and headed for the target early on the morning of 20 December. The poor weather stayed with them and worsened as they approached the coastline until the strike force was confronted with a mass of heavy cloud that reached down to the sea. Try as they might they could find no way round it and so they turned to the secondary target, the port of Belawan Deli near Medan on the north-east coast of Sumatra. When the strike force reached their secondary target they found that this too was largely obscured by heavy

A Grumman TBF Avenger in difficulties

cloud and even when the target could be seen the squalls made things very difficult for the aircrews. The Avengers bombed the harbour installations and the Corsairs set petrol storage tanks and warehouses ablaze. Some of the fighters had a little better luck and were able to strafe airfields at Sabang, destroying a number of enemy aircraft on the ground. The only aircraft in the air was a somewhat surprised bomber that was shot down by the Hellcats that formed the top cover. Two Corsairs became separated from the rest of the planes and actually made their way to one of the major refineries where they set fire to a large storage tank.

The problems created by the weather were compounded by the lack of radio discipline in the general excitement of combat with instructions and advice being given by all and sundry. It became so bad by the time the strike force had reached the form-up area after the raid that the Strike Leader's instructions could not be heard. The CO of 854 Squadron gathered the Avengers from *Illustrious* together and took them from the general mêlée and set course for their carrier. The rest of the strike force and their escort eventually sorted themselves out and they too set course for the fleet.

On 4 January 1945 Pangkalan was attacked again, this time with much better results. The weather was kinder to the attacking aircraft and this made all the difference. Before the strike aircraft went in a group of sixteen Hellcats and

Corsairs carried out pre-emptive attacks on four airfields destroying nine Japanese aircraft on the ground and in the air without loss to themselves.

An hour and a half later thirty-two Avengers and Fireflys carried out rocket and bombing attacks on the same refinery, causing such heavy damage to the installation that its output was greatly reduced. Enemy aircraft flew up to meet the strike force but the fighter escort of Corsairs and Hellcats shot down at least five of them, again without loss to themselves. The Japanese fighters damaged just one Avenger, which made it back to its parent ship and the crew of a Firefly that ran out of fuel and had to ditch was rescued by a destroyer.

With the war in Europe drawing to its close the RN at last had ships to spare for the war in the Far East and agreement had finally been reached with the Americans on how the British ships should be used in the Pacific. As a result the British Pacific Fleet was formed with the four Fleet Carriers *Indefatigable*, *Indomitable*, *Illustrious* and *Victorious*, the battleship *King George V*, three cruisers and ten destroyers. Rear Admiral Vian chose *Indomitable* as his flag ship. On 16 January 1945 this fleet left Ceylon bound for Sydney: en route the carriers were to attack the immense oil refineries in the vicinity of Palembang in southern Sumatra. These refineries, Pladjoe and Soengei Gerong close to the town of Palembang, supplied all the fuel required by the Japanese armed forces in this area. In 1945 these were the two biggest and most important oil refineries in the Far East. Their destruction would ground large numbers of Japanese aircraft and restrict the movement of army and navy units. Not surprisingly the targets were heavily defended both by fighters – at least four airfields within 40 miles – and a considerable array of anti-aircraft fire.

The strike on the Pladjoe refinery at Palembang was scheduled for the 22nd but had to be postponed for two days because of bad weather.

On 24 January over one hundred and forty planes were launched from the carriers. Forty-seven of them were Avengers, each armed with four 500-lb bombs and twelve were Fireflies, each one equipped with eight 60-lb rockets. The remainder of this formidable force consisted of Corsairs and Hellcats that were to act as a fighter escort. Two Hellcats were to fly photo reconnaissance flights and two Walruses acted as air / sea rescue aircraft. Over one hundred and forty planes on one raid plus Combat Air Patrols over the Task Force! Only a few years earlier strike forces were usually numbered in single figures. The major blow suffered by the Italian Fleet at Taranto was delivered by a mere twenty aircraft manned by forty men.

The strike force with its close escort of fighters crossed the 12,000-foot-high coastal mountain range a bit before 0800. It had been intended that there should be a pre-emptive strike on airfields in the area but the Corsairs that had been allotted this task were late arriving, which allowed some Japanese aircraft to get into the air to challenge the main force and to inflict some losses. Despite their late arrival the Corsairs were able to destroy thirty-four Japanese aircraft on the ground.

To reach the Pladjoe refinery it was necessary for the attacking planes to descend closer to sea level and to do this they had to negotiate a balloon barrage that was being raised by the Japanese. When the Avengers reached the balloon barrage it was at about 2,000 feet and rising – probably to some 5,000 feet. On this occasion the balloon barrage caused no losses to the British planes. The ground defences were slow to respond and it was not until the Avengers and Fireflies dived onto their targets that there was a response from the Japanese anti-aircraft defences, but then it was a heavy and persistent barrage. Fifteen to twenty Japanese fighters were in the air and there were engagements taking place all around. Pressing home their attack the Avengers and Fireflies did considerable damage to the refinery and the oil storage tanks and as a bonus one of Japan's biggest remaining tankers was damaged beyond repair.

With the attack completed the Avengers made their way towards the rendezvous and form-up point at which all the returning planes were intended to collect and sort themselves out prior to flying back to their parent ships. The route chosen by the planners took the Avengers over an area in which there was a very heavy concentration of anti-aircraft batteries. To make matters worse

Japanese fighters were lying in wait for them. Most of the British fighter escort planes were still locked in combat with Japanese fighters some thirty or more miles away which left the Avengers with only limited protection. Again shamefully poor RT discipline so filled the air with chatter that the Avengers were not able to call for fighter support when they were in danger of attack. As a consequence a number of Avengers suffered damage and one was shot down whilst running the gauntlet to the rendezvous. In all, nine FAA aircraft were lost and many of the surviving planes damaged.

The oil refinery at Soengei Gerong, not far from Palembang, was the next target of importance to receive the attention of the FAA. On 29 January 1945 a strike force of about the same size used for the raids on Pangkalam and Palembang was in the air on its way to the new target. In view of the hostile reception received by the returning aircraft on the raid on the Pladjoe refinery a different route to the rendezvous point was chosen.

The Ramrod – the pre-emptive fighter sweep – was to be concentrated on two major airfields. Fireflies were to form a close escort throughout and they were also to attack the balloon barrage as they dived to deliver their rocket attacks on the refinery. Despite this two Avengers struck balloon cables and were brought down by them. This strike was more costly than the earlier raids on the Sumatran oil refineries. In all sixteen FAA planes were lost to enemy action; eleven ditched close to the Task Force and fourteen were written off in deck landing accidents, a total of forty-one aircraft. Thirty aircrew members were lost. Once all the returning aircraft had been received the fleet turned and headed towards Freemantle and Sydney.

On the plus side this attack was even more successful than the previous efforts. Production at Pladjoe was stopped totally for two months and even after that production at both refineries was down to a third of their earlier output. In time production was increased but it never exceeded half of its normal output. The fighter sweeps over the airfields had destroyed thirty-eight planes on the ground and the close fighter escort shot down more than thirty.

Meanwhile over the fleet a further eight Japanese aircraft were destroyed by aircraft of the Combat Air Patrols bringing the day's total of enemy aircraft destroyed to more than seventy-six. Of the planes protecting the fleet just one Hellcat was badly damaged – by 'friendly fire' from *King George V. Euryalus* also distinguished herself by hitting *Illustrious* with two 5.25-inch AA shells which killed twelve and wounded twenty one. Apart from these self-inflicted wounds the fleet escaped unscathed.

During the attack on the refinery and in the course of the withdrawal a number of Japanese aircraft attempted to engage the Fleet at different times, including a group of seven suicide bombers that directed their efforts at the aircraft carriers. The kamikaze were destroyed by the FAA close-support fighters and a storm of anti-aircraft fire from all the ships that could bring their guns to bear in an action that lasted just four minutes.

In the course of these three raids about 140 Japanese aircraft were destroyed on the ground and in the air. The four British carriers lost a total of twenty-five aircraft in combat in the attacks on these prime targets. There was also a significant number of aircraft and sometimes crew that were lost for reasons ranging from ditching because of insufficient fuel to deck landing accidents and 'friendly fire'.

At this time Japan was desperately short of all kinds of oil products and depended heavily on the production from Sumatra. Whilst these raids on three of their major refineries may be lacking in glamour they cut the total output of aviation fuel from Sumatra to thirty-five per cent of its usual level. This must have been a major blow to the Japanese campaigns in Asia and the Pacific generally. Indeed these raids have been referred to as a strategic victory and as the FAA's greatest single contribution to final victory in the Pacific war. Certainly they are very high on the list of the FAA's great successes in World War Two and one, oddly enough, that is not often mentioned outside FAA circles.

The British Pacific Fleet reached Sydney early in February but it was to be three or four weeks

The burning oil refinery at Palembang

before a decision was forthcoming on whether Admiral Nimitz was to have the British ships under his command or General MacArthur should have their support in his amphibious assaults that were about to be opened in Borneo and Mindanao. Eventually it was agreed that Admiral Nimitz's need was the greater.

The four Fleet carriers had had a long war and signs of wear and tear were appearing. *Illustrious* was having trouble with her centre prop shaft and when she was dry-docked it was decided that the propeller should be removed from the troublesome shaft. This reduced her top speed to twenty-four knots and if the carriers were to operate as a group the whole group would have to accept this speed restriction. *Formidable* was afflicted by the same trouble and her arrival in the Pacific was delayed to allow repairs to be carried out. It was to be the middle of April before she was able to join the British Pacific Fleet and relieve *Illustrious*.

Naturally there were problems to be overcome in fusing major units of two different navies together. The fact that the American command was split between General MacArthur and Admiral Nimitz, who were both fighting their own corners and both wanted the services of the British Pacific Fleet – after they had managed to shed a measure of Anglophobia that was apparent in the early days – did nothing to help.

The RN had to adopt American methods in signals procedure, operating techniques, for the carriers particularly, and so on. Whilst these changes involved a lot of work they were not insurmountable. The state of the Fleet Train was something else. Its shortcomings posed a serious problem that no amount of hard work could hope to overcome.

To sustain a large fleet of warships requires either bases within reach of the area of operations or a fleet of supply ships, oilers, repair vessels, hospital ship and many others, in short, 'The Fleet Train'. In an ocean as vast as the Pacific the Fleet Train obviously becomes an important part of the operation. Add a number of large aircraft carriers to the equation and the fact that the fleet would need to stay at sea for weeks at a time, and the need for support ships of all kinds is multiplied. Just one figure will perhaps underline this point. The four RN Fleet Carriers that joined Admiral Nimitz's force held a total of 238 operational aircraft between them. Ashore a base that could undertake the supply, the care and the maintenance of that number of aircraft and the men and installations needed to sustain them would be a major operation. To create those facilities afloat in an ocean that measures very roughly 9,000 miles from east to west and over 7,000 north to south is a daunting thought.

There were never enough ships to form an adequate Fleet Train for the British Pacific Fleet. In all fairness after five and a half years of war Britain

and others had lost so many ships that there were never going to be enough to do all that was needed. A motley collection of ships of many nations was pressed into service with the Escort Carriers and a few purpose built auxilaries that were used to attend to the special needs of the aircraft carriers. The transfer of fuel from the tankers was always to be slow; they had not been designed for the speedy refuelling of moving ships.

On 19 March the British Pacific Fleet was in Ulithi atoll in the Carolines. The Fleet had been incorporated into the USN's 5th Fleet which was under the command of Admiral Spruance, as Task Force 57.

The US forces had been driving the Japanese off one island after another on their way to Japan and it was now the turn of Iwo Jima. Sited around Iwo Jima at between 400 and 700 miles distance were a number of major airfields and a large number of aircraft that had the range and ability to interfere with the invasion of Iwo Jima. The USN Fast Carrier Force had been flying sorties against them with the intention of destroying as many aircraft as possible. A very considerable number of enemy aircraft had been destroyed, both in the air and on the ground, but on 19 March three of the American Attack carriers were seriously damaged. *Intrepid* and *Wasp* were out of the fight for the first stages of the invasion of Okinawa and *Franklin* suffered grievously with the deaths of nearly 800 men: she was so badly damaged that she played no further part in the war.

On 23 March the British Pacific Fleet (designated Task Force 57) consisted of *Indefatigable, Indomitable, Illustrious and Victorious* in company with *King George V, Howe, Argonaut, Black Prince, Euryalus, Gambia, Swiftsure* and eleven destroyers. Admiral Rawlins RN was in command of Task Force 57. Admiral Spruance USN was the American officer to whom he was responsible. From the start the two men had the great good fortune to hit it off as if they had worked happily together for years.

The British Pacific Fleet sailed from Ulithi to attack airfields on the Sakishima-Gunto group of islands. The aim was twofold: first, to keep enemy planes based on the islands away from the area of

Kerama-Retto and Okinawa whilst American forces launched amphibious assaults on these islands and, second, to prevent the reinforcement of planes to the area by staging them through the Sakishima Islands.

The Sakishima-Gunto group is at the southern end of the chain of islands that reaches from Kyushu, the southernmost of the main islands that make up Japan, to the north-eastern tip of Taiwan (Formosa). There were six airfields on three of the islands and these were to be the target for the British Pacific Fleet. The plan was to have the Fleet fly strikes against the airfields for two days when they would then retire to refuel, etc. and four American Escort Carriers would take over for the next two days. The two groups of carriers would alternate every two days in this fashion for as long as was deemed necessary.

The first strikes were made on 26 March 1945 from a position one hundred miles to the south of the targets. The main aim was to keep the enemy aircraft grounded and to this end the Avengers each carried four 500-lb bombs to be used to crater the runways, destroy fuel dumps, buildings and hangars. Whilst the Avengers were busy Fireflies attacked the anti-aircraft positions with rockets and cannons. About forty planes attacked the airfields four times a day in this way with the aim of keeping the enemy occupied while daylight lasted. For the same reason single Avenger sorties and Corsair and Hellcat dive-bombing and strafing attacks were also made during the day.

The enemy flak was both accurate and intense and the gunners were enterprising in setting flak traps for the attacking aircraft. Dummy aircraft would be sited so as to lure FAA fighters into a strafing run straight into the barrels of concealed AA guns. The runways were made of compacted crushed coral and although the Avengers were successful in their cratering operations, the Japanese could reinstate the runways quite quickly.

The very first Replenishment At Sea (RAS) took three days instead of the scheduled two, principally because a typhoon warning was in force and the foul weather did nothing to help. However on 31 March the four Fleet Carriers were back on station

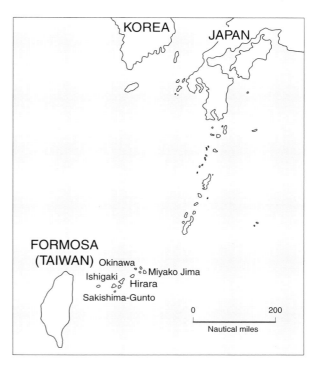

The war approaches Japan

and the strikes on the airfields in the Sakishimas were under way again. Okinawa was invaded the following day and there was a strong response from the Japanese with bombing and kamikaze attacks, the first to be experienced by the British Pacific Fleet. One suicide bomber eluded the Combat Air Patrol and struck *Indefatigable* at the base of her island. Her armoured deck stood her in good stead. What would have been a disaster in an unarmoured vessel put a three-inch deep dent into the flight-deck and started a small fire in the roof of the hangar below the hit. There were casualties, fourteen men killed and sixteen wounded but compared with *Franklin*'s casualty list of nearly eight hundred in similar circumstances...

The damage control parties jury rigged two flight-deck barriers, extinguished the fires and generally tidied up and in less than an hour the first plane was able to land on. Strikes on the Japanese airfields continued throughout the day.

At 1730 four kamikaze used cloud cover to evade the Hellcats that attempted to intercept

USS Sangamon *under suicide bomber attack – the next one hit the flight-deck and caused a number of casualties and extensive damage*

Early morning flights over the enemy airfields found very few planes and almost no activity. During the forenoon of 2 April the Fleet withdrew to the Fleet Train to replenish stores and refuel. An American Task Force took the place of the British ships. In the course of the day the destroyer *Ulster* that had been damaged by a near miss was towed to Leyte.

By 5 April replenishment and refuelling was completed and the Fleet was back on station early on the following day for another three days of attacks on the Sakishimas. The next day there was an attack on the Fleet by a number of kamikaze aircraft. They registered just one strike, *Illustrious* receiving a glancing blow on her island. Two Corsairs on the flight-deck were destroyed and some minor damage was done to the radio aerials but there were no casualties. At the time it seemed to have caused very little damage but in fact plates and frames below the waterline had been cracked. On the 8th the British Pacific Fleet rotated with the American contingent of carriers. It was during this period of refuelling etc. that one of the USN carriers, *Hancock*, was hit by a kamikaze and was so badly damaged that she was out of action. The American carriers had wooden flight-decks which had certain advantages but when one took a direct hit on the flight-deck the damage was usually much more severe than would have been inflicted on the armoured British Fleet Carriers. It was for this reason the British Fleet was asked to take on the job of attacking the kamikaze bases on Formosa.

At daybreak on 11 April the carriers were in position and ready to launch their strike groups at the Formosan bases but the weather was so poor they had to postpone the first strikes for 24 hours. When the aircraft eventually arrived over the airfields they were hampered by a great deal of low cloud. The first attacking force was made up of forty-eight Avengers and forty Corsairs. A few aircraft found an airfield and strafed Japanese planes and installations but the low cloud caused the major part of the force to turn their attention to the port of Kiirun, their secondary target. Although this was not their prime target the Avengers and Corsairs inflicted considerable damage to port

them. As soon as they were sighted by the Fleet they came under heavy fire. Three were shot down and the fourth went for *Victorious* which was able to turn away from the suicide bomber. The Japanese plane's wing tip struck the edge of the flight-deck and the plane dived into the sea about eighty feet from the carrier's side where it exploded harmlessly.

installations, ships in the harbour and a nearby chemical plant.

A second raid that day had better luck with the weather and found the airfields. The strike was unopposed and the Avengers were able to do a useful amount of damage to the runways whilst the fighters shot up parked aircraft and the various facilities around the airfield. Five Japanese bombers on course for Okinawa were spotted by two Fireflies who went in to attack and shot four of them down. Late the same day a Combat Air Patrol attacked a number of Japanese aircraft and destroyed four more, damaged six and drove off the rest.

The following day, 13 April, the weather improved and the replenishment was put off for a day to enable further attacks to be carried out on the kamikaze bases. These two days of raids were most rewarding. In addition to the considerable damage wreaked on the port and shipping at Kiirun and the nearby chemical plant, road and rail targets had been attacked, the airfield runways had been heavily cratered and aircraft on the ground destroyed. In the air sixteen Japanese aircraft were destroyed and six or more damaged. Fleet Air Arm losses were light; three planes were lost to anti-aircraft fire or in aerial combat and two more in accidents.

While the FAA was attacking the kamikaze bases on Formosa suicide bombers from airfields in the Sakishima-Gunto group of islands had been attacking the American Fleet in large numbers with considerable success. Two USN carriers and three battleships were either damaged or put out of action, thirteen destroyers were damaged and seven were sunk. The American Escort Carriers had been doing their best to keep pressure on the airfields that spawned the kamikaze but they did not have the power nor the protection possessed by the British Fleet Carriers and their best efforts were inadequate for the job. Task Force 57 was asked to tackle the Sakishima airfields again.

The British Pacific Fleet spent a few days replenishing their stores and fuel and in the course of this operation *Formidable* relieved *Illustrious*. The damage inflicted by the suicide bomber on *Illustrious* nine or ten days earlier needed attention and her

ship's company were in need of a rest: they had been in action for a long time.

Strikes were mounted against the Sakishima airfields and 50,000 pounds of bombs were dropped on them in the three days of 16, 17 and 20 April. The tankers of the Fleet Train were very nearly empty, as were the ammunition and stores ships. When operations were completed on the 20th the British Pacific Fleet and the Fleet Train set course for Leyte which was reached on 23 April. Fuel and stores were taken aboard and some small measure of rest and relaxation was afforded the ships' companies.

The Fleet was back at sea on 1 May, heading for the Sakishimas yet again. Three days later forty-seven Avengers took off in two groups with an escort of Fireflies. One group was to attack airfields at Ishigaki and Miyako and the other had Hirara and Nobara as their targets. One Avenger was lost to the heavy anti-aircraft fire. Later the same morning ships of the Task Force were spotted by a high-flying Japanese plane that escaped the CAP and the intense barrage thrown at it by the the guns of the fleet.

The AA batteries on Ishigaki Miyako were proving to be a serious problem. They had been bombed repeatedly by Avengers whose efforts had produced no really worthwhile results and so it was decided to subject them to a bombardment by the guns of the ships of the Task Force.

The battleships *King George V* and *Howe*, five cruisers and the 25th Destroyer Flotilla were detached from the aircraft carriers and steamed to a position close to Miyako Shima, from where the bombardment started just after midday. Almost at once the detached carriers came under attack by Japanese aircraft. *Formidable* was struck by a kamikaze and suffered damage that reduced her speed to eighteen knots. The huge cloud of smoke resulting from this hit was clearly visible to the bombarding fleet. Admiral Rawlins ordered that the bombardment should be speeded up and a little before one o'clock the task was completed and the ships turned south to rejoin the carriers.

Well before the bombarding force was in position the carriers were detecting enemy planes at

HMS Formidable *under kamikaze attack*

A kamikaze strikes her flight-deck

about fifty miles to the west. The radars were showing twenty-six of them in four groups.

The first enemy plane was shot down by Seafires, the next fell to the guns of the Corsairs on Combat Air Patrol but a number eluded the fighters and approached the carriers undetected. The radar sets of the missing fleet were sorely needed, as were their AA guns. *Formidable*'s flight-deck was hit by the first kamikaze plane which released a five hundred pound bomb just before the plane itself hit the deck. The explosion blew a hole two feet across in the armoured deck and surrounded it with an indentation that was about two feet deep at its centre and ten feet across. A sizeable piece of the armoured deck was driven through the hangar below, severed a steam pipe in the engine room and ended its travels in the inner bottom of the ship. The damage in the engine room reduced the ship's speed to a maximum of eighteen knots. Eleven aircraft in the deck park were destroyed.

When the bomb exploded *Formidable* was in the throes of launching aircraft and the flight-deck was crowded with aircrew and aircraft handlers. Eight men were killed and forty-seven wounded, of whom thirteen were very badly burned. Both flight-deck barriers were damaged, one beyond repair and only one of the ship's radar sets was still working. Fires raged all over the flight-deck in parked aircraft, flight-deck vehicles, deck machinery and the suicide bomber's aircraft. Below decks there were fires blazing in a number of compartments.

The next carrier to come under attack was *Indomitable*. A suicide bomber approached her and she took evasive action which caused the Japanese plane to skitter across the flight-deck and disappear over the port side where its bomb exploded in the sea close to *Indomitable*'s side. Another kamikaze plane approached *Indomitable* but was shot down in flames by gunfire just off her starboard bow. No serious structural damage was done to *Indomitable* but a new radar was damaged and for lack of spares had to remain unrepaired for a long time. This was the only one of its kind with the Task Force and its special capabilities were greatly missed. Further attacks were made by the enemy but they were all either fought off or

brought down.

Damage control parties worked furiously and one and a half hours after the splinter of armoured deck had been blasted down into the engine room, repairs had been made and *Formidable* was able to make twenty-four knots again. Five and a half hours after the Japanese bomb exploded on her deck the wounded men were settled into the sick bay, fires had been extinguished, decks cleared of the remains of so much equipment, the hole in the deck was repaired and the indentation filled with rapid-hardening cement, a jury-rigged crash barrier was ready to operate and the carrier was back in business, her survival entirely due to her armoured deck.

The next day the first CAP was flown off and they were soon on the trail of a high-flying Japanese reconnaissance plane. They chased it for three hundred miles before they were close enough to shoot it down!

What had become the 'routine bombing attacks' on the airstrips on Ishigaki and Miyako were carried out and returning planes reported an almost total lack of anti-aircraft fire, clearly a result of the bombardment of the day before, so all was not lost. The British Pacific Fleet then retired to refuel and take on essential stores and replacement aircraft whilst US Task Group 52.1 continued the attacks on the Sakishima-Gunto.

Another bombardment of Ishigaki and Miyako had been planned for 8 May. This time it was intended that the carriers should be escorted by the cruisers of the Task Force and that they should remain within easy reach of the bombarding force so that they could come to the support of the carriers, should they suffer another kamikaze attack. Combat Air Patrols ranging ahead of Task Force 57 found the weather over and around the targets so thick that they had difficulty in finding them. With weather as bad as this there was little danger of the enemy aircraft using the airfields and so the operation was cancelled.

The following morning four bombing sorties were launched against the two islands by a considerable number of Avengers, Fireflies and fighters. One plane and its pilot was lost but otherwise the raid was a success with runways cratered and

Parked Corsairs are set ablaze

Fire spreads to nearby aircraft

The aftermath. Note the minimal damage to the armoured deck

Damage control party working to get the debris over the side

The remains of the kamikaze. This picture shows how well the armoured deck withstood the attack

vehicles and aircraft on the ground very soundly strafed. Late in the afternoon four Seafires intercepted five low-flying Japanese aircraft. It seems they concentrated their attention on one of the enemy planes, which they brought down but in doing so allowed the other four to give them the slip. These kamikazes also eluded another flight of Seafires and approached the Fleet at great speed. *Victorious* was struck by two suicide bombers. The first five hundred pound bomb exploded towards the forward end of the flight-deck, creating a hole in the deck and a fire which was quickly extinguished. The catapult and the forward lift were damaged and a 4.5-inch gun was put out of action. Minutes later another suicider approached from astern. Its bomb failed to detonate and the plane slid along the deck in a ball of flame, destroying four Corsairs that were parked on deck and wrecking an anti-aircraft director and an arrester wire unit before it fell over the side. A third kamikaze approached *Victorious* but at the last moment changed course and headed for the battleship *Howe*. It was brought down by gunfire about one hundred yards from *Howe*.

Formidable was the target for the fourth suicide bomber which was hit repeatedly but still managed to dive into the aircraft parked on the after end of her flight-deck. The weapon was

Kamikaze diving on Indomitable

smaller than previous kamikaze bombs and faulty detonation limited its destructive powers but nevertheless fires were started and seven aircraft were destroyed and fourteen damaged. The casualty list was very much smaller than on the earlier occasions. The fires were out in fifteen minutes and *Formidable* was ready for action in less than an hour.

The American Task Group 52.1 took over from the British Task Force to allow them to refuel and restore but the British Fleet was back on station before daybreak on 12 May.

The first flights were flown off just before dawn. When they arrived over their targets they found that several runways were undamaged and it required four more Avenger strikes to make them unserviceable. Overnight the Japanese had repaired the airstrips and it required four more

strikes by the Avengers to render them inoperable again.

By 16 May there was almost no enemy air activity either on or over the Sakishima airfields. The anti-aircraft fire was as heavy as ever.

On 20 May the Task Force was back in action off the Sakishima Islands, this time with rather more emphasis on shipping strikes. Because of the losses *Formidable* had sustained she could only provide Corsairs as fighter protection over the target and the Fleet. The fighter protection sorties *Formidable*'s aircraft flew in these raids were to be her last for some time as it was decided to send her to Sydney for repairs. Damage from enemy attacks, accidents and plain wear and tear was mounting in all the carriers. *Illustrious, Indomitable* and *Victorious* carried out one more series of offensive operations in the area and then, on 25 May they too left. There were to be no more kamikaze attacks on the British Pacific Fleet. The US Fleet had two more major carriers damaged so badly by suicide bombers that they were unable to take any further part in the war. The heavy and protracted FAA assaults on the kamikaze bases had done much to reduce this problem. The cost to the British Pacific Fleet was high but thanks to the armoured flight-decks the price was nothing like as high as it would have been had the task been left to the USN.

The weight of the armoured deck had its disadvantages, for example, an American Attack Carrier could ship twice as many aircraft as a British Fleet Carrier. The lifts in a British Fleet Carrier were about half the size of those in the comparable American ships because of the weight of the armoured plating that formed the floor of the lift, which plugged the hole in the deck when the lift was not in use. Having said this, whenever an American carrier was hit squarely by a kamikaze, its wooden deck was penetrated and the explosion occurred inside the ship with devastating consequences, both to ship and crew. In six weeks in April and May 1945, seven US carriers were hit by suicide attacks and in each case the carrier was rendered unfit for further service in the current campaign. Four RN carriers were hit in this manner, two of them twice. Their loss was primarily in aircraft parked on the flight-deck. The damage to the ships themselves did not penetrate the armoured flight-decks and was of such a limited nature that the damage control parties soon had each of the ships operational again, in at least one case in about half an hour, but they seldom needed more than an hour or two to put things right.

All four carriers needed various degrees of dockyard work to bring them back to full operational trim, after all they had been at sea in a combat zone for more than sixty days. Replenishment Escort Carriers transferred 173 replacement planes to the four Fleet Carriers. The replacement aircraft were to make good the losses from all causes: twenty-six from enemy action during sorties

over enemy territory; forty-three from kamikaze attacks and the remainder from fair wear and tear and accidents.

Implacable had sailed from Europe arrived at Manus Island early in June 1945, and by the 10th she was at sea in company with the Escort Carrier *Ruler* and five cruisers. Her first task was to complete the working-up of her aircrews and deck handling parties. To achieve this she was given two days of raids on Truk in the Carolines, still a legitimate target but one that had been attacked so often that the defence had lost much of its sting. The strikes were carried out with the loss of three Avengers to engine failure, a Walrus that was blown over the side in a squall and one Seafire that was shot down by anti-aircraft fire. There would have been more losses if the philosophy of 'the spare deck' had not been in operation. On 14 and 15 June there were delays in the deck operations on *Implacable* which would have caused some returning aircraft to ditch because of lack of fuel but *Ruler* was on hand to receive them until such time as they could return to their parent ship. Engine failure caused the loss of three Avengers; the cause of the problem was not discovered until a further ten Avengers were lost for the same reason; the wrong spark plugs had been fitted!

These two days of 'active service in training' was completed successfully and *Implacable* was ready to start more serious operations. With this in mind she returned to Manus to await the arrival of the other components of the Fleet. The various units of what was to be called the 11th Aircraft Carrier Squadron assembled at Manus after *Implacable*'s arrival there. *Formidable* and *Victorious*, in company with *King George V* and the usual screen of lesser vessels left Sydney for Manus on 21 June. *Indomitable* was in need of a limited refit before she could sail to join the other vessels and *Indefatigable* remained behind in Sydney for a short time to have defects in her machinery rectified. She then joined the Fleet at Manus but some mechanical problems remained and she was unable to sail with the rest of the 11th Aircraft Carrier Squadron. Four Light Fleet Carriers *Arbiter, Chaser, Speaker* and *Striker* had left the UK some time before and were soon to join the Aircraft Carrier Squadron Fleet Train. Theirs was to be a double role. They were there to defend the Fleet Train but they also carried replacement aircraft for the Fleet Carriers. The airstrip on Manus had been turned into an aircraft repair and assembly depot and anchored in the lagoon were the two aircraft repair carriers *Pioneer* and *Unicorn*, along with a number of other ships with engineering and workshop facilities aboard.

The British Pacific Fleet, of which the Aircraft Carrier Squadron was part, left Manus on 9 July 1945 to join with the American Forces under the command of Admiral Halsey. When *Indefatigable* joined them a little later the FAA added a total of 255 planes to the Americans' 1,200 aircraft and sixteen aircraft carriers.

The Seafires serving with the British Pacific Fleet had, at long last, been fitted with external fuel tanks which increased their range to that of the Corsairs. Until now their limited range had confined their role to that of Combat Air Patrol over the Fleet; now they could also be used offensively.

Whilst typhoons may occur at most times of the year in the North West Pacific they are most likely to develop in the months between May and November. Since operations were recommenced on 17 July 1945, slap in the middle of the typhoon season, bad weather could be expected as a matter of course. Fleet Air Arm Corsairs and Fireflies were given the task of attacking airfields and railway yards on the north coast of Honshu, the largest of the islands that go to make up Japan. The first planes took off from *Implacable* and *Victorious* at 0350, 250 miles from their objectives. They found and attacked their targets despite the weather and the heavy and accurate anti-aircraft fire. Their American counterparts were not so fortunate and were recalled before they reached the target area. That night the Hitachi works in Tokyo was bombarded by American battleships in company with *King George V* and the next day the USN attacked Yokosuka, the largest of the Japanese naval bases. The Americans, still angry from the treatment of Pearl Harbor, looked on this attack on the Japanese naval bases as a 'grudge fight' and used only USN ships in the attack, and who could blame them!

The next day FAA planes were allocated targets to the north of Tokyo. Again bad weather intervened but the Seafires and Corsairs reached their targets and destroyed twelve Japanese aircraft and damaged eighteen others. Two days of replenishment was intended to follow but the weather was so bad with repeated heavy weather and typhoon warnings that it was not to be until the 24th that the carriers were able to resume the offensive. There were nearly 200 anti-aircraft guns defending the airfields at Tokushima and it is remarkable that only two aircraft were lost to the Japanese flak, which was intense. In the interim *Indefatigable* had rejoined the Task Force.

The Americans continued to concentrate on their 'grudge fight' but there was no shortage of targets for the other contenders. The low cloud produced by the adverse weather made airfield and shipping strikes difficult but the day operations were resumed a group of British planes found and attacked a Japanese escort carrier, leaving her with her back broken and in flames.

Japan

American planes were informed and they delivered the *coup de grâce* a little later. At the same time the USN was busy at Kure sinking a Fleet Carrier and three battleships. The FAA flew over 400 sorties on this day, sinking a large number of coastal ships, destroyers and other smaller escort vessels, and also attacked targets in Japan with some measure of success.

The weather on the next day was no better but still the British aircraft were able to find and inflict considerable damage on a large number of targets on and around the Inland Sea. As dusk fell Hellcats from *Formidable* intercepted a number of Japanese torpedo-bombers that were on their way to attack the Task Force, shooting three down and damaging another. The remaining Japanese aircraft were chased off without ever getting near the Task Force.

There followed two days devoted to replenishment and then three days were taken up with more raids on Japanese installations and shipping. The first day, 28 July, the Harima dockyard was hit at sunrise by twenty Avengers. Fighters attacked the naval base at Maizuru on the north coast of Honshu and four destroyers were either sunk or badly damaged. Enemy aircraft were getting harder to find at this time but a few were destroyed; the anti-aircraft fire was as fierce as ever. On the 30th airfields north of Tokyo were scheduled to be attacked but they were found to be shrouded in fog and so it was back to coastal targets again.

When flying ended for the day the Fleet retired for another round of replenishment but instead of the more usual two days this one ran into nine days. Typhoons were passing through the area, which caused difficulties during the replenishment operation but when it was completed there were further delays to allow the first atomic bomb to be dropped on Hiroshima on 6 August.

The next group of raids were scheduled to start on 8 August but had to be postponed to wait for another typhoon warning to be lifted. The following day the weather had improved to the point where flying could take place and attacks were made on targets up and down the east coast of Honshu. Both Japan's naval and merchant fleets were rapidly being destroyed by the constant pressure that was maintained by the US and British Naval Air Arms and this day was no different. In the port of Onagawa all the shipping left afloat, including a naval sloop, was sunk. Lieutenant Hampton Grey, DSC was killed when his Corsair caught fire during the attack on this sloop. He was awarded the Victoria Cross for his action that day, the second to be won by a Fleet Air Arm airman in World War Two. Enemy airfields were attacked and Japanese planes were encountered in greater numbers than had been the case recently. Fleet Air Arm aircraft destroyed more than fifty Japanese aircraft for the loss of seven planes and five pilots.

On 10 August the carrier-borne aircraft were roaming at will over the Japanese mainland attacking and destroying anything of significance they found. The Task Force again destroyed more than fifty enemy aircraft on the ground. Of six destroyers attacked in Maizuru and the Inland Sea three were sunk and the other three sustained serious damage. Shipyards, barracks and factories were also attacked and damaged.

In the two days of 9 and 10 August the Fleet Air Arm and the USN aircraft between them destroyed over 700 Japanese aircraft. During the course of these two days the kamikazes staged their final performance and damaged just one destroyer. With over 100 fighter aircraft in the air over the Fleet, the majority of the enemy aircraft were shot down and the remainder driven off before they could reach the ships of the Task Force.

With the Japanese surrender imminent there was inevitably a degree of confusion as to whether the surrender was on or not. The major part of the British Pacific Fleet returned to Sydney. *Indefatigable, King George V*, two cruisers and ten destroyers remained behind with the American Fleet.

On 15 August there was still no word of a ceasefire agreement and so at dawn further strikes on targets of opportunity were launched. *Indefatigable*'s Avengers, escorted by ten Seafires were intercepted by twelve Zeros. The Seafires tackled the Japanese fighters and destroyed eight of them, losing one Seafire in the course of the dogfight. A Telegraphist Air Gunner in one of the Avengers shot down the ninth. This was to prove to be the last fighter combat of the war. At 0700 that day all further strikes against Japan were cancelled. The war was virtually over, Japan had been humbled and Pearl Harbor and a great many other barbarities had, at least in part, been avenged.

The war was over but the weather was still to be endured. On 26 August _Wasp_ and _Randolph_ and _Indefatigable_ were struck by a typhoon. _Randolph_ suffered some damage and the forward end of _Wasp_'s flight-deck collapsed under the stress of the storm. When Captain Graham was asked to report on the damage suffered by _Indefatigable_ in the course of the typhoon he replied, doubtless with tongue in cheek, 'What Typhoon?'

CHAPTER TWELVE

The Korean War

On 25 June 1950 the communist forces of North Korea mounted a large-scale attack on South Korea. The United Nations voted to go to the help of South Korea.

The major effort was to come from America but other members of The United Nations provided armed forces too and Britain was one of them. A number of RN vessels were in Japanese waters and these ships sailed to join the American Fleet under the command of Admiral Joy USN. *Triumph*, the first of a succession of Light Fleet Carriers that were to serve in the area, with twelve Seafires and twelve Firefly 1s aboard, was the carrier with the British contingent. The FAA was to play a limited but valuable part in the war that followed. *Valley Forge* was the American carrier and the two ships were to work together under the tactical command of Rear Admiral Hoskins USN.

On 2 July 1950 the two carriers joined forces in the Yellow Sea and the next morning flew off the first air strikes. For her part *Triumph* launched nine Seafires and twelve Fireflies. This small force carried out rocket attacks on the buildings and installations on Haeju airfield and followed up the next day by attacking targets of opportunity. Unfortunately the performance of the FAA's aircraft was inferior to that of the USN's planes, which were more versatile and had a greater range

North and South Korea

A general view of the Korean area

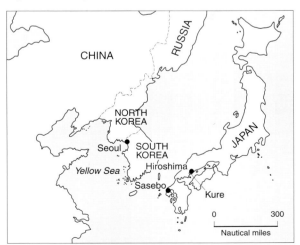

than the Seafires and Fireflies. For this reason, on the next strike _Triumph_'s aircraft flew Combat Air Patrols and Anti-Submarine Patrols while _Valley Forge_'s planes made repeated attacks on the west coast of Korea. Poor aircraft recognition led to an American B-29 shooting down a Seafire but fortunately the pilot was recovered by an American destroyer.

Triumph had trouble with her stern gland (the gland that keeps the sea from entering around the propeller shaft) and on 30 July she sailed for Kure near Hiroshima in Japan in the hope of rectifying the problem in the dockyard there. When the engineers had finished with her she headed back to North Korea.

There was a dearth of shipping in the waters around Korea so _Triumph_ was required to conduct a number of reconnaissance flights and strikes on military objectives on Korea's west coast. Early in September her aircraft were in action again, this time against road and rail targets on the north-east coast of Korea. By now a number of _Triumph_'s elderly Seafires were becoming unserviceable and it became necessary for her to sail to Sasebo Naval Base on the island of Kyushu, the southernmost of the large islands that go to make up Japan, to repair them.

On 12 September _Triumph_ left and headed for the north-west corner of South Korea to provide air cover for the landings at Inch'on. By the end of this operation _Triumph_'s aircraft were on their last legs and she left for the UK.

Triumph's replacement, _Theseus_, arrived in the area on 5 October. She was better equipped than was her predecessor, having on board twelve Firefly AS 5s and twenty-one Sea Fury FB11s Both these planes were better armed and had greater endurance than the aircraft provided by _Triumph_ and this increased performance was to be most welcome. A few days later the Fleet Aviation Officer called on the Air Control Centre at Kimpo to discover that they had no knowledge of the presence of a British aircraft carrier in the area! Despite this, Fireflies from _Theseus_ were in action the next day attacking and destroying a railway bridge while Sea Furies attacked a stores depot. The Sea Furies encountered intense light

anti-aircraft fire and one plane was shot down. Five miles from the target the pilot was picked up under fire by a USAF Helicopter.

It was becoming apparent that the North Korean forces were withdrawing from the area of Haeju and so on 13 and 14 October the aircraft from _Theseus_ shifted their attack further north to the port of Namp'o. The three attacks they made on this port were highly effective. The Fireflies' strikes with bombs and rockets were very accurate and did a large measure of damage to dockside installations. Meanwhile the Sea Furies were able to sink one minelayer and severely damage another. One day's respite was followed by two more days of successful raids again on Namp'o and nearby Mongumpo and Sariwon.

During 18 and 19 October operations were suspended, partly by bad weather and partly because the position ashore was unclear because of the rapid advances that were being made by the UN troops. On 20 and 21 _Theseus_ was able to launch strikes against targets in Sinuiju and the surrounding area.

China and North Korea not only shared a similar political outlook but also a territorial border and it was towards this border that the UN forces were driving the North Koreans. Chinese troops were sent in to bolster the North Korean forces, with such success that the UN forces were in retreat and British and Commonwealth naval units were sent in to lend support and subsequently to evacuate the land forces from the west coast. The evacuation took place on 6 December in dreadful weather conditions; extreme cold, poor visibility and frequent gale force winds.

All the American carriers were committed to operations on the east coast which left _Theseus_ alone to provide air cover for the naval units off the west coast and to carry out reconnaissance ashore and doubtless anything else that was required. In the face of extreme weather conditions in the eight days from 7 to 15 December _Theseus'_ planes conducted 332 sorties without sustaining damage from any cause.

After a few days in the dockyard at Kure, _Theseus_ returned to the west coast of Korea and for the next ten days she continued with air support duties in co-operation with the American 25th Division. In January *Theseus* was joined by USS *Bataan* and it was arranged that they should relieve each other every eight to ten days. In improving weather *Theseus* took over from *Bataan* on the 25th and in the next eight days flew 408 sorties in support of the American 1st Corps.

By early April 1951 it was estimated that China had seventy Divisions in North Korea and was planning another major offensive; there was reason to believe that it would be directed against Formosa. To counter this the US 7th Fleet stationed most of its carriers in the Sea of Japan to the east of Korea and both *Theseus* and *Bataan* joined them. The friendly rivalry generated by aircraft carriers of two nations working side by side speeded up the deck work in both ships. Aircraft from the carriers were kept busy with all the usual requirements, spotting, reconnaissance, attacks on bridges, marshalling yards, rolling stock and road transport, and just about anything that would further the cause of the forces fighting ashore.

On 25 April *Theseus* set sail for England; in seven months her aircraft had flown nearly 3,500 operational sorties and her losses were in single figures, a remarkable achievement. Her place was taken by *Glory* with a complement of twenty-one Sea Fury FB 11s and twelve Firefly 5s. In addition she carried a Dragonfly helicopter that was to be the FAA's first operational rescue helicopter.

The Chinese spring offensive started at about the same time as *Glory* arrived in the area and her aircrews found themselves working hard in support of the forces ashore. It was anticipated that the Chinese forces would have heavy air support but in the event it did not materialise.

Bataan took over from *Glory* on the 19th and it was to be a fortnight before she was back in the area, only to find that her aviation spirit was contaminated which entailed a return to harbour to rectify matters.

Glory was relieved by HMAS *Sydney* after her aircraft had flown nearly three thousand sorties. *Sydney* was equipped with two Sea Fury squadrons and one Firefly squadron. She had no helicopter of her own but the USN loaned her one for the period of her stay. Like the British carriers

before her, the Australian carrier conducted a wide variety of operations but with particular emphasis on ground support for the troops ashore. On one occasion sixteen of her Sea Furies attacked more than two thousand troops who were in the process of digging themselves in on hills overlooking the beaches, killing more than two hundred of the enemy and destroying an ammunition dump. Later *Sydney*'s aircraft were successfully engaged in attacking targets such as coastal shipping, railway bridges and tunnels and concentrations of North Korean ground forces.

After sixty-four very successful days in the operational area *Sydney* was relieved by *Glory*, whose Sea Furies' bombing capacity was particularly useful against the well-constructed Korean gun positions. Initially the Sea Furies had been armed with 60-lb rockets which were limited in the damage they could do to a target of this kind. To overcome this the planes had been modified to carry two 500-lb bombs. With a short delay on the detonation of these bombs the pilots were able to deliver their attack from a low altitude, thereby increasing their accuracy, and have time to escape the blast when the bomb did explode. *Glory*'s aircraft battled on in the bitterly cold winter weather until she was relieved in May by *Ocean*.

Right from the start *Ocean* experienced problems which were really not of her making. She lost a number of aircraft on the first patrol. Her sorties were restricted because bombs and rockets were in short supply and on occasions fog caused problems. Enemy MiG-15s began to put in an appearance and on 26 July a Firefly was shot down. On 9 August four Sea Furies were attacked by eight MiGs. The Sea Furies escaped harm and shot down one of the MiGs. The next day eight MiGs again attacked a flight of four Sea Furies without causing them any damage. Fire was returned and two of the MiGs were hit, one catching fire before they were driven off.

Reconnaissance on 16 September 1952 showed that all the mainline railway bridges between Chinnampo and Pyongyang were destroyed so attention was turned to the sluice gates in three places on the rivers. All the gates were destroyed and delayed-action bombs were dropped to discourage repair work on them.

Fleet Air Arm operations continued in this manner until 27 July 1953, when an armistice was signed signifying the end of hostilities. In the three years of the Korean War FAA casualties were low, twenty-two aircrew being killed by enemy action and another thirteen losing their lives in accidents. Helicopters played an emerging but important part, both as planeguards when the carriers were flying off or receiving aircraft and in the role of short-range rescue aircraft.

CHAPTER THIRTEEN

Helicopters

Helicopters were making their debut well before the end of World War Two. As early as 1943 they were beginning to look as if they could have a useful future and the RN ordered forty-five American-built Sikorsky R4s so that the FAA could investigate their worth in a variety of tasks. The Navy gave them the name of Hoverfly. The first operational experiment by the RN was to use two Hoverflies for convoy protection early in 1944. A platform was built onto a British merchant ship called the *Daghestan* which then took the two helicopters aboard and joined an Atlantic convoy

bound for Britain. The weather was so bad during the crossing that the choppers were able to make only one sortie. The verdict was that helicopters at that stage of development were not suited to hunting submarines in the North Atlantic. Despite this the Admiralty placed an order with Sikorsky for 250 R5s, the next stage in the development of the Sikorsky helicopter. These were not ready when it became apparent that the war was drawing to its

---

Westland Dragonfly landing on HMS Centaur

close so the order was cancelled. One hundred and fifty R6s had also been ordered and that order was reduced to thirty-one. Twenty-eight went to the RAF and three to the Fleet Air Arm – shades of 1918!

Throughout 1945 and '46 the few helicopters available to the Navy were assessed for their suitability for a wide variety of tasks, from torpedo dropping to hydrographic surveying.

Britain had pioneered the early stages of helicopter development as far back as World War One but, as so often happens, it was the Americans who had the foresight to take them seriously, and by the late 1940s they were well ahead with development and it was to the USA we had to turn for the more powerful rotating-wing aircraft that were needed.

In 1947 Westland Aircraft bought six Sikorsky 51s to help with their development work and later took out a licence that would allow them to build Sikorsky 51s at Yeovil in Somerset. From this start they eventually dropped the building of fixed-wing aircraft and worked solely with the development and production of rotating-wing machines.

By October 1948 Westland were able to fly their first British assembled machine which was called the Dragonfly but it was to be a further fourteen months before the first of these helicopters was delivered to the RN. The best part of another year was to pass before the last of the Hoverflies were replaced by Dragonflies. The delay, at least in part, was due to the simple fact that economically the war had cost Britain dearly and there was no money to spare for development of this kind. Although the Dragonfly was bigger and more powerful than its predecessor it was still not man enough for anti-submarine work. The helicopters available at this time did not have the power to carry all the gear, weapons and crew needed for this work, nor did they have the range needed to make them a viable anti-submarine weapon. It was excellent for air/sea rescue duties and it was here that the helicopter made its initial impact.

Air/Sea Rescue, later to become known as Search and Rescue, SAR for short, was usually conducted from shoreside bases. Much of the work involved the rescue of civilians, from holidaymakers and yachtsmen to professional

seamen and over the years this has not changed.

In the late 1940s Westland produced the very successful Wasp. This was a lightweight machine designed specifically to be carried aboard a frigate. It was the RN's intention to get helicopters afloat on every possible ship. The first of the smaller naval vessels to be fitted with a helicopter landing pad was the survey ship _Vidal_. She was equipped with a single Dragonfly. _Protector_, the Antarctic survey ship, was the next to be given a platform and she received two Mk 1 Whirlwind helicopters.

From the Wasp design came the Lynx. Equipped with wire-guided missiles, she had the ability to tackle surface shipping as well as submarines. When it came into service the Lynx was able to operate with the more modern Sea Skua missile, depth bombs and Stingray anti-submarine lightweight torpedoes.

Plane Guard duty was an early task undertaken by helicopters for the RN. It has become standard practice whenever planes are landing on or taking off from the flight-deck of a carrier to have a helicopter airborne and ready to go to the assistance of an aircrew that might get into difficulties and end up in the water.

The first Plane Guard unit was embarked by _Indomitable_, a Fleet Carrier, early in 1951. Three months later the Light Fleet Carrier _Glory_ left the UK to take part in the Korean War. On board was a second Plane Guard unit that was to rescue eight FAA pilots, four from the sea and four from behind the enemy lines.

Closer to home in January 1952 a freighter called _The Flying Enterprise_ broke down in the Western Approaches and went missing in appalling weather. An FAA Dragonfly flew from Culdrose in conditions that were close to impossible in a gallant attempt to rescue the master, Captain Carlson, and his mate, who had remained with her. That the rescue attempt failed was not for the want of trying.

Search and Rescue groups of the FAA experienced their first major test in February 1953 when really fearsome storms battered their way down the North Sea and caused unprecedented flooding of much of the east and south-east coasts of England and the coast of Holland. There was great

Westland Whirlwind ASW helicopter

loss of life on both sides of the North Sea which would have been even worse had it not been for the efforts of the FAA SAR helicopter crews. In the course of two weeks 600 Dutch people were rescued from the floods by the aircrews of the Dragonflies. The effort required to move 600 people to safety is perhaps highlighted when it is realised that the Dragonfly's maximum load was just three passengers. The whole operation was carried out without loss of life but one helicopter was lost when its crew attempted to land on a minor road on the top of a dyke: it skidded and fell into a canal.

By now the need for larger and more powerful machines was beginning to be felt and it was necessary to turn to the USA yet again. Westland

obtained another licence, this time to allow them to produce the Sikorsky 55, to be named the Whirlwind by the British Forces. To fill the gap before Westland Aviation were able to start delivering the British-built S-55s America supplied the RN with twenty-five Sikorskys. The Sikorsky / Whirlwind required a crew of two and could carry up to ten passengers. Ten Whirlwinds were intended to be used for SAR duties and fifteen for Anti-Submarine Warfare. The SAR helicopters arrived in November 1952 and the ASW helicopters eleven months later, in September 1953.

British and Malayan Forces had been fighting off an attempt by Communist guerillas and terrorists to take over Malaya since 1948. The ten Whirlwinds that had arrived and were intended for SAR duties were placed aboard *Perseus* on 10 December 1952 which then headed for Singapore. On arrival the helicopters were put ashore at Sembawang on Singapore Island expecting to have a three-and-a-half-week period in which to work up to operational standards. Because the resident RAF Dragonflies were having extensive mechanical problems the working up period for the FAA helicopter crews was reduced to sixteen days and on 24 January 1953 the Whirlwinds of 848 Squadron became operational. Their first task was to evacuate three casualties from the jungle to the British Military Hospital in Kiurara.

This small unit of helicopters pioneered the way for a variety of operations that have now become commonplace helicopter tasks. For the very first time men and equipment could be transported by air to, or evacuated from, a precise map reference position. No longer would men arrive weary from marching many miles whilst carrying their equipment and hacking their way through areas of dense jungle. If there was a suitable clearing the chopper would land, but if not it would hover at treetop height and lower men and gear in on ropes. Further supplies and reinforcements could be delivered at short notice. The Whirlwinds were able to evacuate men when their task was completed but probably the greatest morale booster for the men on the ground was the ability of the helicopters to pick up casualties and have them in hospital in the shortest possible time.

It was not long before the unique abilities of the helicopter were being built into Commando operations. By the end of their first two years in Malaya these ten modestly sized helicopters had transported 18,000 men and more than 180 tons of stores of all kinds in the course of which they logged some 6,000 hours of operational flying. With the end of the Malayan Emergency in 1956 this pioneering squadron that had contributed so much to the successful conclusion of the campaign was disbanded.

As the Malayan Emergency was coming to a close so the Suez Affair was emerging.

In July 1956 President Nasser nationalised the Suez Canal. French and British interests were at stake; with the result that the politicians of both countries had a rush of Imperialism to their heads and decided to attack Egypt with the aim of securing the Canal Zone and reversing President Nasser's action. Where the arrogance of politicians lead it is the duty of the armed forces to follow, whether they like it or not. With that proviso in place it is fair to say that the FAA acquitted itself well.

If land areas are to be held there is no substitute for armed men on the ground but in the early stages of this conflict at least, naval and air support were essential. Royal Air Force support could only come from Malta and Cyprus so the close support had to be provided by the FAA and by RN ships. A number of carriers were still in service with the RN and *Albion, Bulwark* and *Eagle* were equipped with the most up-to-date fixed-wing aircraft and helicopters available.

The objective of the first phase was the destruction of the Egyptian Air Force and if this could be achieved on the ground, so much the better.

Twelve Sea Hawks from *Bulwark* attacked Cairo West Airfield, destroying installations and a large number of Egyptian aircraft. Further highly successful attacks were carried out on several other airfields. The technique used was to climb to 20,000 feet over the sea and when the target was reached to dive onto it to rain bombs, rockets and gunfire on the ground installations and parked aircraft. The attacking planes would then retire at high speed at ground level and when the coast had been reached they would climb to 5,000 feet and return to their parent ship. The raids were devastating. The initial attacks were made on 1 November and by 5 November the Egyptian Air Force was no longer a fighting entity. Not only had its planes been destroyed but much of the ground equipment, installations and communications systems were wrecked too.

On 5 November parachute troops were dropped and they occupied the outskirts of Port Fouad and Port Said. Throughout the operation the carriers steamed close inshore and their aircraft gave continuous cover and close support to the attacking ground forces. Helicopters from the Light Fleet Carriers *Ocean* and *Theseus* spent the day carrying food, ammunition and stores of all kinds ashore.

At dawn on 6 November FAA aircraft attacked shore defences and put Commando groups ashore. When this was finished 500 men of 45 Marine Commando, complete with all their gear, were airborne and heading for the shore. Their chosen landing zone was obscured by smoke so the helicopters headed westwards looking for a clearer area on which to land. The first plane to land was carrying the reconnaissance party and the pilot put them down in the Egyptian Stadium. As soon as the marines were well clear of the helicopter Egyptian soldiers were seen to be swarming over the stadium walls, causing the British Force to beat a hasty retreat to the helicopter that had thoughtfully relanded for them. Further west still a safer landing spot was found and the marines disembarked.

Things went well for the attacking force and it is highly likely that the Canal Zone could have been taken but international pressure was such that the French and British forces had to be withdrawn. The FAA had dealt competently with every task that had been allocated to it and had, yet again, proved that the Air Arm was an indispensable part of the armed forces with a role to play that could not be fulfilled by other branches of the armed services.

From 1956 to 1962 the FAA found itself 'odd-jobbing' with minor side-shows such as helping with the anti-terrorist campaign in Cyprus, the odd flare-up in the Persian Gulf or Middle East and so on.

Meanwhile the helicopter's Anti-Submarine Warfare role was being explored and developed. It soon became apparent that a second engine would be a very desirable safety factor, especially for helicopters operating over the sea for long periods, and the slow task of replacement began. That it was a slow process is illustrated by the fact that quite a number of Wasp HAS 1s and Wessex HAS 3s, both single-engined helicopters, were employed in the Falklands campaign as late as

1982 and acquitted themselves well.

The Whirlwind HAS 7 was the first FAA helicopter to be used in the anti-submarine role. In the early 1960s *Centaur* embarked a squadron of eight helicopters. The squadron suffered a severe bout of teething troubles, losing thirteen aircraft to accidents mostly caused by engine failures. It would seem that the replacement aircraft were no better than the original eight.

Much of the exploration of the helicopters' role was linked to the new equipment that was being developed specifically for them. Radar in all its varied forms was an important feature. The miniaturisation that became possible with the developments in electronics ensured that the early cumbersome radar sets were indeed a thing of the past. With progress, radar-based equipment had become highly sophisticated and very versatile. Surface search and surveillance was still an important function but now it was enhanced with the ability to detect small targets as far off as fifty nautical miles. An over-the-horizon targetting capability and the ability to lock missiles onto their target were two more features of the much improved radar systems now available.

The so-called Dipping Sonar was made a practical proposition by the helicopter's ability to hover. The FAA installed its first Dipping Sonar in the Whirlwind in 1960. When computers were installed on board the helicopters the crews were able to process the information supplied by the buoys. Hitherto it had been necessary to transmit the data back to their ship to be handled by the shipboard computers.

Submariners have learned to 'hide' below layers of water of different saline density or temperature. To counter this tactic a sonar buoy that could be lowered on a cable from a helicopter to some 1,500 feet below the surface of the sea was developed. When these sonar units were in use the helicopter had to remain stationary directly over the sonar equipment. If the helicopter drifted, it dragged the sonar in the water, which caused the apparatus to tilt and the beams projected by the apparatus would no longer be pointing in the right direction. For the pilot to keep station directly above the sonar gear required constant adjustment of the

controls. In daylight this was difficult and tiring. At night the lack of external references made it impossible and downright dangerous. The first steps taken to help the pilot maintain his position produced visual references in the cockpit that did indeed make his task somewhat simpler. The Auto Stabilisation Equipment, as it was called, went through several stages of development until eventually it was possible to feed in the required information, switch on and let the control system take charge.

Wide-ranging, fast, atomic-powered submarines posed a special detection problem and 'passive sonobuoys' have been deployed as a screen across a wide stretch of ocean, where they listen and relay relevant data by radio to a processor that is carried on board the helicopter.

Helicopters were being given increased lifting

Westland Lynx in flight

and carrying power by the installation of ever more powerful engines in both production and existing aircraft. The Wessex HU 5 twin-engined helicopter was able to lift loads such as a field gun, a Land Rover or sixteen fully armed men.

By now helicopters on Anti-Submarine Warfare duties were laden with electrontic detection gear etc. to the extent that range and the ability to carry weapons were being curtailed. A more powerful helicopter was needed and again Sikorsky in America had produced what was needed. In 1967 Westland Helicopters obtained a licence from the American company to build a version of this aircraft in England. A good deal of British-designed and -produced electronic gear was incorporated and more powerful engines were installed. This new helicopter, given the name Sea King, entered service with the RN in about 1970 and proved to be a great success.

The Sea King can carry up to twenty-five passengers as well as the crew of four. This anglicised version of a Sikorsky S-61 B has twin Rolls-Royce Gnôme engines which drive a five-bladed rotor and give it a range of 690 miles and an endurance of some four hours, five if not heavily laden.

The development of ancillary equipment was keeping pace with the development of the helicopter itself and the Sea King was fitted with a fully automatic flight control system and an integrated sonar and radar tactical display. Her armaments could include four homing torpedoes or a number of depth-charges.

A simple form of in-flight refuelling was dreamed up in which the helicopter would approach a ship that had a supply of suitable fuel and lower its winch cable to that ship, when a refuelling hose would be hooked on and then raised to the hovering aircraft. By this means anti-submarine helicopters could be kept in the air for an almost indefinite period, subject only to the serviceability of the aircraft and aircrew fatigue.

Both *Ark Royal* and *Eagle* had squadrons of Sea Kings aboard and *Tiger* and *Blake* were able to accommodate four of these aircraft. In July 1974 during the Turkish invasion of Northern Cyprus Sea Kings flown from *Hermes* evacuated about 1,500 civilians from a beach near Kyrenia.

As ever with aircraft that were destined to work from the deck of a ship at sea, the landing gear had to be up to the task. The problem was twofold; strength enough to withstand the rugged conditions and, once the helicopter was down, it had to be secured before the movement of the ship's deck threw the aircraft into the sea. Two forms of

The Boeing Vertol CH-47 Chinook ... even bigger and more powerful

securing gear were tried, one of which consisted of four large suction pads on the underside of the skids. Apparatus that was part of the helicopter created a negative pressure at each pad as the aircraft landed. Positive pressure could also be produced in the hope of allowing the helicopter to move around as if it were a hovercraft. The system failed, at least in part because difficulties arose with the sealing of the pads due to the rough surface of the deck and problems with obtaining equal pressures at all the pads. The other system that was under consideration required a grid to be part of the landing pad and a 'harpoon' that was built into the underside of the helicopter. On landing the 'harpoon' was 'fired' to engage with the grid, thereby securing the aircraft in position. This latter system was evaluated but was not put to use until the Lynx came into service early in 1972.

In 1982 naval helicopters were used in large numbers for a multitude of jobs in the Falklands War and were an important factor in evicting the Argentinians from those islands.

CHAPTER FOURTEEN

Carriers

The FAA ended World War Two with more than 72,000 officers and men, about 37,000 aircraft and a large number of aircraft carriers either in being or in the course of construction. This clearly was a naval air arm far in excess of the peacetime needs of a nation that had just endured six years of a very costly war, a nation that had so much to restore and renew in the fabric of its country. Much of the new carrier construction was halted, a large number of the carriers in commission were taken out of service, many to be scrapped, and the Escort Carriers that had been constructed in the USA were returned to the States in accordance with the Lend-Lease Agreement. Shoreside establishments and airfields were either closed or put onto a Care and Maintenance routine and officers and men returned to civilian life.

Work was stopped on the aircraft carriers *Arrogant*, *Hermes*, *Monmouth* and *Polyphemus* and they were dismantled on the slipways on which they were being constructed.

While aircraft were going through the jet revolution and helicopters were being developed, the ships needed to work with them were changing too. This was partly due to economic pressures but a great many changes were required to accommodate the changing needs of the aircraft of the day.

The appearance of the Fleet Carriers just prior to the outbreak of World War Two must be considered to be the aircraft carrier's coming of age. They were designed for the job and served the Navy well. It is fair to say that many later developments stem from the experience gained with those ships.

The Fleet Carriers averaged from about 750 to a little over 800 feet in overall length with a beam of

HMS Ocean, *a Light Fleet Carrier*

95 to 112 feet. The earlier vessels had a fully laden displacement of about 33,000 tons but later ships of this kind were enlarged to more than 50,000 tons.

The first Fleet Carriers were laid down two or three years before the outbreak of World War Two and were commissioned in the first year or so of that conflict. Light Fleet Carriers of about 18,000 tons were laid down during the war but they were not completed in time to see active service, although _Colossus_ did assist with the repatriation of prisoners of war in the Pacific area. The Light Fleet Carriers included the classes _Majestic, Colossus, Centaur_ and _Invincible_.

Unicorn was designed as an aircraft carrier that would operate as a supply and repair ship but saw service as an aircraft carrier proper in the Mediterranean in the course of 1943 and 1944. She reverted to her original duties as a supply and repair ship in 1944 and joined the British Eastern Fleet and then later the British Pacific Fleet.

In 1953 _Centaur_ was commissioned. She had a length overall of 737 feet and a beam of 90 feet; her fully laden tonnage was 24,500 which placed her somewhere between the size of the old Fleet Carriers and the newer Light Fleet Carriers. There were other members of this class and their dimensions were about the same as those of _Centaur_. They had the misfortune to be on the scene at a time of financial stringency and of rapid change. The current jets were both fast and heavy and the ships of the _Centaur_ class were too small to operate with them without considerable modification. As a class they were subjected to a great deal of experimentation. Different ships at different times were involved in the early angled flight-deck trials and the ski-jump ramp. Others had all their fixed-wing aircraft operating gear removed and were converted to handle helicopters.

Bulwark and _Hermes_ were converted to operate as Commando Carriers. _Bulwark_ for example carried up to sixteen helicopters and 900 marines, a full commando. Royal Marine-manned LCVPs (Landing Craft, Vehicle / Personnel) swung from her davits, which would normally have been occupied by the ship's boats.

The _Centaur_ class included the Modified _Centaur_ Class and the Improved _Centaur_ Class. These vessels were laid down in 1944 and 1945 and their construction and completion suffered the natural delays and postponements that were to be expected in the immediate post-war period. _Albion_ for example was launched in 1947 but not commissioned until May 1954. _Bulwark_ was laid down in 1945, commissioned 1954, placed in reserve in 1976, where she stayed until 1979 and was then brought out of reserve in 1981 to 1983 then sold for scrap in 1984.

Hermes, an Improved _Centaur_ Class, entered the service of the RN in November 1959. In late 1973 she was refitted and her role was changed to that of a Commando Carrier.

In 1962 the RN had five carriers suitable for the operation of fixed-wing strike aircraft and two Light Fleet Carriers that had been converted to Commando Carriers and furnished solely with helicopters.

Five years later a major refit was started on _Victorious_ but unfortunately a fire broke out on board which damaged her so badly that it was decided to scrap her.

Ark Royal, which had been laid down in 1943, was the next carrier to go for a much needed refit to bring her up to date. When the work was completed her electrics, engines, armaments and other basic equipment were either modernised or renewed. The angled flight-deck had been strengthened and its angle increased to eight and a half degrees. The starboard catapult was relocated and the opportunity was taken to install an upgraded model with an increased length of 199 feet. The port catapult was also renewed but with one with a length similar to the original 154 feet. She had a number of Phantom aircraft which were an anglicised version of the American McDonnell Douglas F-4. Numerous modifications had been made to the original McDonnell version to fit it for service with the FAA including the substitution of two Rolls-Royce Spey turbojets for its original engines to improve its performance. In 1969 an FAA Phantom won the _Daily Mail_ Trans-Atlantic Air Race with an average true airspeed of 956 knots (1,100 statute miles per hour), an incredible advance on that of the dear old Swordfish that'd had such a distinguished World War Two career!

The name of *Ark Royal* had been given to a succession of ships, this one was unique inasmuch as she was never involved in action. Her end came in 1979, twelve years after the completion of her major refit, when she was decommissioned and then scrapped in 1980. Her sister ship *Eagle* was decommissioned at Devonport in 1972 and spent her next few years with the RN being cannibalised to provide spare parts for *Ark Royal*. She was converted to an Anti-Submarine Warfare Carrier in 1976 and in 1981 she was recommissioned as a carrier and equipped with Sea Harriers. Finally she was sold to the Indian Navy in 1985.

In the early 1960s the Admiralty and its designers were working on plans for a super carrier that was expected to enter the Service in about 1971. CVA-01, as it was designated, was intended to replace the big but ageing carriers that were still in service. The defence cuts made in 1966 were such that the plans for the new Strike Carrier had to be cancelled. She was to have been larger than any carrier that had seen service with the RN. Fully laden her designed weight was to be 54,500 tons; her overall length was intended to be 963 feet with a beam of 191 feet, more than twice that of most of her predecessors. The great beam allowed for two parallel runways to port of the island, so making the angled flight-deck redundant with a full size 'Alaskan Highway' to starboard of the island. She was to be equipped with water spray arrester gear and two new long-stroke steam catapults and a single hangar that measured 660 feet by 80 feet.

The aircraft coming into service with the FAA were faster and heavier than ever before and building a ship to accommodate them pushed the cost beyond the country's purse and heralded the beginning of the end of the era of the big Fleet Carrier. Everything about CVA-01 was to be bigger and better and bang up to date; judging from the artist's impression of her she would have been a beautiful ship and really from a purely Service point of view it was very sad she was not built.

Even major aircraft carriers like *Illustrious* and *Implacable* were becoming unbearably expensive, both to build and to operate. With the cancellation of CVA-01 in 1966 and the decommissioning of *Ark Royal* in 1979 the end of the conventional fixed-wing high-performance aircraft at sea was in sight.

In the mid-1960s it was decided to convert two *Tiger* class cruisers to act as Anti-Submarine Warfare helicopter ships; the after turrets were removed from both vessels and a large helicopter platform built in their place. Four Wessex helicopters made up the initial air group but they were replaced later by Sea Kings. With the commissioning of the new *Invincible* class ASW Light Aircraft Carriers, *Tiger* and *Blake* became redundant and were decommissioned in 1981.

The RN commissioned *Invincible* in July 1980 and *Illustrious* in March 1983. Both carriers had a laden displacement of about 20,000 tons, a length overall of 677 feet and a beam of 90 feet; not quite as big as the old Fleet Carriers that had given such good service but nevertheless a reasonable size. They were initially designed to be through-deck cruisers to serve as escorts to CVA-01 but with the cancellation of that project a new role had to be found for them and they were put into service with NATO in the Atlantic. *Invincible* served in the Falklands action in 1982.

CHAPTER FIFTEEN

The Advent of the Jet

One of the many skills required of an FAA pilot has always been the need to set his plane down safely onto the moving deck of an aircraft carrier. The area in which carrier-borne planes had to land was always restricted, seldom more than 200 feet by 90 feet and often rather less. The tail-down, three-point landing was a prime necessity in getting the landing hook to engage one of the arrester wires. If a tailwheel plane is landed main wheels first the aircraft will almost certainly bounce and 'float' and fail to engage its hook, thereby ending up in the safety barrier. Despite its name, ending up in the safety barrier could be a dangerous way to stop a plane. Naturally it was desirable that the approach speed should be the slowest possible, which is another way of saying as close to stalling speed as possible. More often than not the flight-deck was far from stable. In these circumstances, to arrive close to stalling speed over a heaving round-down left precious little margin for error. If a mistake was made and it was necessary to 'take a wave off' and go round again, additional power had to be applied to regain safe flying speed to enable you to climb away for another approach. This could be a dicey moment because if the throttle was pushed forward too violently to increase power, always a possibility in the heat of the moment, the engine could cut out with disastrous results. Eventually

'Get your wings level'

'That's good, throttle back and land'

'Ah good, we're hooked on'

'Oh dear I've broken it! Never mind, they say a good
landing is one you can walk away from'

'Meteor 3, it is still necessary to catch the wire'

Success!

fuel lines were redesigned to make it impossible to stall the engine by a sudden excessive use of the throttle. Landing on so close to stalling speed meant there was just nothing in hand to help deal with any additional problems. Aboard a well-drilled aircraft carrier planes returning from a mission were expected to land on at about 30-second intervals or less and this did nothing to reduce the tension of the moment.

A further improvement in the landing characteristics was achieved by giving later models large air brakes which helped to slow down the plane more quickly and steepen the descent. When they were lowered these air brakes increased the drag, and to maintain the same speed the application of more power was required which caused the aircraft to fly in a tail-down attitude. At the same time the propeller would be put into fine pitch to allow quicker response to the movement of the throttle,

rather like putting a car into a low gear to help you make a quick get away. This helped but the approach still had to be tail-down to be successful.

The RN received its first jet-engined aircraft, two Meteors and six Sea Vampires, in April 1949. The jets had tricycle undercarriages and quite soon it was found that their landing qualities were a decided improvement on the tail wheel planes pilots had been accustomed to handling. The tricycle undercarriage allowed the plane to sit down without hesitation on landing. The design was such that landings could be made at some fifteen to twenty knots greater than the plane's stalling speed. This safety margin was in welcome contrast to the need to bring a tail wheel plane in much closer to its stalling speed.

A de Havilland Sea Vampire in flight

In theory, if a plane with a tricycle undercarriage is landed clumsily so that the nose wheel touches down first it should 'float' but in fact the aircraft's design is usually such that this does not happen. The tricycle undercarriage offers a number of advantages, amongst which the plane can be braked without the danger of tipping it onto its nose and the nose wheel can be made steerable.

The first deck landing of a jet-propelled aircraft took place on 3 December 1945 when Lt-Cdr Brown successfully set a modified Vampire down on the flight-deck of *Ocean*.

Clearly with such a radical change in the design of aircraft there were bound to be problems; it was not simply a matter of replacing piston-engined planes with jet-propelled aircraft, there being too many differences in handling and performance for that to be possible.

An early difficulty was to design a wing that would maintain the required lift throughout the ever increasing speed range. The cambered upper surface of the wing causes the airflow across it to speed up, thereby reducing the pressure of that air compared with the pressure across the lower surface of the wing. It is this pressure differential that creates the lift that keeps the aircraft in the air. To develop the full potential of this lift it is essential that the air remains in smooth and close contact with the wing's surface. The air flowing over the upper surface of the wing, especially in high-performance aircraft, is always tempted to pull away and so become turbulent and once that smooth airflow is disturbed, lift is progressively reduced.

A lot of work was done on this problem and in 1955 American aeronautical engineers came up with the idea of 'Boundary Layer Control'. By installing athwartships slots across the wing some way back from the leading edge and causing a stream of high pressure air to flow from them, the air passing over the wing is accelerated and this increased airflow speed induces it to cling to the upper surface of the wing. As the air approaches the after edge of the wing it again slows down, creating a further tendency for the airflow to become turbulent. A second set of slots, situated close to the after edge of the wing, were so designed that they sucked the turbulent air from that area thereby smoothing out the airflow, maintaining lift and giving better aileron control. From these measures came a number of advantages: a reduced approach and landing speed, always a welcome factor, and a reduction in catapult launch speeds. As an added bonus it was found that the same Boundary Layer Control slots tended to stop icing on a plane's wings, a tremendous asset. Ice that has formed on a wing obviously alters its shape and probably roughens its surface too, thus spoiling its lift potential on both counts.

The speeds attained by these early jets made it clear that quite soon it would be possible to fly at and beyond the speed of sound. This was unknown territory that had to be explored well before planes with this ability came into general use. Unfortunately the planes available to British test pilots were lacking in power compared to those being used by their American counterparts. To gain the speed required for investigation into the behaviour of planes at speeds that had not hitherto been achieved, it was necessary to put the aircraft into a prolonged dive. For the airman sufficient altitude is his great safety factor and throwing it away in a prolonged dive like this greatly reduces the pilot's chance of recovery should a problem arise or, if things go badly

wrong, baling out. Escape from a high-speed plane by leaping out, as in days gone by, ranges from very difficult to quite impossible and ejector-seats were not available to the pilots who investigated the behaviour of the early jets. Lives were lost because pilots were unable to escape from the cockpit, a number when these high-speed dives got out of hand.

Entry into the denser air of lower altitudes at a very high rate of knots and other high-speed manoeuvres causes the load on the control surfaces to become excessive, on occasion making it impossible for the pilot to operate the controls. On the face of it the answer would seem to be obvious – power-assisted controls. This proved to be the right answer but the application of powered assistance to the controls had to be made with some subtlety. Eventually a system called 'Control harmonisation' was developed that gave adequate powered assistance to the controls in all circumstances without destroying the feedback that came from the all important 'feel'. As aircraft speeds have increased, so power-assisted control has become increasingly important.

Although the jet-propelled plane created a number of problems it also brought in its train some advantages.

The engines in a twin-engined propeller-driven plane had to be placed some distance out on each wing to give the props room to rotate without striking the fuselage. If power was lost from one of the engines the pull of the remaining propeller way out to one side would require the application of considerable rudder control to keep the aircraft on a straight course. As engines became more powerful so the problem increased. Contra-rotating props on the centre line of the plane were sometimes used as a solution. Because jet engines lacked a propeller they could be placed close to the fuselage, so largely doing away with the difficulty.

For some years it had been the custom to use the forward part of the flight-deck when it was not needed for take-off, as a parking space for aircraft and an area in which work on the planes could be carried out. With aircraft landing on the after end of the deck there was always the possibility of an aircraft missing the arrester wires and continuing on through the parked planes and the men working on them to the detriment of both. Protection was provided by the provision of a crash barrier across the deck at about midway along the island structure. Initially these barriers were constructed of steel cables and whilst they did their prime job and also saved rogue aircraft from careering off the flight-deck, an encounter with the crash barrier was not to be taken lightly: planes were damaged and crew members could often be injured or killed.

In piston-engined planes some measure of protection was afforded the crew by the very fact that the propeller and engine were positioned in front of them ready to absorb some of the impact. Jet planes do not usually offer this limited form of protection to their crew as the cockpit is normally situated in the nose of the plane.

In 1956 crash barriers were redesigned and nylon webbing was substituted for the steel cables. Nylon is immensely strong and has the ability to stretch very considerably when it is placed under heavy load, making an encounter with a nylon crash barrier a much more agreeable experience than one with the old unyielding steel barriers.

Ashore it was found that jet-propelled planes required a longer landing strip than did their piston-engined predecessors. To avoid increasing the length of runways at Naval Air Stations, Chain Arrester Gear (CHAG) was rigged when needed. This was a hark back to the earliest days of arrester gear when cables with sand bags attached to either end were laid across the flight-deck to be picked up by the plane's arrester hook. Either someone knew his FAA history or the system was reinvented. In this latter-day version discarded heavy anchor cable was used in place of the sandbags. Four wires were found to be sufficient for the earlier jets but as jet planes became larger and heavier and landing speeds faster something more was needed. The answer was slightly more technical but still blissfully simple.

In this system the weight of the anchor cable at each end of the arrester wire was replaced by pistons that were dragged up enclosed cylinders when their cable was hooked. The horizontally mounted cylinders were filled with water but had

a series of holes bored into their upper surface and as the piston was pulled up, the tube water was forced out from the holes. As the piston travelled up the tube so the number of holes available for the water to escape through was reduced thereby increasing the retarding effect as the plane slowed down. This system, Spray Arrester Gear, rejoiced in the acronym SPRAG. Later SPRAG would be adapted for use on board ship.

By the sixties arrester gear similar to that in use on board aircraft carrriers became a regular feature on all naval airfields, making it possible for FAA planes to use small airfields around the world which were denied to high performance land-based aircraft that had no arrester hooks.

The angled flight-deck that has proved to be so

The angled flight-deck, HMS _Eagle_

successful grew out of a conference held in August 1951 to consider ways and means of eliminating the need for a crash barrier. The meeting was chaired by a Captain Campbell RN and was attended by, amongst others, Professor Lewis Boddington CBE, a government scientist. Captain Campbell displayed some pencil sketches that illustrated his idea for an angled deck without much interest being shown at the time. Later Professor Boddington, having given much thought to the various ideas that were aired at the conference, came to the conclusion that the angled deck was the one most likely to be of value.

The new carrier, *Ark Royal*, was nearing completion and it was agreed that the idea should be tried out in her. The first attempt was with a deck angled at just four degrees to the ship's fore and aft line which was later increased to eight or ten degrees. Arrester wires were set up in the usual way but to serve the angled deck. The barrier became redundant for most operations as any plane that failed to pick up an arrester wire could simply fly off and go round again for another bite at the cherry. For those who landed successfully the lift to the hangars on the lower decks was close to the point at which they had touched down or, if it was more convenient, they could be parked well forward on the fore and aft flight-deck. In either case it was but a moment's work to whisk the aircraft out of the path of the next in line to land.

Angling the deck in this way produced a large working space forward of the island that was no longer immediately ahead of planes that were landing on. This not only allowed aircraft to be parked and crew to work safely at refuelling and rearming etc., but catapults could be installed on the forward end of the fore and aft flight-deck to facilitate the launching of aircraft when, for some reason, the angled deck was not to be the chosen means of getting aircraft into the air. With this layout it became possible to launch and recover aircraft simultaneously.

Even after the appearance of the angled flight-deck special circumstances still demanded the use of crash barriers but this was to be the exception rather than the rule. With the adoption of the angled deck the accident rate was reduced by

something like seventy-five per cent. Other improvements were to bring the accident rate even lower.

As aircraft speeds increased so did their landing speeds until no longer was it enough to be able to land on 'by the seat of your pants'-type flying.

Approach speeds had increased to the point where it was becoming hazardous to take one's eyes off the flight-deck to check the instrument panel for such vital information as the airspeed. In 1945 experiments were carried out with the intention of projecting certain information relating to the aiming of the aircraft's guns onto the windscreen. In 1949 Commander Mike Crosley RN, who was at the time working as a test pilot for Short, submitted a comparatively simple design that would project the image of chosen instruments onto the windscreen, the first 'head-up display' unit which was to become so important to future generations of pilots.

Until a little before the appearance of the jet it was possible for a competent pilot to land on an aircraft carrier's deck by using both his and the batsman's skill and judgement, but with heavier and faster aircraft to handle, a more rapid response was needed and this called for electronics and the like to replace or supplement human judgement and reaction.

'The batsman', or to give him his official title the Deck Landing Control Officer, used oversized 'table-tennis bats' with which to signal to the incoming pilot, hence his unofficial title. Traditionally the pilot had been expected to follow the signals given by the Deck Landing Control Officer (DLCO).

In the RN until 1948 the batsman's signals had indicated what the pilot of the incoming plane should do to correct his approach. If a wing was too low the DLCO would raise the bat on that side, if the approach was considered to be too high both bats would be lowered to tell the pilot to reduce his altitude, and so on.

In 1948 the system was changed to conform with the American Navy's method in which the DLCO's action was a reflection of the incoming plane's attitude and left the correction to the pilot's judgement.

It was not long before the increased landing speeds meant that, by the time the need for a correction was realised by the batsman, and this need was translated into a signal to the pilot and then noted and acted upon by that pilot, precious seconds had been lost.

In the early 1950s initial trials of an invention conceived by Lt-Cdr Nick Goodhart were carried out in *Albion*. The Deck Landing Mirror System (DLMS) as it was called was a gyro-stabilised horizontal concave mirror onto which were projected a number of lights to represent the flight-deck point at which the plane was required to land and a moving light that was an indication of the progress of the aircraft in relation to it. The idea was successful and was installed at the after end of *Ark Royal*'s flight-deck adjacent to the arrester wires and within a year all aircraft carriers with the angled deck were fitted with the device. Now the pilot could not only read his instruments without taking his eyes off the flight-deck he was approaching, but he could follow his flight path and plane's attitude in relation to the flight-deck and react as needed without the delay caused by the transmission of signals by the batsman.

The DLMS was subjected to alteration and improvement until eventually the mirror was dispensed with and the system worked by the projection of lights alone. With the appearance of aircraft with the ability to land vertically a version of the DLMS was designed to help guide them to a safe landing.

As jet engine design progressed so speeds and weight increased and the maintenance of the ideal landing approach speed by adjustment of the throttle became more difficult. It is not simply a question of speed but rather speed in relation to the weight of the plane and sometimes the manoeuvre that is being indulged in, factors which could not readily be known to the pilot. For example, an aircraft returning from a mission would have used much of its fuel and maybe its armaments too, and be lighter by an unknown amount.

The first step was a device that gave audible warning of the actual speed in relation to the desirable speed. One of three tones was fed into the pilot's headphones. If all was well the tone was of a medium level; if the plane was travelling too fast the tone was high-pitched and if the speed was too low a deeper tone was transmitted. Further work in this area produced the 'Auto Throttle', a device that took over the maintenance of the correct speed for landing and left the pilot free to deal with other matters in those few pressing last moments.

Another aspect of the same problem was the fact that different stalling speeds require the wings to be presented to the airstream at different angles of attack. With higher landing speeds and greater aircraft weights it was becoming dangerous to leave this as a 'seat of the pants' decision on the part of the pilot. In 1962 an 'Angle of Attack meter' was devised which solved this problem for the pilot. It was not only of value in landing but in any situation where a stall might be induced, for example, in high speed manoeuvres where the 'G' loading would momentarily 'increase the weight' of the machine.

The Navy had used catapults to launch aircraft from ships that lacked a flight-deck for many years, typically cruisers, battleships, CAM ships and the like. With the exception of the CAM ships where the returning plane was expected to ditch, the other vessels were restricted to the launching of seaplanes and flying boats that could be craned inboard after they had alighted on the sea close to their parent ship. These catapults were operated by a combination of compressed air and hydraulic fluid. Accelerator Catapults, as they were called, produced a launch speed of about sixty-five knots and could handle planes with a maximum all-up weight of 10,000 pounds.

With the appearance of the angled deck, catapults had found their way into aircraft carriers. It was obvious that with the promise of larger, heavier and faster naval planes the compressed air catapults would be inadequate and in 1947 Commander C. Mitchell developed the idea of the 'Direct Acting Steam Catapult'. After successful trials in *Perseus* the steam catapult entered service aboard *Ark Royal* in 1955. This new catapult gave a launch speed of something in excess of ninety knots, depending on the weight of the plane that was to be launched.

Both the Accelerator Catapults and the Steam Catapults required the plane that was to be launched to run its engine at full throttle. The slipstream from a piston-engined plane was bad enough but with the introduction of jets the exhaust gases were a very large part of the slipstream and they were very hot, requiring cooling water devices to protect the deck etc. The jet exhaust was of such power that it could readily pick up equipment or men and blast them overboard. To protect the men who had to work around the catapults, blast-deflector screens were devised and installed.

Now that the angled flight-deck allowed steam catapults to be installed right forward above the stem of the carrier, it became possible to launch a plane every forty seconds from a single catapult, or for those aircraft carriers equipped with two catapults a plane could be launched every twenty seconds.

Malaysia became independent in 1957 and not long afterwards it became apparent that Indonesia was seriously considering invading Malaysia with a view to annexing her territory. Units of the RN were despatched to thwart these ambitions. The aircraft carrier *Victorious* was part of the fleet and the very hot weather she was experiencing caused her catapult tracks to distort, making it impossible to launch her aircraft by this means. The Flight-Deck Engineer, Lt-Cdr D. Taylor put his mind to

A Sea Harrier leaving the angled Ski Jump

the problem and came up with the Ski-Jump Ramp. A wedge-shaped ramp that was constructed at the leading edge of the flight-deck. The first Ski-Jump Ramps to be installed were built with a seven degree slope which in the light of experience was later increased to twelve degrees. Now it was possible for a fully laden Sea Harrier, for example, to take off in less than half the distance required ashore on a conventional runway.

The Ski-Jump Ramp had been invented at just about the right moment. The aircraft carrier that had served the FAA so well had grown to such a size and was so expensive to build and maintain that it was in danger of extinction rather like the dinosaur before it. The Ski-Jump Ramp made the wish for a smaller aircraft carrier become a real possibility. It is highly likely that, without the invention of the Ski-Jump Ramp and a number of other British inventions, namely the angled flight-deck, the mirror/projector landing sight, the head-up display of cockpit instruments, the steam-powered catapult and the vertical take-off Sea Harrier, all carrier aviation, not just in Britain but world-wide, would have come to an end some time in the late 1940s or early 1950s. These and other measures made it possible to operate much smaller carriers, which in turn allowed naval aviation to remain a viable entity.

CHAPTER SIXTEEN

The Sea Harrier and The Falklands War

The Sea Harrier

Somewhere in the 1950s we were seeing television footage of what was dubbed the Flying Bedstead, a name well justified if the pictures we were seeing were anything to go by. This contraption, no other word will serve, consisted of a horizontal rectangle of what appeared to be scaffold poles that supported a Rolls-Royce jet engine, a seat and a collection of controls. A vertical scaffold pole was fixed at each corner, hence the 'bedstead', and a mass of engineering works was draped around and over the engine. It looked like something tossed together by the joint efforts of a scaffolder and a drunken plumber on an off-day. This strange heap staggered into the air more or less vertically and landed in much the same manner; between take-off and landing it was coaxed to move around a short distance in a somewhat erratic manner.

It took ten years to turn this into an aircraft and another ten before it was recognised as the superb flying machine it really is. Perhaps without the Falklands War its true worth would still not be recognised.

Rolls-Royce Flying Bedstead, the start of it all

The end product, a Sea Harrier armed and in flight

The concept is a simple one. The power plant is a Rolls-Royce jet engine with four outlets for the exhaust gases, two on either side of the fuselage. The nozzles of these outlets can be swivelled so that the gases can be expelled in a variety of directions, including directly downwards.

When landing or taking off vertically the Harrier does so literally on a powerful cushion of descending gases from its jet engines. With the nozzles suitably adjusted the plane will behave somewhat like a helicopter and when it is high enough it can change into a modern jet fighter or attack plane. It is also capable of taking off and landing in the conventional manner.

By about the mid-1960s the Harrier was established as the world's first high-performance plane with the ability to take off and land vertically, but no one would buy it. Potential customers seemed

not to believe what was claimed for it, no matter how often these possibilities were demonstrated. It seemed that it was destined to be looked upon as a novelty and not much more; good entertainment at an air show. True it was slower than conventional fighters and its bomb load was smaller than was considered desirable. On the plus side it was nimble in the air, could slow down to force an adversary to overtake it, thereby turning the Harrier into the hunter instead of the quarry, and it needed neither runway, catapult nor vast great flight-deck from which to operate.

The first sales breakthrough came in 1968 when the United States Marines bought a number of Harriers primarily because of its ability to operate without a runway. This prompted NATO to take an interest in this unique machine for the same reason. It had long been understood by NATO that if we were to go to war with the Eastern Bloc countries, NATO Forces would be handicapped by the lack of good runways in eastern Europe.

A year later The RAF formed its first Harrier squadron which was intended to be used in a ground support role. The Harriers quickly found favour with the aircrews who flew them.

In 1970 the RN lost its big aircraft carriers and with them they also lost the ability to operate supersonic jets at sea. In place of the large aircraft carriers the Navy developed smaller carriers designed initially to operate with helicopters. Helicopters are wonderfully versatile machines but by no stretch of imagination could they be thought of as fighter planes suited to the air defence of the Fleet. Once out of the range of RAF fighters the Fleet would be without an airborne defence against enemy aircraft and World War Two had demonstrated that to be a recipe for disaster.

These circumstances forced the RN to consider using the Harrier for air defence. Clearly it could operate from a helicopter carrier and maybe it had some fighter potential. The Harrier's lower speed would perhaps be offset by the fact that attacking aircraft would need to come to them if they wanted to attack the Fleet. Guided missiles were coming onto the scene which might well counter the speed advantage that attacking planes would have. It would be wrong to suggest that the Navy were happy with this solution but they were in a take it or leave it situation. Changes were made to the Harrier to fit it for its role at sea and from those changes came the Sea Harrier.

The new plane, the Sea Harrier, was delivered to the FAA in 1980. The RN was the first Service to accept the Harrier as a fighter plane and now it was down to the pilots of the FAA to prove that the idea was a valid one. It was to be the RN's salvation, indeed eventually it was to be the salvation of many naval air forces around the world.

No longer equipped with large conventional carriers two helicopter carriers were given short, angled flight-decks that ended with Ski-Jump

Ramps. Whilst it is perfectly possible for the Harrier to take off vertically the penalty for this ability is a much reduced pay load. It was the Ski-Jump Ramp that made it possible to fly a fully laden Harrier off the short flight-decks of the smaller carriers that had come into service. Ashore a Harrier with a full load requires about 300 metres to take off into the wind; the ski-jump ramp gets the same plane airborne in about half of that distance. 'Airborne' in that last sentence may offend the purist as the plane behaves in part as a ballistic missile for the first several hundred metres after leaving the ramp before it becomes airborne in the conventional sense.

The Falklands War

On the night of 1/2 April 1982 the Argentinians invaded the Falkland Islands. It would seem that this surprised the British Government. I can't imagine why. There were a number of pointers

Ascension Island in the South Atlantic was a vital staging post

A squadron of Westland Sea Kings served in the Falklands Conflict

that must have suggested to the Argentinians that the British Government had little interest in the Falklands. To give just two, Admiralty charts, in world-wide use, had for some years labelled the Falkland Islands as the Malvinas and _Endurance_, the Navy's Arctic Survey ship that had been in the area for many years was withdrawn; not only was she withdrawn but it was made known that she would not be replaced.

Her Majesty's Government decided to despatch a Task Force to recover the Islands and as an early step announced a 200-mile exclusion zone around the Falkland Islands against Argentinian ships and aircraft.

The Falklands lie some 8,000 miles to the south of Britain and so were far from any hopes of an air-field from which to fly aircraft in support of the

Forces that were to fight the war on land and sea. The air support of these forces was, in the early stages, to fall entirely on the FAA.

Hermes, first commissioned in 1959, had, from her earliest days, undergone a number of refits to enable her to undertake a variety of tasks. In 1980/81 she was converted yet again, this time to enable her to operate Sea Harriers. The much newer carrier _Invincible_ was, for the same reason, given a ski-jump ramp at the forward end of her very slightly angled flight-deck and brought into commission in June 1981.

The two carriers were loaded with all the Sea Harriers the Navy could muster, all twenty of

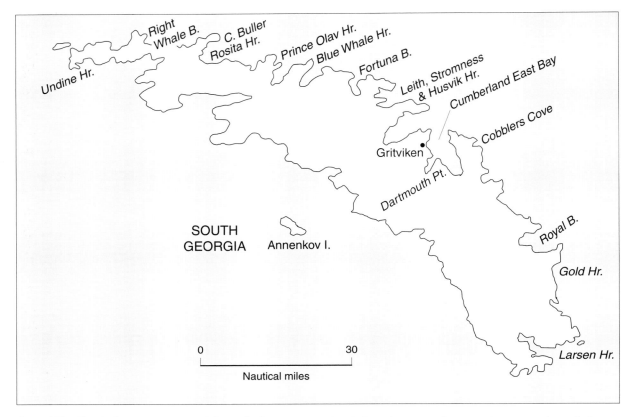

South Georgia was used as a staging post and supply base

them! Until reinforcements could reach the area these two squadrons of Harriers plus forty-five helicopters were the only aircraft the Fleet Air Arm would have to pit against the more than 200 first-line aircraft the Argentine Air Force was known to have. The twenty Sea Harriers were required to be responsible for the air support of the ground forces and the defence of the Fleet. The two carriers sailed for the Falklands on 5 April 1982 with *Hermes* as the flagship. Without the aircraft carriers it is arguable that the Falklands would never have been retaken. Some time later the FAA received a further eight Sea Harriers and the RAF provided fourteen Harriers.

In the South Atlantic midway between Britain and the Falklands lies Ascension Island which has both an anchorage and an airfield. This was an obvious staging post and a Naval Air Support Unit was hastily established there. Helicopters were to be delivered in transport planes by the RAF and by private charter companies. Two Wessex HU.5s

were the first to arrive from Britain in a chartered Belfast.

Meanwhile another squadron of Sea Harriers, a squadron of Sea Kings and two squadrons of Wessex helicopters, all second-line training squadrons, started working-up exercises to fit them for active service. Two container ships, *Atlantic Conveyer* and *Atlantic Causeway*, underwent some measure of conversion to enable them to fulfil the role of aircraft transporters. As soon as all was ready the aircraft, which included a squadron of RAF Harriers and a squadron of Chinook helicopters, were loaded aboard. The two aircraft transporters and other vessels arrived at Ascension Island on 16 April having continued with working-up exercises en route and the helicopters were put to work at once. In the first twenty-four hours after their arrival they flew more than 300 sorties, shifting men and gear into the ships from which they would make their initial landings. The carriers' visit was brief and they, with their escorts, were away on 18 April. Three days later the Sea Harriers made their first contact with an Argentinian Air Force plane. It was a Boeing 707 and the Sea Harriers escorted it from the area.

It had been decided that South Georgia, some 750 nautical miles to the east of the Falklands had to be secured to deny the Argentine Forces the use of those islands and to provide a base for the British forces closer than Ascension Island. On the morning of 21 April three Wessex helicopters from the destroyer *Antrim* and the Royal Fleet Auxiliary *Tidespring* started to ferry groups of Special Forces ashore but the weather soon became impossible, causing the loss of two of the Wessex helicopters. Fortunately the crew and passengers escaped serious injury. Conditions became so bad that the SAS had to be evacuated, as did a group of SBS that had landed from the Survey Ship *Endurance*. The next day both groups were back again and this time things went better for them.

In the course of the morning of 25 April a radio signal was picked up suggesting that the Argentinian submarine *Santa Fe* was leaving South Georgia, having put stores and troop reinforcements ashore. The Wessex 5 helicopter from *Antrim* spotted the submarine and attacked it with depth-charges, causing damage that prevented her diving. Soon afterwards the Lynx from *Brilliant* carried out a further attack and this was followed by the Wasp from *Endurance* attacking the submarine with anti-submarine missiles. One missile struck the fin of the submarine but failed to explode. The helicopters continued to harass the submarine with light machine-gun fire and further missile attacks. By this time *Santa Fe* was no longer seaworthy and sought refuge in Cumberland East Bay on South Georgia, where she beached herself alongside the jetty at Gritviken. With this threat removed the helicopters started to ferry the main assault force ashore whilst *Antrim* and *Plymouth* maintained a deterrent barrage from their 4.5-inch guns. Helicopters spotted the fall of the shot and carried

out reconnaissance and a variety of support missions. By 1730 that day South Georgia was recaptured. The importance of South Georgia was to be its use as a staging post and a supply base for the Royal Fleet Auxiliaries and troopships that were part of the main Task Force.

The Task Force now had to establish both air and naval superiority throughout the area to facilitate the amphibious assault that was intended to lead to the retaking of the Falklands.

The question in everone's mind was, 'how would the Sea Harrier fare against the enemy fighters?' The Argentine Air Force was well equipped, in part with one of the great military jets of the post-war period, the French-built Mirage, a fine aircraft that was considerably faster than the Sea Harrier. It had long been argued that the Harrier was no match for planes of this kind. Fortunately these arguments were to be proved wrong.

On 1 May the opening moves in the air war began. *Hermes* launched nine Sea Harriers to bomb Port Stanley Airport and three more to attack the grass airstrip at Goose Green. These air strikes were covered by six more Sea Harriers from *Invincible*, armed with Sidewinder missiles ready to deal with any Argentine fighters that might appear. Anti-aircraft fire was heavy at both targets but the only damage sustained was from a single 20-mm shell that passed through the fin of one of the Sea Harriers. A number of Argentinian aircraft took off with the intention of attacking the Task Force but they failed to penetrate the screen provided by the six Sea Harriers that were on Combat Air Patrol. The Harriers shot down an Argentinian Canberra, a Dagger bomber and two Mirage fighters and one close-support Pucara was destroyed on the ground.

A bombardment of the airfield at Port Stanley was carried out by three Navy ships that afternoon. Whilst the airport was not put out of action enough damage was done to cause the Argentinians to cease using it for their more important aircraft. From here on the major part of the Argentinian airstrikes had to fly some 400 miles from the mainland before reaching their targets.

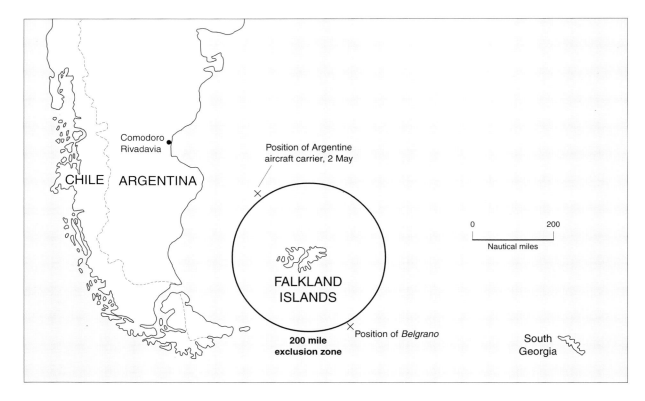

Map labels:
Comodoro Rivadavia
Position of Argentine aircraft carrier, 2 May
CHILE
ARGENTINA
0   200
Nautical miles
FALKLAND ISLANDS
200 mile exclusion zone
Position of *Belgrano*
South Georgia

This map shows the exclusion zone and the position of the Belgrano *as she lay in wait for vessels moving between South Georgia and the Falklands*

Glamorgan, Arrow and *Alacrity* returning from bombarding the airfield had a narrow escape. A group of three Daggers attacked them, coming in fast and low, which allowed them to penetrate the ships' radar screen. The three vessels were thoroughly raked with cannon fire and *Alacrity* took a shaking from a bomb that exploded too close for comfort. This incident led to all future vessels that were to be deployed on bombardment being provided with an escort in the shape of a modern frigate armed with Sea Wolf SAM guided missiles. Before the day was finished there were more raids by Argentinian planes with the result that the Argentine Air Force lost another Dagger and a Canberra and the rest were driven off by the FAA Combat Air Patrols of Sea Harriers.

Two things had been established on the first full day of action. The FAA pilots had greater air to air combat skills than their adversaries and the Sea Harrier was more than a match for the Dagger fighter plane at medium altitudes.

Whilst these preliminaries were under way the

Argentine Navy was preparing a two-pronged attack on the Task Force. To the north-west in the sea area close to their base at Comodoro Rivadavia the aircraft carrier *Veintecinco de Mayo*, with a large escort of surface vessels, was setting out with the intention of conducting a major air strike against the British Task Force on 2 May.

Daybreak on 2 May found *Veintecinco de Mayo* at a point 200 miles north-west of the Task Force, just outside the exclusion zone, from where she planned to launch her air strike against the British ships. To get airborne carrying two 500-pound bombs and enough fuel for the 400-mile round trip the Argentinian Skyhawks needed a wind of at least fifteen knots. Unfortunately for them there was almost no wind at all and so the strike was cancelled.

To the south-east of the Task Force the *General Belgrano,* a heavy cruiser, and *Hipolito Bouchard* and *Piedrabuena*, two modern destroyers armed with Exocet missiles, were in a position to intercept any reinforcements from South Georgia and to attack any damaged vessels from the Task Force that might attempt to reach the security of South Georgia.

Belgrano had been shadowed for two days or more by the submarine *Conqueror* as she sailed back and forth about thirty-six miles outside the exclusion zone. The threat she posed was considered to be so serious that she was torpedoed by the *Conqueror* on instructions from the government in London.

It took *Conqueror* two hours to shake off the attentions of *Belgrano*'s destroyer escort.

There has been a great deal of controversy about the sinking of *Belgrano*, just outside the then exclusion zone. If in fact she was waiting in that position hoping to destroy any damaged British vessels that came her way then surely her sinking must have been justified. Indeed why should the Argentinian aircraft carrier be considered free from the danger of attack when she was sitting just outside the exclusion zone with the intention of launching aircraft to attack the Task Force? War is not a game, if you lie in wait to kill me there can be no grounds for complaint if I manage to kill you first. It is interesting to note that, despite the fuss that was made in some quarters in Britain over this sinking, the Argentinians accepted it without complaint as a reasonable act of war. Shortly after *Belgrano* was sunk *Veintecinco de Mayo* put her aircraft ashore and most of the Argentine Fleet spent the rest of the conflict in shoal water close to Argentina to escape the attention of British submarines.

Constant anti-submarine sweeps were carried out in defence of the Task Force by ASW Sea King helicopters while others joined with the frigates *Brilliant* and *Yarmouth* in a search for *San Luis*, an Argentinian submarine, known to be operating in the area.

The Argentine Air Force staged another heavy raid later that day. The force consisted of Canberra bombers, Daggers and Skyhawks. One Dagger was shot down with a heat-seeking missile and another was so badly damaged that it returned to Port Stanley Airfield to attempt an emergency landing, only to be shot down by trigger-happy Argentinian gunners as it made its approach.

Two days later it was the turn of the RN to suffer. The modern guided missile destroyer *Sheffield* was to be the target. Super Etendards armed with anti-ship missiles conducted a faultless attack, one missile striking the *Sheffield* amidships. The missile failed to explode but the heat created by its passage through the side of the vessel was enough to ignite the contents of a fuel tank. With so many materials used in her fittings that were plastic-based, vast clouds of deadly gases were given off. Crew members in the Machinery Control Room, the Galley and the Damage Control Room were asphyxiated almost at once and a number of others died in the same way. In all twenty men were killed. Great efforts were made to get the fires under control but the crew were fighting a losing battle and on 10 May the gutted hull sank.

The loss of *Sheffield* underlined the disadvantage suffered by the Sea Harrier Combat Air Patrols when attempting to defend the Fleet against low-level attacks of this kind without an airborne early warning system. It was only a short time earlier that the RN's airborne early warning capability had been abolished. This short sighted decision was to remain a problem throughout the campaign.

The first Sea Harrier was lost along with its pilot Lt Nick Taylor in the course of a bombing attack on the airstrip at Goose Green on 4 May. On 6 May two Sea Harriers failed to return from a Combat Air Patrol and it is believed that the pilots were lost when their planes collided in foul weather.

Two remarkable nonstop flights were made between the end of April and 6 May; the first by eight FAA Sea Harriers and the second by nine RAF Harriers from Britain to Ascension Island. The aircraft in both the flights were refuelled in the air by Handley Page Victor tankers.

Atlantic Conveyor arrived at Ascension Island on 5 May, embarked the Sea Harriers and RAF Harriers and then departed on 7 May for the Falklands. She joined the Carrier Battle Group off

the Falklands on 18 May and transferred the Sea Harriers and Harriers to *Hermes* and *Invincible*. The Royal Fleet Auxiliary *Fort Austin* arrived with four Lynx helicopters which were equipped with specialist electronics that would allow them to act as decoys for Exocet missiles. Two were placed aboard *Hermes* and the other pair went to *Invincible*.

There was a period of really bad weather that lasted until 11 May. With the improvement in conditions on 12 May, Sea Harriers were launched to attack Port Stanley airfield with both high- and low-level bombing raids. The Argentinian Air Force had also responded to the improvement in the weather. Two groups of four Skyhawks attacked *Brilliant* and *Glasgow*, inflicting sufficient damage on *Glasgow* to force her withdrawal from the area of operations.

A Victor tanker refuelling a Harrier in flight

By mid-May the RN had gained control of the seas in the vital areas and the necessary ground forces were in position and waiting to be put ashore. The first and main objective was to be East Falkland. The capital, Port Stanley, on the north-east coast of East Falkland, was the obvious objective but the ground around it was heavily defended. For this reason it was decided to stage the initial amphibious landings on the coast of San Carlos Water on the north-west side of the island, where the defences were more thinly spread. Pucara strike aircraft were stationed on the airfield on nearby Pebble Island and represented a threat to troops landing in the San Carlos Water area. Sea Kings transported SAS men there and they

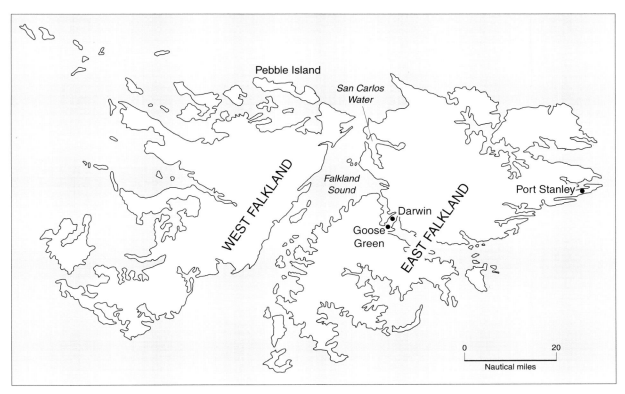

The Falklands

destroyed eleven of the aircraft in a brilliant raid on the night of 14/15 May. Two Argentinian supply ships in Falkland Sound, the water that separates East and West Falkland, were attacked by four Sea Harriers and so badly damaged that they were abandoned.

On 19/20 May the amphibious assault on San Carlos went ahead with the Navy giving covering fire. Sea King helicopters from the RFA *Fort Austin* provided anti-submarine patrols and kept watch for the appearance of surface vessels. Wessex and Sea King helicopters laboured away transporting all the stores, ammunition and weapons that were needed by the troops ashore. Wasp and Lynx helicopters from some of the frigates in the fleet were patrolling the coastal waters to make sure the invasion was not disturbed by Argentinian vessels that might be hiding in the deep coastal indentations.

The initial Argentinian reaction came from Pucaras, ground attack aircraft that were based locally, and Macchi 339s that carried out reconnaissance missions. During the following forenoon sixteen enemy Skyhawks with an escort of Dagger fighters attacked the ground forces in waves of four aircraft. Numerous fierce air attacks were made on the landing area for three days but the defenders destroyed twenty-three of the Argentinian aircraft and the enemy forces were unable to prevent the establishment of the beachhead. During the same period British aircraft losses amounted to one Sea Harrier, one RAF Harrier and three helicopters.

Nevertheless nothing is for free. Attacks on the ships continued throughout that day and those that followed, with some ships sustaining damage. Fortunately a notable number of the bombs dropped on them failed to explode. This did not mean that the vessels got off scot-free. If you drop half a ton of ironmongery from a great height onto a ship it will do damage in its own right without the aid of explosives! The frigate *Ardent* was the worst casualty: she took seven 1,000 lb and five 500-lb bombs, all of which exploded and two more that failed to detonate. Not surprisingly she was reduced to little more than a useless hulk and those of her crew that survived were taken off by *Yarmouth*.

Two British frigates, a cruiser and the container ship *Atlantic Conveyor* were lost between 21 and 25 May.

On 25 May the Task Force operating to the north-west of the Falkland Islands was attacked by two Argentine Navy Super Etendards armed with Exocet missiles. They came in low and launched their missiles at the carriers, who launched Chaff Decoys in an effort to confuse the missiles. One missile was deflected from its target but as it turned away it unfortunately 'found' *Atlantic Conveyor* and locked onto her. The missile exploded between decks, starting a fierce fire which spread rapidly and was soon out of control, so much so that the ship had to be abandoned.

The container ship, in addition to losing nineteen men, took ten sorely needed helicopters to the bottom with her. Three of the helicopters that were lost were Chinooks. They are large helicopters and were due to ferry troops ashore for the attack on Fitzroy. As a direct consequence the RFA *Sir Galahad* and *Sir Tristram* were called upon to transport those troops. Both ships were hit and disabled during an Argentinian air strike. *Sir Galahad*, carrying the First Battalion of the Welsh Guards, burned furiously, with smoke and flames pouring from her. Naval helicopters were on the scene and made repeated sallies to both ships, venturing into the smoke-laden air to take off survivors. It was largely due to the courage and skill of the helicopter crews that the death toll for the two ships was kept as low as fifty. *Sir Tristram* was later salvaged but *Sir Galahad* was too badly damaged and she was taken offshore and sunk as a war grave.

The only real threat to the British landings had been the determined and courageous efforts of the Argentine aircrews. The Sea Harriers in particular outfought the Argentinian Air Force and reduced their future efforts to limited and occasional operations. This is not to belittle the courage and determination shown by the Argentinian aircrews. Sadly the propaganda services of the Galtieri dictatorship besmirched their efforts by reporting their exploits with more imagination than fact. For example, it was claimed that the aircraft carrier *Invincible* had been subjected to a successful attack when the ship attacked was in fact the frigate *Avenger*, which was some thirty miles away.

The ground forces made good progress ashore, taking Darwin and Goose Green and then on towards Port Stanley, all the time receiving major support from FAA aircraft. The advance continued with the ground forces closing in on Port Stanley.

On 14 June British ground forces were on the outskirts of the capital when the white flags of surrender started to appear: Argentinian resistance was at an end.

The weather throughout the campaign had been dreadful. Dense fog was not unusual. Very strong winds that raised heavy seas were commonplace and the winds were often accompanied by heavy rain or thick snow. Photographs taken at the time show Sea Harriers landing on in vast clouds of spray that almost obliterate the planes.

Despite the weather and the fact that at that time of the year there were just three hours of daylight the FAA, in addition to all their other tasks, maintained constant air cover for the Task Force 24 hours a day throughout the conflict.

The little band of Sea Harriers had proved its worth beyond any shadow of doubt, and once more the Fleet Air Arm had underlined the importance of a well equipped and highly trained naval air arm.

Sources

Apps, Mike (1976) *Four Ark Royals*. William Kimber and Co.

Beaver, Paul (1987) *Encyclopedia of FAA since 1945*. Patrick Stevens.

Beaver, Paul (1987) *Fleet Air Arm since 1945*. Patrick Stevens.

Brown, David (1974) *Carrier Operations in World War Two*. Ian Allen.

Busch, Fritz-Otto (1991) *The Drama of the Scharnhorst*. Robert Hale.

Crosley, Mike (1995) *Up in Harm's Way*. Airlife.

Dimott, Roderick (1981) *Fleet Air Arm 1939 to 1945* (Portfolio). Ian Hamilton Ltd.

Burden Draper, Rough, Smith and Wilton *Falklands, The Air War*. British Aviation.

Freidman, Norman *Post War Naval Revolution*. Conway Maritime Press.

Hanson, Norman *Carrier Pilot*. Patrick Stevens.

Harrison, W. (1987) *Swordfish at War*. Ian Allen.

Harrison, W. (1992) *Fairey Firefly*. Airlife.

Hezlet, Vice-Admiral Sir Arthur (1970) *Aircraft and Sea Power*. Ian Allen.

Hoare, John (1976) *Tumult in the Clouds*. Michael Joseph Ltd.

Kemp, P. K. (1954) *Fleet Air Arm*. Herbert Jenkins.

Liskeard *Flashing Blades over the Sea*. Maritime Books.

Longstaff, Reginald (1981) *The Fleet Air Arm, a pictorial history*. Robert Hale.

Mercer, Neil (1994) *Fleet Air Arm*. Airlife.

Middlebrook, Martin (1989) *The Fight for the Malvinas*. Penguin Books.

Munson, Kenneth (1967) *Aircraft of World War One*. Ian Allen Ltd.

Preston, Anthony *History of the Royal Navy in the 20th Century*. Hamlyn (a Bison Book).

Sayer and Ball *Tag on a Stringbag*. Aspen Publications.

Sturtivent, Ray *British Naval Aviation*. Arm and Armour Press.

Welham, John (1995) *With Naval Wings*. Spellmount Ltd.

The Falklands Campaign — the lessons. (1982) HMSO.

The Fleet Air Arm. (1943) HMSO.

BBC Panorama.

Channel 4 TV.

Index

The numbers in **bold type** are the page numbers of illustrations.